World Gazetteer

World Gazetteer

Antony Mason

GEDDES&
GROSSET

First published 1992

Cover design by Cameron Graphics Ltd,
Glasgow, Scotland.

ISBN 1 85534 093 3

Printed and bound in Great Britain.

A

Aachen (Aix-la-Chapelle) A historic university city and spa town in western GERMANY. (Pop. 250 000)

Aarhus *see* Århus.

Aba A industrial town in southern NIGERIA. (Pop. 210 700)

Abadan An major oil-refining port on an island in the SHATT AL ARAB waterway, southern IRAN. (Pop. 296 000)

Abeokuta An industrial town in western NIGERIA. (Pop. 310 100)

Aberdeen A city and fishing port in north-east SCOTLAND, and the admisnistrative centre of the GRAMPIAN region. (Pop. 214 000)

Aberdeenshire *see* Grampian.

Abidjan A major port and the chief city of COTE D'IVOIRE. (Pop. 1 850 000)

Åbo *see* Turku.

Abruzzi A region of southern central ITALY; its capital is Aquila. (Pop. 1 246 600)

Abu Dhabi The largest sheikhdom of the UNITED ARAB EMIRATES, of which the city of Abu Dhabi is the capital. (67 350 sq km/26 000 sq miles; pop. emirate 535 700/city 244 000)

Abuja The new capital of NIGERIA, in the centre of the country, still under construction but inaugurated in 1992. (Forecast population of 2 000 000 by the year 2000)

Abu Simbel The celebrated site of temples of ancient EGYPT, by Lake NASSER.

Acapulco A large port and beach resort on the PACIFIC coast of MEXICO. (Pop. 800 000)

Accra The capital and main port of GHANA. (Pop. 1 045 400)

Aconcagua The highest mountain of the ANDES, in ARGENTINA. (6960 m/22 835 ft)

Adana A city and province in southern TURKEY. (Pop. city 776 000)

Ad Dawhah *see* Doha.

Addis Ababa The capital of ETHIOPIA, in the centre of the country. (Pop. 1 500 000)

Adelaide The state capital of SOUTH AUSTRALIA. (Pop. 969 000)

Aden A major port on southern YEMEN, formerly the capital of SOUTH YEMEN. (Pop. 264 326)

Adirondack Mountains A mountain range in NEW YORK State, U.S.A. The highest peak is Mount Marcy. (1629 m/5344 ft)

Adriatic Sea A branch of the MEDITERRANEAN SEA, between ITALY and YUGOSLAVIA.

Aegean Sea A branch of the MEDITERRANEAN SEA, between GREECE and TURKEY.

Afghanistan A landlocked republic in central ASIA. It is generally arid, with high mountains to the centre and east. Traditional exports include carpets and foodstuffs, but since 1979 it has been tormented by war. The main languages are Pushtu and Dari (Persian), and the capital is KABUL. (652 090 sq km/251 772 sq miles; pop. 15 040 000; cur. Afghani = 100 puls)

Africa The second largest continent in the world, with the MEDITERRANEAN SEA to the north, the ATLANTIC OCEAN to the west and the INDIAN OCEAN to the east. There are 47 nations within Africa.
Agadir A port and popular tourist resort in MOROCCO. (Pop. 111 000)
Agra A city in central INDIA, and site of the Taj Mahal. (Pop. 747 000)
Ahmadabad (Ahmedabad) An industrial city in western INDIA. (Pop. 2 548 000)
Ahvaz A port on the Karun River in southern IRAN. (Pop. 471 000)
Aix-en-Provence A university city in southern FRANCE. (Pop. 129 000)
Aix-la-Chapelle *see* Aachen.
Ajman The smallest emirate of the UNITED ARAB EMIRATES. (65 sq km/25 sq miles; pop. emirate 42 000/town 27 000)
Akron A city in north-east of the state of OHIO, U.S.A. (Pop. city 226 900/metropolitan area 650 100)
Alabama A state in southern U.S.A. The state capital is MONTGOMERY. (133 667 sq km/51 606 sq miles; pop. 4 021 000)
Alamein *see* El Alamein.
Alamo, The An old Spanish mission near SAN ANTONIO, Texas, U.S.A. Davy Crockett and 186 other Texans died defending the fort here against a Mexican army in 1836.
Alaska The largest and most northerly state of the U.S.A. The state capital is JUNEAU. (1 518 800 sq km/586 400 sq miles; pop. 521 000)

Albacete A town and province of south-eastern SPAIN. (Pop. town 177 100)

Albania A republic in south-east EUROPE on the BALKAN peninsula, with a coast on the ADRIATIC SEA. Owing to its repressive Communist regime, it was completely isolated from the outside world until 1991. A relatively poor country with mountains and forests, it exports very little. Albanian is the official language and TIRANA is the capital. (28 748 sq km/11 100 sq miles; pop. 3 033 300; cur. Lek = 100 quintars)

Albany The capital city of NEW YORK State, U.S.A. (Pop. 95 500)

Albert, Lake A lake in the GREAT RIFT VALLEY in East Africa, shared between UGANDA and ZAIRE. (Also known as Lake Mobuto Sese Seko.) (5180 sq km/ 2000 sq miles)

Alberta A province of western CANADA; EDMONTON is its capital. (661 190 sq km/255 285 sq miles; pop. 2 238 000)

Ålborg A city and port in northern DENMARK. (Pop. 160 000)

Albuquerque A university city on the RIO GRANDE in NEW MEXICO, U.S.A. (Pop. 350 600)

Alcala de Henares A town in southern SPAIN, birthplace of Miguel de Cervantes (1547–1616), author of *Don Quixote*. (Pop. 142 900)

Alderney One of the CHANNEL ISLANDS.

Aleppo (Halab) An industrial city of ancient origins in SYRIA. (Pop. 905 944)

Alexandria The main port of EGYPT, on the NILE delta. (Pop. 2 320 000).

Al Fujayrah The second smallest emirate in the UNITED ARAB EMIRATES and also the name of a small town in the emirate. (117 sq km/45 sq miles; pop. emirate 38 000/town 760)

Al Furat *see* Euphrates, River.

Algarve The southern province of PORTUGAL.

Algeria A republic in north-west AFRICA, with a coast on the MEDITERRANEAN SEA. It became independent of FRANCE in 1962. It consists almost entirely of desert, with the ATLAS MOUNTAINS in the north. Oil is the most important export. Arabic is the main language and ALGIERS is the capital. (2 381 741 sq km/919 590 sq miles; pop. 22 710 000; cur. Dinar = 100 centimes)

Algiers (El Djazair, Alger) The capital of ALGERIA, on the MEDITERRANEAN coast. (Pop. 1 800 000)

Aliákmon, River The longest river in GREECE. (Length 297 km/184 miles)

Alicante A port and popular beach resort, and also the name of the surrounding province, on the MEDITERRANEAN coast of SPAIN. (Pop. town 251 400)

Alice Springs A desert settlement in the NORTHERN TERRITORY of AUSTRALIA. (Pop. 18 400)

Aligarh A university town in central INDIA. (Pop. 321 000)

Allahabad A holy city in INDIA on the conflunece of the rivers GANGES and YAMUNA. (Pop. 650 000)

Alma-Ata A trading and industrial city and capital of KAZAKHSTAN. (Pop. 1 046 100)

Al Manamah The capital and main port of BAHRAIN. (Pop. 115 054)

Alps, The A mountain range in southern central

EUROPE that spans the borders of SWITZERLAND, FRANCE, GERMANY, AUSTRIA, YUGOSLAVIA and ITALY.

Alsace A region and former province of FRANCE.

Altai An area of high mountain ranges in central Asia on the borders where CHINA and the U.S.S.R. meet at the western end of MONGOLIA.

Amager A fertile island to the south of COPENHAGEN, in DENMARK.

Amalfi A small, picturesque town on a spectacular part of the west coast of ITALY. (Pop. 6100)

Amarillo An industrial city in north-west TEXAS. (Pop. 162 900)

Amazon, River With the River NILE, one of the world's two longest rivers. It rises in the ANDES of PERU and flows east through BRAZIL to the ATLANTIC. (Length: 6440 km/4000 miles)

Amboina *see* Ambon.

Ambon (Amboina) An island and the capital of the so-called Spice Islands in the MALUKU group in eastern central INDONESIA. (813 sq km/314 sq miles; pop. 73 000)

America The continent lying between the ATLANTIC and the PACIFIC OCEANS. For convenience it is divided into three zones: North America (U.S.A. and CANADA), Central America (the area between the U.S.A.–MEXICO border and the PANAMA–COLOMBIA border), and South America (the area to the south of the PANAMA–COLOMBIA border).

American Samoa *see* Samoa, American.

Amiens An industrial city and capital of the SOMME department of northern FRANCE. (Pop. 159 600)

Amman The capital of JORDAN, in the north-east of the country. (Pop. 1 232 600)

Ammindivi Islands *see* Lakshadweep.

Amritsar An industrial city in northern INDIA and home of the Golden Temple, the most sacred shrine of the Sikhs. (Pop. 595 000)

Amsterdam The capital and commercial centre of the NETHERLANDS, a historic port set on the IJSSELMEER. (Pop. 712 300)

Amudar'ya, River A central Asian river forming much of the border between the TAJIKISTAN and AFGHANISTAN before flowing through UZBEKISTAN into the ARAL SEA. (Length: 2620 km/1630 miles)

Amundsen Sea An arm of the South PACIFIC in ANTARCTICA.

Amur, River (Heilong Jiang) A river which runs along the border between CHINA and RUSSIA, flowing east into the PACIFIC. (Length 4510 km/2800 miles)

Anatolia The historical name for the Asian part of TURKEY.

Anchorage The largest city and port in ALASKA, U.S.A., on its southern coast. (Pop. 226 700)

Andalusia (Andalucía) A region of south-western SPAIN, with a coast on the MEDITERRANEAN SEA and ATLANTIC OCEAN. (Pop. 6 441 800)

Andaman and Nicobar Islands Two groups of islands in the bay of Bengal, administered by INDIA. (Pop. 188 700)

Andaman Sea A branch of the Bay of BENGAL, lying between the ANDAMAN Islands and BURMA.

Andes A high mountain range that runs down the

entire length of the western coast of South AMERICA. The highest peak is Mount ACONAGUA, in ARGENTINA (6960 m/22 835 ft).

Andhra Pradesh A state in south-east INDIA. The capital is HYDERABAD. (275 088 sq km/106 184 sq miles; pop. 53 549 700)

Andorra A landlocked coprincipality lying in the PYRENEES between FRANCE and SPAIN. It is jointly administered by the French head of state and the Bishop of Urgel in Spain. Tourism throughout the year sustains the economy. Catalan, French and Spanish are the chief languages, and the capital is ANDORRA LA VELLA. (464 sq km/179 sq miles; pop. 49 500; cur. Spanish peseta, French franc)

Andorra la Vella The capital of ANDORRA. (Pop. 14 000)

Andros The largest of the islands of the BAHAMAS (4144 sq km/1600 sq miles; pop. 8900)

Angara, River A river in RUSSIA flowing from Lake BAIKAL into the YENISEY River. (Length: 1825 km/ 1135 miles)

Angel Falls A narrow band of water falling 979 m (3212 ft) from a high plateau in south-eastern VENEZUELA to form the world's highest waterfall.

Angkor The ruined ancient capital of the Khmer empire in CAMBODIA.

Anglesey An island off the north-western tip of WALES. (715 sq km/276 sq miles; pop. 69 000)

Angola A republic in south-west Africa, with a coast on the ATLANTIC OCEAN. Formerly a possession of PORTUGAL, it gained independence in 1975 but has subsequently been ravaged by civil war. A coastal plain rises to a plateau in the centre and east. Exports include oil, diamonds, coffee and fish. Portuguese is the official language, and LUANDA is the capital. (1 246 700 sq km/481 350 sq miles; pop. 8 170 000; cur. Kwanza = 100 lwei)

Anguilla An island in the LEEWARD ISLANDS group of the CARIBBEAN, now a self-governing British dependency. (91 sq km/35 sq miles; pop. 6500)

Angus *see* Tayside.

Anhui (Anhwei) A province of eastern CHINA. Its capital is HEFEI. (130 000 sq km/50 000 sq miles; pop. 48 030 000).

Anjou A former province of western FRANCE, in the valley of the River LOIRE.

Ankara The capital of TURKEY, in the eastern central part of Asian Turkey. (Pop. 2 252 000).

Annaba (Bone) A historic town and seaport on Mediterranean coast of ALGERIA. (Pop. 245 000)

Annam The old name used by the French for the central MIEN TRUNG region of VIETNAM.

Annapolis The capital of the state of MARYLAND, U.S.A. (Pop. 31 900)

Annapurna A mountain of the HIMALAYAS, situated in NEPAL (8172 m/26 810 ft)

Anshan An steel-manufacturing city in LIAONING province, northern CHINA. (Pop. 11 000 000)

Antakya (Antioch) A city of ancient origins in southern TURKEY. (Pop. 109 200)

Antalya A port and resort on the MEDITERRANEAN coast of TURKEY. (Pop. 258 100)

Antananarivo The capital of MADAGASCAR, in the centre of the island. (Pop. 663 000)

Antarctic Circle Latitude 66° 32′ south. At the winter solstice, the sun does not rise above this line, nor does it set below it at the summer solstice.

Antarctic Ocean (Southern Ocean) The waters which surround ANTARCTICA.

Antarctica An ice-covered continent around the SOUTH POLE.

Antigua and Barbuda A state in the WEST INDIES which became independent of the U.K. in 1981. Tourism is a major industry. English is the principal language and the capital is ST JOHN'S. (442 sq km/171 sq miles; pop. 80 000; cur. East Caribbean dollar = 100 cents)

Antioch *see* Antakya

Antilles The major chain of islands in the CARIBBEAN SEA, divided into two groups: the Greater Antilles (which includes CUBA and PUERTO RICO) to the west; and the Lesser Antilles (including e.g. MARTINIQUE and BARBADOS) to the east.

Antrim A county and town in NORTHERN IRELAND. (2 831 sq km/1093 sq miles; pop. county 642 267/ town 22 242)

Antwerp (Antwerpen, Anvers) The capital of the province of Antwerp and the main port of BELGIUM. (Pop. 488 000)

Anvers *see* Antwerp.

Anyang A city of ancient origins in the HENAN province of eastern CHINA. (Pop. 500 000)

Aomori A port on HONSHU island, JAPAN. (Pop. 294 000)

Apennines The mountain range which forms the 'backbone' of Italy. The highest peak is Monte Corno (2912 m/9554 ft).

Apia The capital of WESTERN SAMOA. (Pop. 34 000)

Appalachian Mountains A chain of mountains which stretches 2 570 km (1600 miles) down eastern NORTH AMERICA from CANADA to ALABAMA in the U.S.A. The highest peak is Mount MITCHELL (2037 m/6684 ft).

Apulia *see* Puglia.

Aqaba The only port in JORDAN, situated on the Gulf of Aqaba in the RED SEA. (Pop. 35 000)

Aquitaine A region and former kingdom of south-western FRANCE.

Arabian Gulf *see* Gulf, The.

Arabian Sea A branch of the INDIAN OCEAN between INDIA and the Arabian Peninsula.

Arafura Sea A stretch of the PACIFIC OCEAN between NEW GUINEA and AUSTRALIA.

Aragon A region and former kingdom of north-east SPAIN.

Aral Sea A large, salty lake, to the east of the CASPIAN SEA, which lies on the border between UZBEKISTAN and KAZAKHSTAN. (64 750 sq km/25 000 sq miles)

Aran Islands (Oileáin Arann) Three small islands – Inishmore, Inishmaan and Inisheer – off County GALWAY in the Republic of IRELAND. (44 sq km/18 sq miles; Pop. 1380)

Ararat, Mount (Büjük Agri Dagi) The mountain peak in eastern TURKEY where Noah's Ark is said to have come to rest after the Great Flood. (5165 m/12 818 ft)

Arauca, River A major tributary of the ORINOCO River which forms part of the border between COLOMBIA and VENEZUELA. (Length: 1000 km/620 miles)
Archangel (Arkhangel'sk) A port on the DVINA Delta on the WHITE SEA in RUSSIA. (Pop. 403 000)
Arctic The regions that lie to the north of the ARCTIC CIRCLE.
Arctic Circle Latitude 66° 32′ north. The sun does not set below this line at the summer solstice, nor does it rise above this line at the winter solstice.
Arctic Ocean The ice-laden sea to the north of the ARCTIC CIRCLE.
Ardabil A town in Iran, famous for its knotted carpets. (Pop. 222 000)
Ardennes A hilly and forested region straddling the borders BELGIUM, LUXEMBOURG and FRANCE.
Arequipa A city and department of PERU. (Pop. city 448 000)
Argentina A republic in southern South AMERICA, with a coast on the ATLANTIC OCEAN. The ANDES lie to the west, forests to the north, fertile plains to the east, and deserted wastelands to the south (Patagonia). Exports include meat, grain, wool and other farm produce. Spanish is the principal language. The capital is BUENOS AIRES. (2 766 889 sq km/1 068 296 sq miles; pop. 31 700 000; cur. Peso = 100 centavos)
Århus A port and the second largest city in DENMARK. (Pop. 246 700)
Arizona A state in the south-west of the U.S.A. The capital is PHOENIX. (295 024 sq km/113 902 sq miles; pop. 3 137 000)

Arkansas A state in the south of the U.S.A. The state capital is LITTLE ROCK. (137 539 sq km/53 104 sq miles; pop. 2 359 000)

Arkansas, River A tributary of the River MISSISSIPPI in the U.S.A., flowing from the ROCKY MOUNTAINS through the states of KANSAS, OKLAHOMA and ARKANSAS. (Length 2335 km/1450 miles)

Arkhangel'sk *see* Archangel.

Armagh A county and city in NORTHERN IRELAND. (1254 sq km/484 sq miles; pop. county 118 820/city 12 700)

Armenia **1** The former independent kingdom which straddles the borders of modern TURKEY, IRAN and the U.S.S.R. **2** That part of Armenia which forms the Republic of Armenia in the U.S.S.R. The capital is YEREVAN. (Pop. 3 267 000)

Arnhem A town in the NETHERLANDS, scene of a battle in 1944 between British (and Polish) paratroops and the German army. (Pop. 128 600)

Arnhem Land An Aboriginal reserve in the NORTHERN TERRITORIES of AUSTRALIA.

Arno, River The main river of TUSCANY in ITALY, flowing westwards through FLORENCE to PISA on the coast. (Length 245 km/152 miles)

Aruba A CARIBBEAN island off the coast of VENEZUELA, formerly one of the NETHERLANDS ANTILLES. The capital is ORANJESTAD. (193 sq km/75 sq miles; pop. 67 000; cur. Aruba guilder = 100 cents)

Arunachal Pradesh A union territory of northern INDIA, bordering TIBET. The capital is Shillong. (Pop. 631 800)

Ascension Island A tiny volcanic islands in the South ATLANTIC OCEAN, forming part of the ST HELENA DEPENDENCIES. (Pop. 1625)

Ashkhabad The capital of TURKMENISTAN. (Pop. 347 000)

Asia The largest continent, bounded by the ARCTIC, PACIFIC and INDIAN OCEANS, plus the MEDITERRANEAN and RED SEAS. East Asia is taken to mean those countries to the north-east of BANGLADESH (e.g. CHINA); South Asia refers to the countries on the Indian subcontinent (e.g. INDIA); and South-East Asia includes those countries to the south-east of CHINA, including the islands to the west of NEW GUINEA (e.g. INDONESIA).

Asmara The main city of ERITREA in ETHIOPIA. (Pop. 430 000)

Assam A state in north-eastern INDIA (99 680 sq km/ 38 476 sq miles; pop. 19 900 000)

Assisi A small town in UMBRIA, central ITALY, and birthplace of St Francis (1182–1226). (Pop. 24 400)

Assyria An empire of ancient MESOPOTAMIA founded in around 3000 BC and reaching the height of its power in the 7th century BC. Its main cities were Assur and NINEVEH on the River TIGRIS, now in modern IRAQ.

Astrakhan A port near the CASPIAN SEA in southern RUSSIA, situated on the delta of the River VOLGA. (Pop. 487 000)

Asturias A region of northern Spain. the capital is OVIEDO. (Pop. 1 227 000)

Asunción The capital and the only major city of PARAGUAY. (Pop. 456 000)

Aswan A city in southern EGYPT by the River Nile. The Aswan High Dam, completed 1971, is 13 km (8 miles) to the south. (Pop. 200 000)

Atacama Desert An extremely dry desert lying mainly in northern CHILE.

Athabasca, River A river in CANADA which flows north from the ROCKY MOUNTAINS to Lake Athabasca. (Length 1231 km/765 miles)

Athens (Athinai) The historic capital, and the principal city, of GREECE. (Pop. city 885 700/metropolitan area 3 027 300)

Athos A group of monasteries on Mount Athos (2 033 m/7770 ft) on a peninsula in central GREECE.

Atlanta The capital and largest city of the state of GEORGIA in the U.S.A. (Pop. 426 100)

Atlantic Ocean The second largest ocean, lying between North and South AMERICA, EUROPE and AFRICA.

Atlas Mountains A series of mountain chains stretching across NORTH AFRICA from MOROCCO to TUNISIA.

Auckland The largest city and chief port of NEW ZEALAND, on North Island. (Pop. 769 6000)

Augsburg A historic city in BAVARIA, GERMANY. (Pop. 245 000)

Augusta 1 A city and river port on the Savannah River in GEORGIA, U.S.A. (Pop. city 46 000/metropolitan area 368 300). **2** The state capital of MAINE, U.S.A. (Pop. 22 000)

Auschwitz A small town in POLAND and site of the biggest of the Nazi concentration camps 1940–45. (Pop. 35 6000)

Austin The capital city of the state of TEXAS, U.S.A. (Pop. city 397 000/metropolitan area 645 400)

Australasia A general term for AUSTRALIA, NEW ZEALAND and neighbouring islands.

Australia An island continent, with shores on the INDIAN and PACIFIC OCEANS, and a Commonwealth country. The centre and west are vast areas of desert or semi-desert; to the north lie tropical forests; to the east there are subtropical mountain ranges; and to the south and south-east lie plentiful grasslands. Exports include meat, wool, iron ore and minerals. The capital is CANBERRA. (7 682 300 sq km/2 966 140 sq miles; pop. 17 000 000; cur. Australian dollar = 100 cents)

Australian Capital Territory The small region which surrounds CANBERRA, the capital of AUSTRALIA. (2 432 sq km/939 sq miles; pop. 240 000)

Austria A landlocked republic in the centre of EUROPE, with the ALPS in the west and the DANUBE basin in the east. Tourism (skiing) is a major industry, and exports include iron and steel, timber and chemicals. German is the dominant language and VIENNA is the capital. (83 853 sq km/32 375 sq miles; pop. 7 540 000; cur. Schilling = 100 groschen)

Auvergne A mountainous region of central FRANCE.

Avignon A historic city on the River RHONE in southern FRANCE, the seat of the Pope 1309–77. (Pop. 177 500)

Avila A town and province in the mountainous central region of SPAIN, famous as the birthplace of St Teresa (1515–82). (Pop. town 41 800)

Avon A county in the west of ENGLAND; the county

town is BRISTOL. (1338 sq km/517 sq miles; pop. 936 000)

Axios, River A river flowing through the BALKANS and MACEDONIA from YUGOSLAVIA to GREECE and the AEGIAN SEA. (Length: 388 km/241 miles)

Axum An important historic town in ETHIOPIA, once a royal capital where the Queen of Sheba is said to have ruled. (Pop. 20 000)

Ayers Rock A huge rock, sacred to the Aborigines, rising sharply out of the plains in the NORTHERN TERRITORY of AUSTRALIA. (348 m/1142 ft)

Ayrshire *see* Strathclyde.

Ayutthaya A town with the extensive ruins of the city that was the capital of THAILAND from 1350 to 1767. (Pop. 113 300)

Azarbaijan A region of northern IRAN. Its population share the same language as the people of neighbouring AZERBAIDZHAN. (Pop. 4 613 000)

Azerbaidzhan (Azerbaijan) A former republic of the U.S.S.R., which declared its independence in 1991. It borders AZARBAIJAN in IRAN and the CASPIAN SEA. The capital is BAKU. (Pop. 6 506 000)

Azores Three groups of small islands in the North ATLANTIC OCEAN, belonging to PORTUGAL. The capital is Ponta Delgada. (2335 sq km/901 sq miles; pop. 336 100).

B

Baalbek A ruined city dating back to Phoenician and Roman times in the BEQA'A VALLEY in LEBANON.

Babylon One of the great cities of ancient MESOPOTAMIA, situated in modern IRAQ.

Baden-Baden A famous spa town in south-west GERMANY dating from Roman times. (Pop. 50 000)

Baden-Württemburg The southern state of GERMANY bordering FRANCE and SWITZERLAND. (Pop. 9 241 000)

Baffin Bay A huge bay within the ARCTIC CIRCLE between BAFFIN ISLAND in CANADA and GREENLAND.

Baffin Island A large, mainly ice-bound island in north-east CANADA (507 451 sq km/195 927 sq miles)

Baghdad The capital of IRAQ, in the centre of the country, on the River TIGRIS. (Pop. 3 300 000)

Bahamas A group of some 700 islands which were a British colony until 1964, when they became independent and a member of the Commonwealth. The islands have few natural resources but they have prospered thanks to a booming tourist industry. English is the dominant language. The main islands are Andros, Grand Bahama, Great Abaco, Cat Island, Eleuthera and Great Inagua. The capital NASSAU is on the central island of New Providence. (13 935 sq km/5380 sq miles; pop. 237 000; cur. Bahamian dollar = 100 cents)

Bahrain An independent sheikdom comprising several islands off the western side of the GULF (the main island also being called Bahrain). It was a British protectorate until 1971, when it became independent.

Most of the land is barren, but Bahrain is an oil-rich state. Arabic and English are the main languages. AL MANAMAH is the capital. (661 sq km/255 sq miles; pop. 443 200; cur. Bahrain dinar)

Baikal, Lake The world's deepest freshwater lake, and the largest by volume, situated in south-east SIBERIA in RUSSIA. (31 500 sq km/12 150 sq miles)

Baile Atha Cliath *see* Dublin.

Baja California A huge 1300-km (800-mile) long peninsula belonging to MEXICO which stretches south from CALIFORNIA in the U.S.A. into the PACIFIC OCEAN. (Pop. 1 400 000)

Bakhtaran Formerly called Kermanshah, a large city in IRAN on the old trading routes between TEHRAN and BAGHDAD. (Pop. 531 000)

Baku A port on the CASPIAN SEA and the capital of the republic of AZERBAIDZHAN. (Pop. 1 661 000)

Balaklava *see* Sevastopol.

Balaton, Lake A lake in western HUNGARY, famous as a tourist resort. (601 sq km/232 sq miles)

Bâle *see* Basle.

Balearic Islands A group of islands in the western MEDITERRANEAN SEA belonging to SPAIN and famous as tourist resorts. The main islands are Majorca (Mallorca), Minorca (Menorca), Ibiza (Iviza), Formentera and Cabrera. (Pop. 685 000)

Bali A small island of the eastern tip of JAVA, distinguished by being the only island in INDONESIA to have preserved a predominantly Hindu culture intact. The main town and capital is DENPASAR. (5 591 sq km/ 2159 sq miles; pop. 2 470 000)

Balkans The south-eastern corner of EUROPE, a broad, mountainous peninsula bordered by the ADRIATIC SEA, the IONIAN SEA, the AEGEAN SEA and the BLACK SEA. ALBANIA, BULGARIA, GREECE, ROMANIA, YUGOSLAVIA and the European part of TURKEY are all in the Balkans.

Balkhash, Lake A massive lake in central-southern RUSSIA, near the border with CHINA. (22 000 sq km/ 8500 sq miles)

Ballarat A historic gold-mining town in VICTORIA, AUSTRALIA, the scene of the 1854 rebellion known as the Eureka Stockade. (Pop. 62 600)

Baltic Sea A shallow sea in northern EUROPE, completely surrounded by land masses except for the narrow straits that connect it to the NORTH SEA.

Baltimore The largest city in the state of MARYLAND, U.S.A. (Pop. city 763 000/metropolitan area 2 244 700)

Baluchistan A province of south-western PAKISTAN, bordering IRAN and AFGHANISTAN. (Pop. 4 332 000)

Bamako The capital of MALI. (Pop. 405 000)

Banda Sea A part of the PACIFIC OCEAN, in eastern INDONESIA.

Bandar Abbas A port in southern IRAN on the Strait of HORMUZ, at the neck of the GULF. (Pop. 89 200)

Bandar Seri Begawan The capital of BRUNEI. (Pop. 50 000)

Bandung A large inland city in western JAVA, INDONESIA. (Pop. 1 46 700)

Banffshire *see* Grampian.

Bangalore A large industrial city in central southern India.·(Pop. 2 921 800)

Bangkok (Krung Thep) The capital of Thailand, on the River CHAO PHRAYA. (Pop. 5 900 000)

Bangladesh A republic in South ASIA with a coast on the Bay of BENGAL. It was formerly known as East PAKISTAN but became independent in 1971 and joined the Commonwealth in 1972. It occupies the low-lying deltas of the Rivers GANGES and BRAHMAPUTRA and is prone to destructive floods and cyclones. The principal exports are jute and textiles. The dominant religion is Islam, and the main language is Bengali. The capital is DHAKA. (144 000 sq km/55 598 sq miles; pop. 104 250 000; cur. Taka = 100 paisa)

Bangui The capital of the CENTRAL AFRICAN REPUBLIC, in the south of the country. (Pop. 387 000)

Bangweulu, Lake A large lake in Northern ZAMBIA. (9800 sq km/3784 sq miles)

Banja Luka A city of ancient origins on the Vrbas River in north-west BOSNIA HERZEGOVINA, YUGOSLAVIA. (Pop. 183 000)

Banjarmasin A port on the southern coast of KALIMANTAN, INDONESIA. (Pop. 381 300)

Banjul The capital of the GAMBIA. Formerly called Bathurst (Pop. 42 000)

Barbados An island state in the WINDWARD ISLANDS of the southern CARIBBEAN. A former British colony, it became an independent Commonwealth country in 1966. Tourism is a major industry, and sugar and sugar-products are important exports. The main language is English, and the capital is BRIDGETOWN. (430 sq km/166 sq miles; pop. 253 000; cur. Barbados dollar = 100 cents)

Barbuda *see* Antigua and Barbuda.
Barcelona The second largest city in SPAIN, and the name of the surrounding province. It is a major port on the MEDITERRANEAN SEA. (Pop. city 1 754 900)
Barents Sea A part of the ARCTIC OCEAN to the north of NORWAY.
Bari A major port on the ADRIATIC coast of ITALY. (Pop. 370 000)
Baroda *see* Vadodara.
Barossa Valley A wine-producing region in SOUTH AUSTRALIA, 50 km (30 miles) north of ADELAIDE.
Barquisimeto An industrial city in western VENEZUELA. (Pop. 600 000)
Barranquilla The largest port on the CARIBBEAN coast of COLOMBIA. (Pop. 1 067 000)
Basel *see* Basle.
Bashkiria (Baskir Republic) A republic of the RUSSIAN FEDERATION, in the southern URALS. The capital is UFA. (143 500 sq km/55 400 sq miles; pop. 3 860 000)
Basle (Basel, Bâle) A city in northern SWITZERLAND and the name of the surrounding canton. (Pop. city 200 000)
Basque Region An area straddling the border of SPAIN and FRANCE on the ATLANTIC coast.
Basra The second city of IRAQ, and its main port. (Pop. 1 200 000)
Bassein A trading city on the delta of the IRRAWADDY River in BURMA. (Pop. 355 600)
Bass Strait The stretch of water spanning the 290 km (180 miles) which separate the mainland of AUSTRALIA from TASMANIA.

Basseterre The capital of ST KITTS AND NEVIS. (Pop. 16 000)

Basse Terre The capital of the French island of GUADELOUPE, situated on the island called Basse Terre. (Pop. town 14 000/island 141 000)

Bath A beautifully preserved spa town in the county of AVON, south-west ENGLAND. (Pop.85 000)

Bathurst *see* Banjul.

Baton Rouge The state capital of LOUISIANA, U.S.A., situated on the MISSISSIPPI River. (Pop. city 238 900/ metropolitan area 538 000)

Bavaria (Bayern) The largest state in GERMANY (70 553 sq km/27 241 sq miles; pop. 10 958 000)

Bayern *see* Bavaria.

Bayeux A market town in NORMANDY, FRANCE, and the home of the huge 11th-century Bayeux tapestry depicting the Norman conquest of England. (Pop. 15 300)

Bayonne The capital of the French BASQUE region. (Pop. 129 730)

Bayreuth A town in BAVARIA, GERMANY, famous for the theatre built by the composer Richard Wagner (1813–83), where his operas are still staged every summer. (Pop. 71 800)

Beaufort Sea A part of the ARCTIC OCEAN to the north of North AMERICA.

Beaujolais A famous wine-producing region of FRANCE situated on the River SAONE between LYONS and Macon.

Bechuanaland The former name of BOTSWANA (until 1966).

Bedfordshire A county in central southern ENGLAND; the county town is Bedford. (1 235 sq km/477 sq miles; pop. 75 000)

Beijing (Peking) The capital of CHINA, situated in the north-east of the country. (Pop. 9 231 000)

Beirut The capital and main port of LEBANON. (Pop. 938 000)

Belarus *see* Belorussia.

Belau A republic consisting of a group of islands in the western PACIFIC. It has an agreement of free association with the U.S.A. Copra is the chief export and the main language is English. The capital is KOROR. (494 sq km/191 sq miles; pop. 14 000; cur. U.S. dollar = 100 cents)

Belém A major port of BRAZIL situated to the north of the mouth of the River AMAZON. (Pop. 934 000)

Belfast The capital and by far the largest city of NORTHERN IRELAND. (Pop. 360 000)

Belgium A kingdom in north-western EUROPE with a coast on the NORTH SEA. Most of the land comprises fertile plains rising to mountains in the south-east. The nation is divided into two main communities: the Flemish-speakers in the north and the French-speakers (Walloons) in the south. It is a member of the European Community, and it exports foodstuffs, iron and chemicals. BRUSSELS is the capital. (30 513 sq km/11 781 sq miles; pop. 9 860 000; cur. Belgian franc = 100 centimes)

Belgrade (Beograd) The capital of SERBIA and of YUGOSLAVIA, on the confluence of the Rivers DANUBE and Sava. (Pop. 1 407 100)

Belize A state in Central AMERICA with a seaboard on the ATLANTIC. It is a former British colony and became independent, and a member of the Commonwealth, in 1981. Much of the country is forested, with mountains to the south. Exports include sugar and bananas. The main language is English. BELMOPAN is the capital. (22 963 sq km/8866 sq miles; pop. 165 000; cur. Belize dollar = 100 cents)

Bellinghausen Sea A part of the PACIFIC OCEAN off ANTARTICA, due south of South AMERICA.

Belmopan The capital of BELIZE. (Pop. 5000)

Belo Horizonte An industrial city, and the third largest city of BRAZIL, in the south-east of the country. (Pop. 1 777 000)

Belorussia (Belarus, Byelorussia) A former republic of the U.S.S.R. which declared itself independent in 1990. It borders POLAND on its western side, and lies to the south of LATVIA and LITHUANIA. The capital is MINSK. (207 600 sq km/80 150 sq miles; pop. 9 878 000)

Belostock *see* Bialystok.

Benares *see* Varanasi.

Bengal A former Indian state which was divided at the partition of India in 1947 into two parts: WEST BENGAL in INDIA, and East Pakistan (now BANGLADESH).

Bengal, Bay of The massive bay occupying the broad sweep of the INDIAN OCEAN between INDIA and BURMA, to the south of BANGLADESH.

Benghazi A major port at the eastern end of the Gulf of SIRTE in LIBYA. (Pop. 266 1960)

Benidorm One of the most popular MEDITERRANEAN seaside resorts of SPAIN. (Pop. 25 600)

Benin A republic in West AFRICA with a coast on the Gulf of GUINEA. It was a French colony until 1960, when it gained independence. Swamps on the coast give way to fertile plains in the centre of the country, and there are mountains to the north. Exports include cotton, palm oil and cocoa. The official language is French. The capital is PORTO NOVO. (112 622 sq km/ 43 484 sq miles; pop. 4 140 000; cur. CFA franc = 100 centimes)

Ben Nevis *see* Grampian Mountains.

Benue, River A river which flows through CAMEROON and NIGERIA to the Gulf of GUINEA. (Length 1390 km/ 865 miles)

Benxi An industrial city in LIAONING province in northern CHINA. (Pop. 1 200 000)

Beograd *see* Belgrade.

Beqa'a A long, fertile valley running north to south in LEBANON, between the Lebanon and Anti-Lebanon Mountains.

Bergamo A historic and industrial city in northern ITALY. (Pop. 121 000)

Bergen 1 An old port in south-west NORWAY, and now that country's second largest city. (Pop. 181 000). **2** *See* Mons.

Bering Sea A part of the PACIFIC OCEAN between ALASKA and eastern RUSSIA.

Bering Strait The stretch of sea, 88 km (55 miles) wide, that separates RUSSIA from ALASKA in the U.S.A.

Berkshire A county of central southern England; the county town is Reading. (1256 sq km/485 sq miles; pop. 708 000)

Berlin The capital of GERMANY, situated in the north of the country on the River Spree. Until 1990 it was divided in two by the infamous Berlin Wall. (Pop. 3 097 000)
Bermuda A group of 150 small islands in the western ATLANTIC OCEAN which form a self-governing British colony. (53 sq km/21 sq miles; pop. 55 000)
Berne (Bern) The historic capital of SWITZERLAND, and also the name of the surrounding canton. (Pop. city 150 000)
Berwickshire *see* Borders.
Besançon A town of ancient origins in the JURA region of eastern France. (Pop. 120 800)
Bethlehem A town in the WEST BANK area of ISRAEL, celebrated by Christians as the birthplace of Jesus Christ. (Pop. 30 000)
Béthune An industrial town in north-eastern FRANCE. (Pop. 259 700)
Beuten *see* Bytom.
Beyrouth *see* Beirut.
Bhopal An industrial city in central INDIA. It was the scene of a massive industrial accident in 1984 in which some 3000 people were killed by gas leaking from the Union Carbide chemical plant. (Pop. 671 000)
Bhutan An isolated, landlocked kingdom in South ASIA, sandwiched between INDIA and CHINA in the eastern HIMALAYAS. It has few exports. The principal religion is Buddhism; Dzongkha, Nepali and English are all official languages. The capital is THIMPHU. (47000 sq km/18 000 sq miles; pop. 1 447 000; cur. Ngultrum (paper), tikehung (silver), Indian rupee)

Biafra *see* Iboland.
Bialystok (Belostock) An industrial city in north-east POLAND producing primarily textiles. (Pop. 240 000)
Bianco, Monte *see* Blanc, Mont.
Bielefeld An industrial city in western GERMANY. (Pop. 310 000)
Bielsko-Biala (Bielitz) An industrial city in southern POLAND. (Pop. 172 000)
Bihar A state in north-east INDIA. The capital is PATNA. (Pop. 69 914 700)
Bikini An atoll in the MARSHALL ISLANDS famous as the site of US nuclear weapons tests between 1946 and 1962. This invited joking comparison with the effect on male onlookers of women's two-piece swimwear, to which the name bikini was applied.
Bilbao A port and industrial city in the BASQUE region of northern SPAIN. (Pop. 433 000)
Bioko An island in the Gulf of GUINEA, formerly called Fernando Póo, and now governed by EQUATORIAL GUINEA. (2017 sq km/780 sq miles; pop. 57 000)
Birmingham 1 The main city of the industrial West MIDLANDS and the second largest city in the U.K. (Pop. 976 000). **2** The largest city in the state of ALABAMA, U.S.A. (Pop. city 279 800/metropolitan area 895 200)
Biscay, Bay of The broad bay, notorious for its rough weather, formed by the ATLANTIC OCEAN between northern SPAIN and BRITTANY in north-west FRANCE.
Bismarck The state capital of NORTH DAKOTA, U.S.A. (Pop. city 47 600/metropolitan area 86 100)
Bismarck Sea A branch of the PACIFIC OCEAN to the north of PAPUA NEW GUINEA.

Bissau (Bissão) A port and the capital of GUINEA-BISSAU. (Pop. 109 000)
Black Country The industrial area of the British MIDLANDS around BIRMINGHAM.
Black Forest (Schwarzwald) An extensive area of mountainous pine forests in south-west GERMANY.
Black Hills A range of hills rising to 2207 m (7242 ft) on the border between the states of SOUTH DAKOTA and WYOMING in the U.S.A.
Black Sea A sea lying between south-east EUROPE and western ASIA; it is surrounded by land except for the BOSPHORUS channel, leading to the MEDITERRANEAN SEA.
Blackpool The largest seaside holiday resort in the U.K., in LANCASHIRE. (Pop. 147 000)
Blanc, Mont (Monte Bianco) The highest mountain in Western EUROPE, on the border between FRANCE and ITALY, just to the south of Chamonix (4807 m/ 15 770 ft)
Blantyre The largest city in MALAWI. (Pop. 333 800)
Bloemfontein The judicial capital of SOUTH AFRICA, and the capital of the ORANGE FREE STATE. (Pop. 256 000)
Blue Mountains **1** A range of mountains rising to 1100 m in NEW SOUTH WALES in AUSTRALIA, some 65 km (40 miles) from SYDNEY. **2** The mountains in eastern JAMAICA rising to 2256 m (7402 ft) at Blue Mountain Peak. The region has given its name to the high-quality coffee produced there.
Bochum An industrial city in the RUHR region of western GERMANY. (Pop. 410 000)

Bodensee *see* Constance, Lake.
Bodh Gaya A small town in eastern INDIA which is the site of Buddhism's most revered shrine. Gautama, the Lord Buddha, achieved enlightenment here in about 500 B.C. (Pop. 15 700)
Bodrum A port on the south-eastern Mediterranean coast of TURKEY. Known in the ancient world as Halicarnassus, its Mausoleum (since destroyed) was once of the Seven Wonders of the Ancient World. (Pop. 13 090)
Bogotá The capital of COLOMBIA, set on a plateau of the eastern ANDES in the centre of the country. (Pop. 5 789 000)
Bohemia Formerly an independent kingdom (9th to 13th centuries), now a region of western CZECHOSLOVAKIA which includes the capital PRAGUE. In the mistaken belief that gipsies came from Bohemia, the term Bohemian came to be applied to artists and writers with unconventional lifestyles.
Bohol One of the VISAYAN ISLANDS in the central area of the PHILIPPINES. (3 862 sq km/1491 sq miles; pop. 759 370)
Boise The state capital of IDAHO, U.S.A. (Pop. city 107 200/metropolitan area 189 300)
Bolivia A landlocked republic in the central part of South AMERICA. The high ANDES to the west drop to low plains in the east. Bolivia is one of the world's largest producers of tin and other metals. Languages include Spanish, Quechua and Aymara. The capital is LA PAZ. (1 098 581 sq km/424 163 sq miles; pop. 6 360 000; cur. Peso = 100 centavos)

Bologna The capital of the EMILIA ROMAGNA region in north-eastern ITALY. (Pop. 455 900)

Bolton A textile manufacturing town in the county of LANCASHIRE, ENGLAND. (Pop. 147 000)

Bombay A major port, the capital of MAHARASHTRA state in central western INDIA, and now India's most important industrial city. (Pop. 8 234 400)

Bonaire A CARIBBEAN island off the coast of VENEZUELA but formerly administered by the Dutch and still a part of the NETHERLANDS ANTILLES (288 sq km/ 111 sq miles; pop. 9 700)

Bondi Beach A famous surfing beach in the suburbs of SYDNEY, AUSTRALIA.

Bone *see* Annaba.

Bonin Islands A group of small volcanic islands in the PACIFIC OCEAN belonging to JAPAN. (Pop. 2300)

Bonn The former capital of West GERMANY, which will remain the administrative centre of Germany until the government moves to BERLIN. (Pop. 300 000)

Bophuthatswana One of the homelands declared by the government of SOUTH AFRICA to be an independent republic in 1977. It consists of seven separate territories. (44 109 sq km/17 030 sq miles; pop. 1 935 000)

Bordeaux A major port on the GIRONDE estuary in south-western France. The region is famous for its wines, called Bordeaux or claret. (Pop. 650 125)

Borders An administrative region of southern SCOTLAND, created in 1975 out of the former counties of Berwickshire, Peeblesshire, Roxburghshire, Selkirkshire and Midlothian. (4662 sq km/1800 sq miles; pop. 101 000)

Borkum *see* Friesian Islands.

Borneo One of the largest islands in the world, now divided between three countries. Most of the island is known as KALIMANTAN, a part of INDONESIA. The northern coast is divided into the two states of SARAWAK and SABAH, which are part of MALAYSIA, and the small independent Sultanate of BRUNEI (751 900 sq km/290 320 sq miles)

Borobodur The great Buddhist temple near YOGYAKARTA in southern central JAVA, INDONESIA, dating from about A.D. 750.

Bosnia Herzegovina One of the six former republics of YUGOSLAVIA. In 1991 it declared its intention to become an independent state. The capital is SARAJEVO. (51 129 sq km/19 736 sq miles; pop. 4 124 000)

Bosphorus The narrow strip of water, some 29 km (18 miles) long and no more than 4 km (2.5 miles) wide, which provides the navigable link between the MEDITERRANEAN SEA and the BLACK SEA by way of the Sea of MARMARA. The Bosphorus separates the European part of TURKEY from its Asian part.

Boston An ATLANTIC port and the state capital of MASSACHUSETTS, U.S.A. (Pop. city 570 700/metropolitan area 2 820 700)

Botany Bay A bay now in the suburbs of SYDNEY, AUSTRALIA, discovered by Captain James Cook in 1770.

Bothnia, Gulf of The most northerly arm of the BALTIC SEA, bordered by FINLAND and SWEDEN.

Botswana A landlocked republic in central southern AFRICA, formerly a British protectorate known as

Bechuanaland, which became independent in 1966. It occupies an extensive plateau, with the mosquito-infested Okavango swamp to the north and the KALAHARI DESERT to the south. Meat and diamonds are its few exports. English is the official language and the capital is GABORONE. (600 372 sq km/231 805 sq miles; pop. 1 100 000; cur. Pula = 100 thebe)

Bouaké The second largest city of the COTE D'IVOIRE. (Pop. 640 000)

Bougainville The easternmost island belonging to PAPUA NEW GUINEA, and a part of, though politically separate from, the chain of islands forming the SOLOMON ISLANDS.

Bournemouth A coastal resort on the county of DORSET in southern ENGLAND. (Pop. 145 000)

Boyne, River A river flowing into the IRISH SEA on the east coast of the Republic of IRELAND. It is famous for for its extensive prehistoric remains (notably at Newgrange); and also as the site of the battle in which Protestant William of Orange defeated Catholic James II in 1690. (Length: 115 km/70 miles)

Boyoma Falls A series of seven cataracts over 90 km (56 miles) where the LUALABA River beomes the ZAIRE River. They were formerly called Stanley Falls after the British explorer Sir Henry Morton Stanley.

Brabant The central province of BELGIUM around the capital, BRUSSELS. (3358 sq km/1297 sq miles; pop. 2 200 000)

Brac *see* Dalmatia.

Bradford A city in the county of WEST YORKSHIRE, ENGLAND, which came to prominence as the centre of the woollen industry in the 19th century. (Pop. 281 000)

Bragança A small inland town of medieval origins in PORTUGAL, and the original home of the family which ruled Portugal from 1640 to 1910. (Pop. 13 900)

Brahmaputra A major river of South ASIA, flowing from the HIMALAYAS in TIBET through ASSAM in northern INDIA to join the River GANGES in BANGLASDESH. (Length 2900 km/1802 miles)

Braila A port in ROMANIA on the River DANUBE, 140 km (87 miles) inland from the BLACK SEA. (Pop. 214 000)

Brasília The capital, since 1960, of BRAZIL. (Pop. 412 000)

Brazov An industrial city in central ROMANIA. (Pop. 304 000)

Bratislava (Pressburg) The second largest city in CZECHOSLOVAKIA, and the capital of SLOVAKIA. (Pop. 402 000)

Braunschweig *see* Brunswick.

Brazil A republic occupying the greater part of eastern South AMERICA, with an extensive coastline on the ATLANTIC OCEAN. A vast forested region drained by the AMAZON basin lies to the north, and grasslands (Mato Grosso) to the south. Exports include foodstuffs (coffee and cocoa), machinery and iron ore. The national language is Portuguese, and the capital is BRASILIA. (8 511 965 sq km/3 286 488 sq miles; pop. 140 650 000; cur. Cruzado = 100 cruzeiros)

Brazzaville The capital of the CONGO, on the River Congo. (Pop. 425 000)

Breconshire *see* Powys.
Breda A historic and manufacturing city in the NETHERLANDS. (Pop. city 118 000/Greater Breda 153 000)
Bremen A major port on the River WESER, near to the NORTH SEA coast of GERMANY, and also the name of the surrounding state. (Pop. 550 000)
Bremerhaven A port on the NORTH SEA coast of GERMANY, 55 km (34 miles) to the north of BREMEN. (Pop. 135 000)
Brescia A city in northern ITALY. (Pop. 206 000)
Breslau *see* Wroclaw.
Brest 1 A important naval port situated on an inlet on the tip of the FINISTERE cape in north-western FRANCE. (Pop. 205 000). **2** (Brześć) An inland port in BELORUSSIA situated on the River BUG on the border between Belorussia. and POLAND. (Pop. 205 600)
Brezhnev An industrial town in eastern central RUSSIA, formerly Naberezhnyye Chelny, but renamed in 1984 after the President Leonid Brezhnev (1906–82). (Pop. 414 000)
Bridgeport A manufacturing city on the coast of the state of CONNECTICUT, U.S.A. (Pop. city 142 000/ metropolitan area 441 500)
Bridgetown The capital of BARBADOS. (Pop. 97 000)
Brighton A famous seaside resort on the south coast of England in the county of EAST SUSSEX. (Pop. 149 000)
Brindisi A port on the east coast of ITALY at the southern end of the ADRIATIC SEA. (Pop. 92 000)
Brisbane A port on the east coast of AUSTRALIA, and the state capital of QUEENSLAND., (Pop. 942 400)

Bristol A major city and port in south-west ENGLAND, and the administrative centre of the county of AVON. (Pop. 399 000)

Britain *see* Great Britain.

British Columbia The western seaboard province of CANADA. The capital is VICTORIA. (929 730 sq km/ 358 968 sq miles; pop. 2 744 000)

British Indian Ocean Territory The Chagos Archipelago, a group of five coral atolls in the middle of the INDIAN OCEAN. (52 sq km/20 sq miles)

British Isles The name given to the group of islands in north-western EUROPE formed by GREAT BRITAIN and IRELAND, and the surrounding islands.

British Virgin Islands *see* Virgin Islands.

Brittany (Bretagne) The region of FRANCE which occupies the extreme north-western peninsula, overlooking the ATLANTIC OCEAN.

Brno (Brünn) An industrial city in the centre of CZECHOSLOVAKIA. (Pop. 381 000)

Bromberg *see* Bydgoszcz.

Bruges A historic town and capital of the province of West FLANDERS, BELGIUM. (Pop. 120 000)

Brunei An islamic sultanate occupying two small segments of the coast of north-west BORNEO. Formerly a British protectorate, it became independent in 1984. Most of the country is forested, but oil has been discovered and Brunei now has one of the highest *per capita* incomes in the world. Malay, Chinese and English are all widely spoken. The capital is BANDAR SERI BEGAWAN. (5765 sq km/2226 sq miles; pop. 230 000; cur. Brunei dollar = 100 cents)

Brünn *see* Brno.

Brunswick (Braunschweig) A historic town in northern GERMANY, and the capital of the Dukes of Saxony. (Pop. 255 000)

Brussels (Brussel, Bruxelles) A historic city and the capital of BELGIUM. It plays a central role in EUROPE as the administrative headquarters for the European Community. (Pop. 1 000 000)

Bryansk An industrial city in central western RUSSIA. (Pop. 424 000)

Bubiyan Island A large island belonging to KUWAIT situated in the very north of the GULF and close to the border with IRAQ.

Bucaramanga A city in the north of COLOMBIA, close to the border with VENEZUELA. (Pop. 516 000)

Bucharest (Bucureşti) The capital of ROMANIA, in the south-east of the country. (Pop. 1 861 000)

Buckinghamshire A county in central southern ENGLAND; the county town is Aylesbury. (1883 sq km/727 sq miles; pop. 609 000)

Budapest The capital of HUNGARY, comprising Buda and Pest, which lie on opposite sides of the River DANUBE. (Pop. 2 064 400)

Budweiss *see* Ceské Budejovice.

Buenos Aires The capital of ARGENTINA. (Pop. city 3 325 000/metropolitan area 9 948 000)

Buffalo A city and port in NEW YORK state situated at the eastern end of Lake ERIE. (Pop. city 339 000/metropolitan area 1 205 000)

Bug, River A river which flows north-west from the UKRAINE, forming the border with POLAND before turning west into Poland and joining the Narew and VISTULA rivers. (Length: 813 km/480 miles)

Büjük Agri Dagi *see* Ararat, Mount

Bujumbura The capital of BURUNDI, situated at the northern end of Lake TANGANYIKA. (Pop. 180 000)

Bukhara An old trading city in UZBEKISTAN. (Pop. 204 000)

Bulawayo The second city of ZIMBABWE, in the south-west of the country. (Pop. 414 000)

Bulgaria A republic and former Communist state in south-eastern EUROPE. It forms part of the BALKANS and has a shoreline on the BLACK SEA. To the north is the valley of the River DANUBE, while a series of mountains and troughs occupy the south. Exports include farm products and machinery. Bulgarian is the main language, and the capital is SOFIA. (Pop. 9 000 000; cur. Lev = 100 stotinki)

Burgas A major port on the BLACK SEA coast of BULGARIA. (Pop. 183 000)

Burgos An industrial town in northern SPAIN, and the name of the surrounding province. (Pop. town 156 000)

Burgundy (Bourgogne) A region of central FRANCE, famous for its wine.

Burkina (Burkina-Faso) A landlocked republic in West AFRICA which became independent of FRANCE in 1960 and was known as Upper Volta until 1984. The land comprises an arid plateau which is chronically over-populated and Burkina struggles to feed its people. Exports are minimal, but include cotton and food-stuffs. French is the official language; OUAGADOUGOU is the capital.(274 200 sq km/105 869 sq miles; pop. 7 080 000; cur. CFA franc = 100 centimes)

Burma (Myanmar) A republic in south-eastern ASIA with an extensive coast on the Bay of BENGAL. It became an independent country in 1948 after over a century of rule by Britain. Its mountainous and thickly forested landscape is drained by a range of major rivers with fertile valleys, including the IRRAWADDY. The government has persistently closed Burma off to the outside world and exports are minimal. The main religion is Buddhism; the main language is Burmese. The capital is RANGOON. (676 552 sq km/261 217 sq miles; pop. 37 660 000; cur. Kyat = 100 pyas)

Bursa A city in north-western TURKEY, and also the name of the surrounding province, of which it is the capital. (Pop. city 614 100)

Burundi A landlocked republic towards the east of central AFRICA. It won its independence from BELGIUM in 1962, but has subsequently suffered from bitter internal conflict. The country consists of high plateaux to the west, which descend to grasslands in the east. Exports include cotton, tea and coffee, and other foodstuffs. The principal languages are Kirundi, French and Swahili. The capital is BUJUMBURA. (27 834 sq km/10 746 sq miles; pop. 4 910 000; cur. Burundi franc = 100 centimes)

Buryat Republic An autonomous republic of the RUSSIAN FEDERATION, situated in the south-east, between Lake BAIKAL and MONGOLIA. (351 300 sq km/135 600 sq miles; pop. 985 000)

Bute *see* Strathclyde.

Bydgoszcz (Bromberg) A historic and industrial city in central POLAND. (Pop. 357 700)
Byelorussia *see* Belorussia.
Bytom (Beuthen) An industrial city in south-west POLAND. (Pop. 238 100)
Byzantium *see* Istanbul.

C

Cadiz A port of Phoenician origins on the Atlantic coast of southern SPAIN; also the name of the surrounding province. (Pop. town 157 800)
Caen A city in the NORMANDY region of northern FRANCE. (Pop. 187 600)
Caerdydd *see* Cardiff.
Caernarfonshire *see* Gwynedd.
Cagliari The capital of the Italian island of SARDINIA. (Pop. 232 800)
Cairngorm Mountains A range forming part of the GRAMPIAN MOUNTAINS in SCOTLAND.
Cairns A port on the north-east coast of QUEENSLAND, AUSTRALIA and a tourist resort catering for visitors to the GREAT BARRIER REEF. (Pop. 48 000)
Cairo (El Qahira) The capital of EGYPT, in the north of the country on the River NILE; it is the largest city in AFRICA. (Pop. 8 540 000)
Caithness *see* Highland Region.
Calabria The region which occupies the southern 'toe' of ITALY. The main town is REGGIO DI CALABRIA. (Pop. 1 121 700)

Calais An old port in nothern FRANCE situated on the narrowest part of the ENGLISH CHANNEL, opposite DOVER in ENGLAND. (Pop. 101 500)

Calcutta The largest city in India, a major port and industrial centre situated in the north-east of the country, on the HUGLI River. (Pop. 9 194 000)

Calgary The second largest city in the province of ALBERTA, CANADA. (Pop. 593 000)

Cali An industrial city in southern COLOMBIA. (Pop. 1 755 000)

Calicut (Kozhikode) A port on the west coast of southern INDIA. (Pop. 546 100)

California A state of the U.S.A. on the PACIFIC coast. The state capital is SACRAMENTO, but LOS ANGELES is the biggest city. (411 015 sq km/158 693 sq km; pop. 26 365 000)

California, Gulf of The narrow inlet which separates the mainland part of MEXICO from peninsula of BAJA CALIFORNIA. It is also known as the Sea of Cortes.

Callao The port serving LIMA, the capital of PERU. (Pop. 440 500)

Calvados A department of northern FRANCE, a part of the region of NORMANDY. It is famous for its apple-based liqueur called Calvados. (Pop. 590 000)

Cam Ranh Bay A naval base in VIETNAM developed by the U.S. Navy and which subsequently played an important part in the Soviet military presence in South-East Asia.

Camargue The broad, flat area of sea-marshes in the delta of the River RHONE in the centre of the MEDITERRANEAN coast of FRANCE.

Cambodia A state in south-east ASIA, with a coast on the Gulf of THAILAND. With its fertile lands and tropical climate it is potentially rich, but has suffered untold damage since the 1960s through invasion and internal strife, and now struggles to support itself. Most of the population is Buddhist and the main language is Khmer. The capital is PHNOM PENH. (181 035 sq km/69 898 sq miles; pop. 6 380 000; cur. Riel = 100 sen)

Cambrian Mountains A range of mountains which forms the 'backbone' of WALES.

Cambridge 1 A famous university city in eastern ENGLAND. **2** A city in MASSACHUSETTS, U.S.A., home of Harvard University and the Massachusetts Institute of Technology. (Pop. 95 300)

Cambridgeshire A county in eastern ENGLAND; the county town is CAMBRIDGE. (3409 sq km/1316 sq miles; pop. 578 700)

Cameron Highlands An upland area of MALAYSIA where tea and and vegetables are grown.

Cameroon A republic in West AFRICA with a coast on the Gulf of GUINEA. A single nation was finally forged from French and British protectorates in 1972. The north is desert, the central area is fertile highland and the south is tropical jungle. The main exports are coffee, cocoa and cotton. French and English are the primary languages, and the capital is YAOUNDE. (475 439 sq km/183 570 sq miles; pop. 10 035 000; cur. CFA franc = 100 centimes)

Cameroon, Mount An active volcano in northern CAMEROON. (4095 m/13 435 ft)

Campania A region of central southern ITALY, on the west coast around NAPLES. (Pop. 5 623 400)
Campinas A modern industrial town 75 km (47 miles) north of SAO PAULO in BRAZIL. (Pop. 665 000)
Canada A Commonwealth country occupying the northen part of North AMERICA (with the exception of ALASKA to the north-west). To the north lie ARCTIC wastelands, to the west are the ROCKY MOUNTAINS, the south-east borders the GREAT LAKES, and the central south is occupied by the plentiful prairies. Most of the population lives in a belt along the southern border with the U.S.A. Exports include include grain, timber, coal and mineral ores. English is the main language (although French is spoken by the people of QUEBEC in the east). The capital is OTTAWA. (9 976 139 sq km/ 3 851 793 sq miles; pop. 25 650 000; cur. Canadian dollar = 100 cents)
Canary Islands A group of islands belonging to SPAIN situated some 95 km (60 miles) off the coast of the Western SAHARA (southern MOROCCO). The main islands are Gran Canaria, Tenerife, La Palma, Fuerta-ventura, Gomera, Lanzarote. (7273 sq km/2808 sq miles; pop. 1 444 600)
Canaveral, Cape A long spit of land on the east coast of the state of FLORIDA, U.S.A. It is the U.S.A.'s main launch site for space missions and the home of the John F. Kennedy Space Center. For a time it was known as Cape Kennedy.
Canberra The capital of AUSTRALIA, lying about half-way between SYDNEY and MELBOURNE in the south-east of the country. (Pop. 255 900)

Cancún A tiny island just off the YUCATAN coast of MEXICO, connected to the mainland by a causeway, and now a popular holiday resort. (Pop. 70 000)
Cannes A famous beach resort on the COTE D'AZUR in southern FRANCE. (Pop. 72 800)
Cantabria A province on the Atlantic coast of northern Spain. (Pop. 510 000)
Canterbury A small cathedral city in the county of KENT in southern ENGLAND. (Pop. 36 000)
Canton *see* Guangzhou.
Cape Breton Island An island of the eastern coast of CANADA which forms part of the province of NOVA SCOTIA. (10 349 sq km/3970 sq miles; pop. 170 000)
Cape Town A major port on the south-western tip of SOUTH AFRICA, and the country's legislative capital. (Pop. 213 800)
Cape Verde A republic in the eastern ATLANTIC, off the coast of West AFRICA, comprising some 15 islands. It gained independence from PORTUGAL in 1975. Reliant on aid, the islands have yet to exploit their tourism potential. Portuguese is the official language. The capital is PRAIA. (4033 sq km/1557 sq miles; pop. 321 000; cur. Cape Verde escudo = 100 centavos)
Cappadocia An area of eastern TURKEY to the south-east of ANKARA, noted for the extraordinary sugar-loaf shapes of its volcanic rock formations, into which cave houses have been carved.
Capri A rocky island at the southern end of the Bay of NAPLES on the west coast of ITALY, famous as a fashionable holiday retreat. (10.4 sq km/4 sq miles; pop. 16 500)

Caprivi Strip A narrow corridor of land, 450 km (280 miles) long, which belongs to NAMIBIA and gives it access to the ZAMBEZI River along the border between BOTSWANA to the south and ANGOLA and ZAMBIA to the north.
Caracas The capital of VENEZUELA, in the north-east of the country. (Pop. 3 500 000)
Cardamom Mountains A range of mountains rising to 1813 m (5948 ft) which line the coast of CAMBODIA and separate the interior from the Gulf of THAILAND.
Cardiff (Caerdydd) The capital of WALES, situated in the south-east of the principality, in SOUTH GLAMORGAN. (Pop. 218 000)
Cardiganshire *see* Dyfed.
Cardigan Bay The long, curving bay which, as part of the IRISH SEA, forms much of the west coast of WALES.
Caribbean, The A term that refers to the islands lying within the compass of the CARIBBEAN SEA.
Caribbean Sea A part of the western ATLANTIC OCEAN, bounded by the east coast of Central AMERICA, the north coast of South AMERICA and the WEST INDIES.
Carinthia (Kärnthen) The southern state of AUSTRIA, which borders ITALY and YUGOSLAVIA. (9533 sq km/ 3681 sq miles; pop 536 730)
Carlow A landlocked county in the south-east of the Republic of Ireland. The county town is also called Carlow. (Pop. county 39 000)
Carlsbad *see* Karlovy Vary.
Carmarthenshire *see* Dyfed.
Carmel, Mount A ridge of land rising to 528 m (1746 ft)

in northern ISRAEL, mentioned in the Bible, and the place where the Carmelite Order of mendicant friars originated in the 12th century.

Caroline Islands A scattered group of islands in the western PACIFIC OCEAN which now make up the Federated States of MICRONESIA and the separate state of BELAU.

Carpathian Mountains A broad sweep of mountains stretching for nearly 1000 km (625 miles) down the border between CZECHOSLOVAKIA and POLAND and into central ROMANIA. They rise to 2663 m (8737 ft) at their highest point.

Carpentaria, Gulf of The broad gulf of shallow sea between the two horn-like peninsulas of northern AUSTRALIA.

Carrara A town 50 km (31 miles) north of PISA in ITALY, famous for centuries for its marble quarries. (Pop. 68 500)

Carson City The state capital of NEVADA, U.S.A. (Pop. 35 900)

Cartagena 1 A major port on the CARIBBEAN coast of COLOMBIA. (Pop. 548 0000). **2** A port of ancient origins on the MEDITERRANEAN coast of SPAIN. (Pop. 172 800)

Carthage The site of a great trading port of the ancient MEDITERRANEAN world, now in modern TUNISIA.

Casablanca (Dar el Beida) The main port and largest city of MOROCCO. (Pop. 2 140 000)

Cascade Range A range of mountains stretching some 1125 km (700 miles) parallel to the coast of northern CALIFORNIA in the U.S.A. and into southern CANADA.

The highest point is at Mount Rainier (4392 m/ (14 410 ft) in WASHINGTON State.

Caspian Sea The largest inland (salt) sea in the world, supplied mainly by the River VOLGA. It lies to the north of IRAN, which shares its coasts with AZERBAIDZHAN, GEORGIA, KAZAKHSTAN and TURKMENISTAN.

Cassai *see* Kasai.

Cassel *see* Kassel.

Castile (Castilla) A former kingdom of SPAIN, occupying most of the central area, now divided into two regions, Castilla-La Mancha and Castilla-León.

Castries The capital of ST LUCIA. (Pop. 45 000).

Catalonia (Cataluña) An autonomous region of SPAIN, in the north-east, centring on BARCELONA. (Pop. 5 958 000)

Catania A major port and the second largest city in SICILY. (Pop. 378 500)

Catskill Mountains A range of mountains in NEW YORK State, U.S.A., famed for their scenic beauty. The highest peak is Slide Mountain (1281 m/4204 ft).

Caucasus (Kavkaz) The region between the BLACK SEA and the CASPIAN SEA in the U.S.S.R.

Cauvery *see* Kaveri.

Cavan A county in the north of the Republic of IRELAND, part of the ancient province of ULSTER; Cavan is also the name of the county town. (1890 sq km/730 sq miles; pop. county 53 900)

Caveri *see* Kaveri.

Cawnpore *see* Kanpur.

Cayenne The capital of GUYANE. (Pop. 38 000)

Cayman Islands A group of three islands in the

CARIBBEAN SEA which form a British Crown colony. The capital is George Town, on Grand Cayman. (260 sq km/100 sq miles; pop. 19 100)

Cebu One of islands in the central PHILIPPINES, forming part of the VISAYAN group; also the name of its capital city. (5088 sq km/1964 sq miles; pop. island 2 092 000/city 490 231)

Celebes *see* Sulawesi.

Celebes Sea A sea between the islands of eastern INDONESIA and the PHILIPINNES.

Central African Republic A landlocked republic in the heart of central AFRICA. Poverty-stricken and tragically ruled since it gained independence from FRANCE in 1960, the country exports little besides some animal produce and timber (from its forests in the south). French is the official language; the capital is BANGUI. (622 984 sq km/240 535 sq miles; pop. 2 740 000; cur. CFA franc = 100 centimes)

Central Region A local government area of SCOTLAND formed in 1975 out of the old counties of Clacmannanshire and parts of Perthshire and Stirlingshire. (2590 sq km/1000 sq miles; pop. 273 000)

Cephalonia *see* Ionian Islands.

Ceram *see* Seram.

Ceské Budejovice (Budweiss) A historic town in the south of BOHEMIA, CZECHOSLOVAKIA, famous for its Budvar beer. (Pop. 92 800)

Ceuta An Spanish enclave in northern MOROCCO administered by SPAIN. (Pop. 80 000)

Cévennes The name given to the southern part of the MASSIF CENTRAL in FRANCE.

Ceylon *see* Sri Lanka.

Chad A republic in northern central AFRICA which became independent of French rule in 1960. Much of the country is desert, but Lake CHAD, lying to the west, provides some irrigation. Exports are minimal, and civil conflict has worsened the fragile economy. French and Arabic are spoken, and the capital is NDJAMENA. (1 284 000 sq km/496 000 sq miles; pop. 5 380 000; cur. CFA franc = 100 centimes)

Chad, Lake A large lake in western CHAD, on the border with NIGER and NIGERIA. (26 000 sq km/ 19 040 sq miles)

Chamonix A winter sports resort in FRANCE, just to the north of Mont BLANC. (Pop. 11 000)

Champagne A region of north-eastern FRANCE famous for the sparking wine called champagne. It now forms part of the administrative region called Champagne-Ardennes.

Chandigarh A modern city 230 km (143 miles) north of DELHI, INDIA, planned by the French architect Le Corbusier (1887–1965). (Pop. 422 800)

Chang Jiang (Yangtze) The world's third longest river. It rises in TIBET and flows across central CHINA into the East China Sea. (Length 6380 km/3965 miles)

Changchun The capital of JILIN province, CHINA. (Pop. 1 604 000)

Chang-hua A historic city situated near the west coast of TAIWAN. (Pop. 1 206 400)

Changsha The capital of HUNAN province, CHINA. (Pop. 2 638 000)

Channel Islands A group of islands in the ENGLISH

CHANNEL, close to the coast of FRANCE, which are British Crown dependencies. The main islands are JERSEY and GUERNSEY, but the group also includes the smaller inhabited islands of Alderney, Sark and Herm. (Pop. 134 700)

Chao Phrya, River A river running from north to south down the west side of THAILAND and through its capital, BANGKOK. (Length 100 km/620 miles)

Chapala, Lake The largest lake in MEXICO, near GUADALAJARA. (2460 sq km/950 sq miles)

Charleroi A industrial city in central BELGIUM. (Pop. 213 000)

Charleston 1 The state capital of WEST VIRGINIA, U.S.A. (Pop. city 59 400/metropolitan area 267 000). **2** An old port on the ATLANTIC coast of SOUTH CAROLINA, U.S.A. (Pop. city 67 100/metropolitan area 472 500)

Charlotte Amalie The capital of the U.S. VIRGIN ISLANDS, on St Thomas. (Pop. 11 800)

Charlottetown A port and the provincial capital of PRINCE EDWARD ISLAND, CANADA. (Pop. 15 300)

Chartres A market town, capital of the department of Eure-et-Loir, in northern FRANCE, 80 km (50 miles) west of PARIS. It is famous for its early 13th-century cathedral, with original stained-glass windows. (Pop. 80 340)

Chattanooga A industrial city and railway town in TENNESSEE, U.S.A. (Pop. city 164 400/metropolitan area 422 500)

Chechen-Ingush Republic One of the 16 autonomous republics of the RUSSIAN FEDERATION. (19 300 sq km/ 7450 sq miles; pop. 1 204 000)

Cheju Do An island belonging to SOUTH KOREA, lying some 90 km (56 miles) off its southern tip, and dominated by the sacred volcano, Mount Halla (1950 m/ 6398 ft) (1828 sq km/706 sq miles; pop. 463 000)

Chelyabinsk An industrial city in central RUSSIA. (Pop. 1 086 000)

Chemnitz An industrial city in south-east GERMANY, named Karl-Marx-Stadt during the period of Communist rule in East Germany (until 1990). (Pop. 319 000)

Chengdu The capital of SICHUAN province, CHINA. (Pop. 2 470 000)

Chenstokhov *see* Czestochowa

Chernobyl' A city about 90 km (55 miles) north of KIEV, in the UKRAINE. In April 1986 one of the reactors in its nuclear power station exploded, causing the world's worst nuclear accident.

Chesapeake Bay An inlet, 314 km (195 miles) long, on the east coast of the U.S.A., shared by the states of VIRGINIA and MARYLAND.

Cheshire A county in north-west ENGLAND; the county town is Chester. (2322 sq km/897 sq miles; pop. 933 000)

Cheviot Hills A range of hills, 60 km (37 miles) long, which line the border between SCOTLAND and the county of NORTHUMBERLAND in ENGLAND.

Cheyenne The state capital of WYOMING, U.S.A. (Pop. 50 900)

Chiang Mai *see* Chieng Mai.

Chianti The wine-making region of central TUSCANY, ITALY.

Chiba A large industrial city on HONSHU island, JAPAN. (Pop. 788 900)

Chicago The largest city on the state of ILLINOIS, and the third largest city in the U.S.A. (after NEW YORK and LOS ANGELES). (Pop. city 2 992 500/metropolitan area 8 035 000)

Chichén Itzá A village in YUCATAN, MEXICO, which is the site of a complex of major ruins of the Mayans and Toltecs.

Chieng Mai The second largest city in THAILAND, in the north-west of the country, famous for its temples and the crafts produced in the surrounding villages. (Pop. 200 700)

Chihuahua A city in northern central MEXICO, and the name of the surrounding province, of which it is the capital. (Pop. city 410 000)

Chile A republic of South AMERICA which consists of a long, ribbon-like strip of land bordering the PACIFIC OCEAN. The landscape is dominated by the ANDES to the east, the ATCAMA DESERT to the north, and desolate wastelands to the south; the remainder is a fertile region in the centre. Exports include copper, iron and nitrates. The principal language is Spanish. The capital is SANTIAGO. (756 945 sq km/292 256 sq miles; pop. 12 060 000; cur. Peso = 1000 escudos)

Chiltern Hills A range of hills to the north-west of LONDON, ENGLAND, rising to 260 m (850 ft)

Chi-lung *see* Keelung

China A vast republic in East ASIA and the most populous in the world. It has a formidable history that predates most Western civilizations. To the west lie the Tibetan plateaux; to the north, arid wastelands; and to the south-east, fertile plains. Largely self-sufficient by dint of economic programmes organized centrally by the Communist government, China exports fabrics, coal and machinery. Many languages are spoken, including the official language, Mandarin. The capital is BEIJING. (9 596 961 sq km/3 705 387 sq miles; pop. 1 090 000 000; cur. Yuan = 100 fen)

China Sea A part of the PACIFIC OCEAN, off the east coast of CHINA.

Chindwin, River A river in BURMA, flowing parallel to the north west border before joining the IRRAWADDY River in the centre of the country. (Length 1130 km/ 700 miles)

Chios (Khios) An island in the AEGIAN SEA, belonging to GREECE but lying only 8 km (5 miles) from the coast of TURKEY. It is said to have been the home of the poet Homer (*c.* 800 BC). (904 sq km/349 sq miles; pop. 49 900)

Chişinău *see* Kishinev.

Chittagong The main port of BANGLADESH and its second largest city. (Pop. 1 392 000)

Cholula A town in south-east MEXICO famous for its extensive Toltec ruins dating from 500 BC. (Pop. 160 000)

Chongqing (Chungking) An industrial city on the CHANG JIANG river, CHINA, and the largest city in SICHUAN province. (Pop. 2 650 000)

Chonju An historic city in the south-west of SOUTH KOREA. (Pop. 367 100)

Chonnam *see* Kwangju.

Christchurch The largest city on South Island, NEW ZEALAND. (Pop. 300 000)

Christmas Island 1 An island in the eastern INDIAN OCEAN, 400 km (250 miles) to the south of JAVA, administered by AUSTRALIA since 1958. (142 sq km/ 55 sq miles; pop. 3500). **2** (Kiritimati) The PACIFIC OCEAN's largest coral atoll, situated at the north-eastern end of the KIRIBATI group. (432 sq km/ 167 sq miles; pop. 1300)

Chubu Sangaku A national park in central HONSHU island which contains two of the highest mountains in JAPAN, Mount Hotaka (3190 m/10 466 ft) and Mount Yari (3180 m/10 434 ft)

Chungking *see* Chongqing.

Churchill, River A river which flows into the HUDSON BAY at the port of Churchill after a journey through SASKATCHEWAN and MANITOBA. (Length 1600 km/ 993 miles)

Chuvash Republic One of the 17 autonomous republics of the RUSSIAN FEDERATION. (18 300 sq km/7050 sq miles; pop. 1 314 000)

Cincinnati A city in the south-west of the state of OHIO, U.S.A., on the OHIO RIVER. (Pop. city 370 500/metropolitan area 1 673 500)

C.I.S. *see* Commonwealth of Independent States.

Ciskei A Bantu homeland for the Xhosa people declared independent by the SOUTH AFRICA in 1981. (8300 sq km/3205 sq miles; pop. 728 400)

Citaltépetl A volcanic peak to the south-east of MEXICO CITY, and at 5747 m (18 855 ft) the highest point in MEXICO.

Clare A county on the west coast of IRELAND; the county town is Ennis. (3188 sq km/1230 sq miles; pop. 87 500)

Clermont-Ferrand A city in the AUVERGNE region of central FRANCE. (Pop. 262 175)

Cleveland 1 A county of north-east ENGLAND created in 1974 out of Durham and Yorkshire to administer the industrial region along the River Tees, known as Teeside (583 sq km/225 sq miles; pop. 565 000). **2** A port and industrial city on the southern side of Lake ERIE, in OHIO, U.S.A. (Pop. city 546 500/metropolitan area 1 867 000)

Cluj-Napoca A city of ancient origins in central ROMANIA. (Pop. 260 000)

Clwyd A county in north-east WALES created in 1974 out of the county of Flintshire and parts of Merionethshire and Denbighshire. (2425 sq km/ 936 sq miles; pop. 395 000)

Clyde, River A river of the STRATHCLYDE region in south-west SCOTLAND which flows north west to form an estuary 100 km (60 miles) long, called the Firth of Clyde, with GLASGOW at its head. (Length 170 km/ 105 miles)

Coast Ranges A range of mountains lining the western coast of the U.S.A., stetching 1600 km (1000 miles) from the borders with CANADA to LOS ANGELES. The highest point is in the San Jacinto Mountains (3301 m/ 10 831 ft)

Cobh A town and port in Cork Harbour on the south coast of IRELAND, some 10 km (6 miles) from the city of CORK. (Pop. 6600)

Cochin A port on the south-western tip of India. (Pop. 551 600)
Cochin China The name given to the region around the MEKONG delta during the French occupation of VIETNAM.
Cockburn Town The capital of TURKS AND CAICOS. (Pop. 3200)
Cocos Islands (Keeling Islands) A cluster of 28 small coral islands in the eastern INDIAN OCEAN, equidistant from SUMATRA and AUSTRALIA, and administered by Australia since 1955. (14 sq km/6 sq miles; pop. 700)
Cod, Cape A narrow, low-lying peninsula of sand-dunes and marshland on the coast of MASSACHUSETTS, U.S.A., where the Pilgrim Fathers landed in 1620.
Cologne (Köln) A city and industrial centre on the River RHINE, GERMANY. (Pop. 932 400)
Colombia A republic in north-west South AMERICA with coasts on the PACIFIC OCEAN and CARIBBEAN SEA. Coastal plains to the west are separated from the grasslands to the east by the ANDES. Exports include coffee and sugar, but there is also a powerful black economy based on exports of illegal drugs. Spanish is the principal language and the capital is BOGOTA. (1 138 914 sq km/456 535 sq miles; pop. 30 125 000; cur. Peso = 100 centavos)
Colombo A major port and the capital of SRI LANKA. (Pop. 600 000)
Colorado An inland state of central western U.S.A.; the state capital is DENVER. (270 000 sq km/104 247 sq miles; pop. 3 231 000)
Colorado, River A river which rises in the ROCKY

MOUNTAINS in the state of COLORADO, U.S.A., and flows south-west to the Gulf of CALIFORNIA, forming the GRAND CANYON on its way. (Length 2330 km/ 1450 miles)

Colorado Springs A spa and resort city in the state of COLORADO, U.S.A. (Pop. city 247 700/metropolitan area 349 100)

Columbia The state capital of SOUTH CAROLINA. (Pop. city 98 600/metropolitan area 433 200)

Columbia, District of *see* Washington D.C.

Columbia, River A river which flows northwards from its source in BRITISH COLUMBIA, CANADA, before turning south into WASHINGTON STATE, U.S.A. and entering the PACIFIC at PORTLAND, OREGON. (Length 1950 km/1210 miles)

Columbus The state capital of OHIO, U.S.A. (Pop. city 566 100/metropolitan area 1 279 000)

Commonwealth of Independent States (C.I.S.) An organization created in 1991 to represent the common interests of the independent states of the former U.S.S.R. The name is a translation of *Sodruzhestvo Nezavisimikh Gosudarstv*. There are eleven member states: ARMENIA, AZERBAIDZHJAN, BELORUSSIA, KAZAKHSTAN, KIRGHIZIA, MOLDAVIA, The RUSSIAN FEDERATION, TADZHIKISTAN, TURKMENISTAN, UKRAINE, and UZBEKISTAN.

Comorin, Cape The southern tip of INDIA.

Comoros A republic comprising three volcanic islands in the INDIAN OCEAN off the north-west coast of MADAGASCAR. Formerly a French territory, it became independent in 1976. Exports include vanilla and copra. French and Arabic are the main languages. The capital is MORONI. (1862 sq km/719 sq miles; pop. 422 000; cur. CFA franc = 100 centimes)

Conakry The capital of GUINEA, a port partly located on the island of Tumbo. (Pop. 763 000)

Concord The state capital of NEW HAMPSHIRE, U.S.A. (Pop. 30 900)

Congo A republic in West AFRICA with a small coastline on the Gulf of GUINEA. Formerly a part of French Equatorial Africa, it gained independence in 1960. The country is largely forested, and it exports timber, oil, coffee and cocoa. French is the official language, and the capital is BRAZZAVILLE. (342 000 sq km/ 132 000 sq miles; pop. 1 850 000; cur. CFA franc = 100 centimes)

Congo, River *see* Zaire, River.

Connaught (Connacht) One of the four old provinces into which Ireland was divided.

Connecticut A state on the north-eastern seaboard of the U.S.A., in NEW ENGLAND; the capital is HARTFORD. (12 973 sq km/5009 sq miles; pop. 3 174 000)

Connemara A famously beautiful part of County GALWAY on the west coast of IRELAND centring upon the distinctive peaks of the Twelve Bens.

Constanta A major port on the BLACK SEA coast of ROMANIA. (Pop. 283 600)

Constantine (Qacentina) An ancient walled city in the north-eastern corner of ALGERIA. (Pop. 430 500)

Constantinople *see* Istanbul.

Cook, Mount The highest mountain in NEW ZEALAND, on South Island. (3765 m/12 352 ft)

Cook Islands A group of 15 islands in the South PACIFIC, independent since 1965 but associated with NEW ZEALAND. The capital is Avarua. (240 sq km/ 93 sq miles; pop. 17 700; cur. Cook Islands dollar/ New Zealand dollar = 100 cents)

Cook Strait The strait that separates North Island and South Island of NEW ZEALAND, 26 km (16 miles) across at its widest point.

Cooper Creek A river flowing into Lake EYRE in SOUTH AUSTRALIA from its source in central QUEENSLAND. The upper stretch is known as the Barcoo River. (Length 1420 km/800 miles)

Copacabana A famous beachside suburb of RIO DE JANEIRO, BRAZIL.

Copán A village in HONDURAS which is the site of a great Mayan city which flourished between AD 450 and 800 before being abandoned.

Copenhagen (København) A port and the capital of DENMARK, located on the islands of ZEALAND and AMAGER. (Pop. 641 900)

Coral Sea A part of the PACIFIC OCEAN, off the north-east coast of AUSTRALIA.

Cordoba (Cordova) 1 A city in southern Spain, famous for its cathedral which was built originally as a mosque; also the name of the surrounding province. (Pop. city 284 700) **2** The second city of ARGENTINA, and the name of the surrounding province. (Pop. city 969 000)

Corfu (Kérkira) The most northerly of the IONIAN ISLANDS, in western GREECE; the capital is also called Corfu. (592 sq km/229 sq miles; pop. 97 100)

Corinth (Korinthos) A town in the PELOPONNESE in western GREECE, built near the Corinth Ship Canal. (Pop. 22 700)

Cork The second largest city in the Republic of IRELAND, at the head of a large natural harbour which cuts into the southern coast. Also the name of the county of which it is the county town. (County 7459 sq km/2880 sq miles; pop. county 402 400; pop. city 136 300)

Cornwall The county occupying the south western tip of ENGLAND; the county town is Truro. (3546 sq km/1369 sq miles; pop. 432 000)

Coromandel Coast The coast of south-eastern INDIA around MADRAS.

Coromandel Peninsula The central peninsula reaching northwards from North Island, NEW ZEALAND.

Corpus Christi A port in TEXAS on the Gulf of MEXICO. (Pop. city 258 100/metropolitan area 361 300)

Corsica (Corse) A large island in the MEDITERRANEAN SEA lying to the north of SARDINIA, governed by FRANCE. (8680 sq km/3350 sq miles; pop. 240 000)

Corunna (La Coruña) A port and manufacturing town in north-west Spain, and also the name of the surrounding province. (Pop. town 232 400)

Costa Brava A strip of coastline to the north-east of BARCELONA in SPAIN, famous for its beaches and its popular resorts.

Costa Rica A republic in Central AMERICA with coasts on the CARIBBEAN SEA and PACIFIC OCEAN. It is a mountainous country, with extensive forests. Exports include coffee and bananas. Spanish is the main language and the capital is SAN JOSE. (50 700 sq km/ 19 575 sq miles; pop. 2 720 000; cur. Colon = 100 centimos)

Costa Smeralda The 'emerald coast' on the north-east side of the MEDITERRANEAN island of SARDINIA, famed for its watersports and its up-market resorts.

Côte d'Azur The coast of south-east FRANCE, famous for its beaches and resorts such as ST TROPEZ, CANNES and NICE.

Côte d'Ivoire A republic in West AFRICA with a coast on the Gulf of GUINEA. Formerly referred to in English as the Ivory Coast, it was a French protectorate and became independent in 1960. Humid coastal plains rise to grasslands in the north. Cocoa, coffee, cotton and timber are the main exports. French is the principal language and YAMOUSSOUKRO is the capital. (322 463 sq km/124 503 sq miles; pop. 10 460 000; cur. CFA franc =100 centimes)

Cotonou A port and the main business centre of BENIN. (Pop. 488 000)

Cotswold Hills A range of hills in western central ENGLAND, lying to the east of the River SEVERN.

Coventry An industrial city in the West MIDLANDS of ENGLAND. (Pop. 315 900)

Cracow (Krakow) The third largest city in POLAND, and the capital during medieval times. (Pop. 520 700)

Craiova An industrial city in south-west ROMANIA. (Pop. 228 000)

Cremona A town on the River PO in central northern ITALY, famous for its violins, especially those of Antonio Stadivari (?1644–1737). (Pop. 80 800)

Crete (Kriti) The largest and most southerly of the islands of GREECE, with important ruins of the Minoan civilization at KNOSSOS. The capital is HERAKLION. (8366 sq km/3229 sq miles; pop. 502 100)

Crimea (Krym) A diamond-shaped peninsula jutting out into the northern part of the BLACK SEA and part of the UKRAINE. (25 900 sq km/10 000 sq miles; pop. 2 309 000)

Croatia (Hrvatska) A former republic of YUGOSLAVIA which became an independent state in 1991. The capital is ZAGREB. (56 538 sq km/21 824 sq miles; pop. 4 601 500)

Crozet Islands A group of some 20 islands and islets in the SOUTHERN OCEAN, forming part of the FRENCH SOUTHERN AND ANTARCTIC TERRITORIES. (300 sq km/ 116 sq miles)

Cuango, River *see* Kwango, River.

Cuba A republic in the CARIBBEAN which has been ruled as a Communist state since 1960. Cuba is largest island of the WEST INDIES; it is a fertile country, with mountains rising to the south-east. Sugar, tobacco (cigars) and minerals are the main exports. Spanish is the official language and the capital is HAVANA. (114 524 sq km/44 218 sq miles; pop. 10 215 000; cur. Peso = 100 centavos)

Cubango, River *see* Kavango, River.

Cúcuta A city in northern COLOMBIA on the border with VENEZUELA. (Pop. 516 000)

Cuenca A city in southern ECUADOR, founded by the Spanish in 1557, but also the site of a number of important Inca ruins. (Pop. 272 500)

Cuernavaca An old resort town in the mountains 80 km (50 miles) to the south of MEXICO CITY. (Pop. 557 000)

Culloden An area of moorland about 8 km (5 miles) to the east of INVERNESS in SCOTLAND, the scene of a bloody battle in 1746 in which the forces of the Young Pretender, Bonnie Prince Charlie, were defeated by the English under the Duke of Cumberland.

Cumberland *see* Cumbria.

Cumbria A county in north-west ENGLAND, created in 1974 from the old counties of Cumberland, Westmoreland and a part of LANCASHIRE. (6809 sq km/ 2629 sq miles; pop. 483 000)

Curaçao An island in the CARIBBEAN lying just off the coast of VENEZUELA, but a part of the NETHERLANDS ANTILLES. (444 sq km/171 sq miles; pop. 170 000)

Curitaba An industrial city in southern BRAZIL. (Pop. 1 442 000)

Cuzco A city set in the ANDES mountains in PERU, and the name of the surrounding province. It was a centre of the Inca empire, and there are numerous Inca remains in the region, including MACHU PICCHU. (Pop. city 184 600)

Cyclades (Kikládhes) A group of some 220 islands in the middle of the AEGIAN SEA and belonging to GREECE. The best known are Tinos, Andros, Milos, Mikonos, DELOS, Naxos, Paros, Kithnos, Serifos, Ios and Síros. (Pop. 88 400)

Cyprus An island in the eastern MEDITERRANEAN which was a British colony until 1960, when it became an independent republic. In 1974 TURKEY invaded the island, which effectively became divided in two, with the north-eastern part coming under Turkish control. The land is fertile and there are high mountains to the south-west. Tourism is a major industry, and fruit and vegetables are among the exports. Greek, Turkish and English are the principal languages. The capital is NICOSIA. (9251 sq km/3572 sq miles; pop. 678 000; cur. Cyprus pound = 100 cents)

Czechoslovakia A landlocked republic in central EUROPE bordering the UKRAINE, HUNGARY, AUSTRIA, GERMANY and POLAND. In 1989 the ruling Communists lost control of the country and were replaced by democratic government. Mountains lie to the west and east with plains in the centre. Exports include machinery, chemicals and coal. Czech, Slovak and Hungarian are the main languages. The capital is PRAGUE. (127 889 sq km/49 378 sq miles; pop. 15 550 000; cur. Koruna (crown) = 100 halers)

Częstochowa (Chenstokhov) An industrial city in southern POLAND. Its Jasna Gora Monastery is a national shrine and pilgimage centre. (Pop. 244 100)

D

Dacca *see* Dhaka.

Dachau A market town in BAVARIA, GERMANY, and the site of the first concentration camp to be built by the Nazis, in 1935. (Pop. 35 000)

Daejeon *see* Taejon.

Dagestan An autonomous republic of the RUSSIAN

FEDERATION lying to the west of the CASPIAN SEA. The capital is MAKHACHKALA. (50 300 sq km/19 400 sq miles; pop. 709 000)

Dakar The main port and capital of SENEGAL. (Pop. 1 000 000).

Dakota *see* North Dakota; South Dakota.

Dal, Lake The most famous of the lakes of KASHMIR, INDIA, by SRINAGAR.

Dallas A city in north-east TEXAS, U.S.A. (Pop. city 974 200/metropolitan area 2 203 700)

Dalmatia (Dalmacija) The coast of CROATIA, on the ADRIATIC SEA. The main islands of the coast are Krk, Rab, Lošinj, Brac, Hvar, Korcula and Mljet. The principal tourist centre is DUBROVNIK.

Damascus The capital of SYRIA, an oasis town. (Pop. 1 042 000)

Damavand, Mount An extinct volcano, and the highest peak in the ELBURZ MOUNTAINS, IRAN. (5670 m/ 18 600 ft)

Danube, River The longest river in Western Europe, rising in the BLACK FOREST in GERMANY, and passing through AUSTRIA, CZECHOSLAVAKIA, HUNGARY and YUGOSLAVIA, forming much of the border between BULGARIA and ROMANIA before turning north and forming a delta on the BLACK SEA. (Length 2850 km/ 1770 miles)

Danzig *see* Gdansk.

Dar el Beida *see* Casablanca.

Dar es Salaam The former capital of TANZANIA and still its largest town. (Pop. 757 346)

Dardanelles The narrow ribbon of water, some 80 km

(50 miles) long, in TURKEY which connects the AEGEAN SEA to the Sea of MARMARA (and from thence the BLACK SEA). GALLIPOLI is on the peninsula to the north. The Dardanelles were known as the Hellespont to the ancient Greeks.

Darién The eastern province of PANAMA, a narrow neck of land on the border with COLOMBIA, and the only gap in the Pan-American Highway, which otherwise runs from ALASKA to CHILE.

Darjiling (Darjeeling) A town in WEST BENGAL, INDIA near the border with NEPAL, famous for its tea. (Pop. 282 200)

Darling, River A river flowing from southern QUEENSLAND through NEW SOUTH WALES in AUSTRALIA before converging with the MURRAY RIVER. (Length 3057 km/ 1900 miles)

Dartmoor An area of remote moorland in the county of DEVON, ENGLAND. (945 sq km/365 sq miles)

Darwin The capital of the NORTHERN TERRITORY, AUSTRALIA. (Pop. 50 000)

Datong (Tatung) An industrial city in SHANXI province, CHINA. (Pop. 800 000)

Davao A city in the southern part of the island of MINDANAO, PHILIPPINES, and now that country's second largest city. It is also the name of the surrounding region. (Pop. city 540 000)

Davis Strait The broad strait, some 290 km (180 miles) across at its narrowest, separating BAFFIN ISLAND in CANADA and GREENLAND.

Dayr az Zawr The largest town in eastern SYRIA, on the River EUPHRATES. (Pop. 332 000)

Dead Sea A small sea on the border between ISRAEL and JORDAN into which the River JORDAN flows and does not exit. It is one of the lowest places on Earth (396 m/1299 ft below normal sea level) and the body of water with the world's highest salt content. (1049 sq km/395 sq miles)

Death Valley A low-lying area of desert and salt beds in eastern CALIFORNIA, U.S.A.

Debrecen An agricultural and industrial centre in eastern HUNGARY, which has grown up around the original medieval town. (Pop. 207 000)

Deccan The broad, triangular peninsula which forms much of the southern part of INDIA.

Dehra Dun A town in northern INDIA, in the foothills of the HIMALAYAS. It is famous as the supposed home of the Hindu god SHIVA, and also for the military academy established by the British in the 1930s. (Pop. 293 000)

Delaware A state on the east coast of the U.S.A., and the second smallest in the U.S.A. after RHODE ISLAND. The capital is DOVER. (5328 sq km/2057 sq miles; pop. 622 000)

Delft A small city in central western NETHERLANDS, famous since the 16th century for its distinctive blue and white pottery. (Pop. 86 300)

Delhi The capital of INDIA, in the north of the country, on the YAMUNA River. (Pop. 5 729 300)

Delos The smallest of the islands in the CYCLADES group, GREECE, said to be the birthplace of the god Apollo.

Delphi The ruins of the Temple of Apollo on Mount

Parnassus, 166 km/102 miles north-west of ATHENS, GREECE. It was the seat of the most important oracle of ancient Greece.

Demerara, River A river in central GUYANA which flows through the capital, GEORGETOWN. It has given its name to the type of brown sugar which is grown in the region. (Length 320 km/200 miles)

Den Haag *see* Hague, The.

Denbighshire *see* Clwyd; Gwynedd.

Denmark A kingdom in northern EUROPE occupying the JUTLAND peninsula and a number of islands between the BALTIC and NORTH SEA. The land is generally flat and used for farming, but there are a number of important industries. A member of the European Community, Denmark exports meat, dairy products and machinery. The capital is COPENHAGEN. (43 000 sq km/16 629 sq miles; pop. 5 100 000; cur. Krone = 100 øre)

Denmark Strait The arm of the North ATLANTIC OCEAN which separates ICELAND from GREENLAND, some 290 km (181 miles) away.

Denpasar The capital of the island of BALI, INDONESIA. (Pop. 82 140)

Denver The state capital of COLORADO, U.S.A. (Pop. city 504 600/metropolitan area 1 582 500)

Derby A city of Saxon and Danish origins in the county of DERBYSHIRE, ENGLAND. (Pop. 215 000)

Derbyshire A county in north central ENGLAND; the county town is MATLOCK. (2631 sq km/1016 sq miles; pop. 911 000)

Derry *see* Londonderry.

Des Moines The state capital of IOWA, U.S.A. (Pop. city 190 800/metropolitan area 377 100)

Detroit A major industrial city and GREAT LAKE port in the state of MICHIGAN, U.S.A. (Pop. city 1 089 000/ metropolitan area 4 315 800)

Devon A county in south-west England; the country town is EXETER. (6715 sq km/2593 sq miles; pop. 980 000)

Dhahran A commercial centre with an important international airport in eastern SAUDI ARABIA. It is also a centre for petroleum extraction business. (Pop. 25 000)

Dhaka (Dacca) The capital of BANGLADESH, on the delta of the Rivers GANGES and BRAHMAPUTRA. (Pop. 3 458 600)

Dhanbad A city in north-east India and a centre for the coal-mining industry of the Damodar Valley. (Pop. 433 100)

Dhaulagiri, Mount A mountain peak of the Great HIMALAYAS in NEPAL. (8172 m/26 810 ft)

Dhodhekanisos *see* Dodecanese.

Dien Bien Phu A small town in north-west VIETNAM where the French army was decisively defeated by the Communist and Nationalist Vietminh forces in 1954, effectively forcing the French to leave Vietnam.

Dijon The historic capital of the Bourgogne region (BURGUNDY) in western central FRANCE, famous in particular for its mustard. (Pop. 221 900)

Diyarbakir A city on the River TIGRIS in south-eastern TURKEY, and the name of the province of which it is the capital. (Pop. city 305 300)

Djerba *see* Jerba.

Djibouti A republic in East AFRICA with a coast on the Gulf of ADEN (a branch of the ARABIAN SEA). Formerly an French overseas territory, it became independent in 1977. Most of the land is desert and there are few exports. Arabic and French are the official languages. The capital (pop.200 000) is also called Djibouti. (23 200 sq km/9000 sq miles; pop. 305 000; cur. Djibouti franc = 100 centimes).

Dnepr, River *see* Dnieper, River.

Dnepropetrovsk An industrial and agricultural city on the River DNIEPER in the UKRAINE. It was formerly (1787–96 and 1802–1920) known as Ekaterinoslav. (Pop. 1 140 000)

Dnestr, River *see* Dniester, River.

Dnieper (Dnepr), River The third longest river in Europe after the VOLGA and the DANUBE, flowing south through RUSSIA and the UKRAINE to the BLACK SEA via KIEV. (Length 2285 km/ 1420 miles)

Dniester (Dnestr), River A river flowing through the UKRAINE and MOLDAVIA to the BLACK SEA. (Length 1411 km/877 miles)

Dodecanese A group of twelve islands belonging the GREECE in the eastern AEGEAN SEA near the coast of TURKEY. They are scattered between Samos in the north and Karpathos in the south and include Patmos, Kalimnos, Kos and RHODES, the largest in the group. They are also called the Southern Sporades. (Pop. 145 000)

Dodoma The capital (since 1975) of TANZANIA, in the centre of the country. (Pop. 45 700)

Doha (Ad Dawhah) The capital of QATAR. (Pop. 180 000)

Dolomites A range of mountains in north-eastern ITALY, near the border with AUSTRIA. The highest point is Mount Marmolada (3342 m/10 964 ft)

Dominica A republic in the WINDWARD ISLANDS of the CARIBBEAN which was a British colony until it gained independence in 1978 and joined the Commonwealth. It comprises a mountainous volcanic island which is thickly forested. Exports include bananas and copra. English is the official language and the capital is ROSEAU. (751 sq km/290 sq miles; pop. 74 000; cur. East Caribbean Dollar = 100 cents)

Dominican Republic A republic occupying the eastern part of the island of HISPANIOLA in the WEST INDIES. The landscape is mountainous, with some fertile plains. Exports include sugar, gold and other metals, and coffee. Spanish is the official language, and the capital is SANTO DOMINGO. (48 442 sq km/18 703 sq miles; pop. 6 766 000; cur. Peso = 100 centavos)

Don, River A river flowing southwards into the SEA OF AZOV from its source to the south of MOSCOW. (Length 1870 km/1165 miles)

Donbass *see* Donets Basin.

Donegal The northernmost county of the Republic of IRELAND, on the west coast. The county town is also called Donegal. (Pop. county 125 100)

Donets Basin (Donbass) A coalmining region and major industrial area in the eastern UKRAINE.

Donetsk The main industrial centre of the DONETS BASIN. (Pop. 1 064 000)

Dongbei (Manchuria) The north-eastern region of CHINA, covering part of the NEI MONGOL AUTONOMOUS REGION and the three provinces, HEILONGJIANG, JILIN and LIAONING. (1 300 000 sq km/502 000 sq miles; pop. 87 962 000)

Dordogne, River A river of south-western FRANCE which rises in the MASSIF CENTRAL and flows west to the GIRONDE estuary. (Length 475 km/ 295 miles)

Dordrecht A river port and industrial city of medieval origin 19 km (12 miles) south-east of ROTTERDAM in the NETHERLANDS. (Pop. 199 200)

Dorset A county of south-west ENGLAND; the county town is Dorchester. (2654 sq km/1025 sq miles; pop. 618 000)

Dortmund A major city in the industrial RUHR region of western GERMANY. (Pop. 620 000)

Douala The main port of CAMEROON, on the Gulf of GUINEA. (Pop. 800 000)

Douro (Duero), River A river flowing west from its source in northern central SPAIN and across northern PORTUGAL to the ATLANTIC OCEAN near OPORTO. (Length 895 km/555 miles)

Dover 1 A port in the county of KENT, ENGLAND overlooking the ENGLISH CHANNEL at its narrowest point, opposite CALAIS, FRANCE. (Pop. 33 000). **2** The state capital of DELAWARE, U.S.A. (Pop. 22 500)

Dover, Strait of The stretch of water separating ENGLAND and FRANCE, where the ENGLISH CHANNEL meets the NORTH SEA. The ports of DOVER and CALAIS are situated on either side of its narrowest point, 34 km (21 miles) across.

Down A county of NORTHERN IRELAND, on the east coast; the county town is Downpatrick. (2448 sq km/ 945 sq miles; pop. 362 100)
Drake Passage The broad strait, some 640 km (400 miles) wide, which separates Cape HORN on the southern tip of SOUTH AMERICA and the ANTARCTIC.
Drakensberg Mountains A range of mountains which stretch 1125 km (700 miles) across LESOTHO and neighbouring regions of SOUTH AFRICA. The highest point is Thabana Ntlenya (3482 m/11424 ft).
Drava (Drau), River A river flowing from eastern AUSTRIA to YUGOSLAVIA, where it forms much of the border with HUNGARY before joining the DANUBE. (Length 718 km/447 miles)
Dresden A historic city on the River ELBE in the south of eastern GERMANY. Formerly the capital of SAXONY, it was noted particularly for its fine porcelain. (Pop. 522 500)
Duarte, Pico A mountain peak in central DOMINICAN REPUBLIC which is the highest point in the WEST INDIES. (3175 m/10 417 ft)
Dubai (Dubayy) The second largest of the UNITED ARAB EMIRATES, at the eastern end of the GULF. Most of the population lives in the capital, also called Dubai. (3900 sq km/1506 sq miles; pop. emirate 296 000/city 265 700)
Dublin (Baile Atha Cliath) The capital of the Republic of IRELAND, on the River LIFFEY, and also the name of the surrounding county. Its main port area is at Dun Laoghaire. (Pop. county 1 002 000/city 525 400)
Dubrovnik (Ragusa) A pretty medieval port on the

ADRIATIC coast of CROATIA, for long a popular tourist destination. (Pop. 31 200)

Duero, River *see* Douro, River.

Duisburg A major inland port situated at the confluence of the Rivers RHINE and RUHR in Germany. (Pop. 541 800)

Duluth A port and industrial centre on Lake SUPERIOR, in the state of MICHIGAN, U.S.A. (Pop. city 85 600/ metropolitan area 253 800)

Dumfries and Galloway A region of south-west SCOTLAND created out of the old counties of Dumfriesshire, Kirkudbrightshire and Wigtownshire. The regional capital is Dumfries. (6370 sq km/2459 sq miles; pop. 145 200)

Dun Laoghaire *see* Dublin.

Dunbartonshire *see* Strathclyde.

Dundee A port on the east coast of SCOTLAND, on the north side of the Firth of Tay, and the administrative centre of TAYSIDE region. (Pop. 180 000)

Dunfermline *see* Fife.

Dunkirk (Dunkerque) A port and industrial town in north-eastern France, close to the border with BELGIUM. It was virtually destroyed in 1940 when British, French and Belgian forces were trapped by the advancing German army, but were successfully evacuated to Britain in a fleet of small boats. (Pop. 196 600)

Durango A mineral-rich state in northern MEXICO, with a capital called (Victoria de) Durango. (Pop. state 1 200 000/city 209 000)

Durban A port on the east coast of SOUTH AFRICA, and

the largest city of the province of NATAL. (Pop. 960 800)

Durham A city of north-east England, and the name of the county of which it is the county town. (County 2436 sq km/940 sq miles; pop. county 607 000/city 26 000)

Dushanbe An industrial city and the capital of TADZHIKISTAN. (Pop. 539 000)

Düsseldorf A major commercial and industrial centre in the RUHR region of western Germany, situated on the River RHINE 34 km (21 miles) north of COLOGNE. (Pop. 579 800)

Dvina, River The name of two quite separate rivers. The West (Zapadnaya) Dvina flows from its source to the west of MOSCOW into the BALTIC SEA at RIGA in LATVIA. The North (Severnaya) Dvina flows through north-western RUSSIA to the WHITE SEA at ARCHANGEL. (Length: West Dvina 1020 km/635 miles; North Dvina 1320 km/820 miles)

Dwarka One of the seven holy cities of the Hindus, situated on the tip of the peninsula to the south of the Gulf of KUTCH, in north-west INDIA. It is said to be the capital of the god Krishna. (Pop. 21 400)

Dyfed A county in south-west WALES, created in 1974 out of the old counties of Cardiganshire, Carmarthenshire and Pembrokeshire. Carmarthen is the county town. (5765 sq km/2226 sq miles; pop. 377 000)

Dzungaria *see* Xinjiang Uygur Autonomous Region.

E

East Anglia An old Anglo-Saxon kingdom occupying the bulge of the east coast of ENGLAND between the THAMES estuary and The WASH, and now covered by the counties of NORFOLK, SUFFOLK and parts of CAMBRIDGESHIRE and ESSEX.

Easter Island (Isla de Pascua) A remote and tiny island in the South PACIFIC OCEAN annexed by CHILE in 1888. About 1000 years ago it was settled by Polynesians who set up over 600 huge stone statues of heads on the island. (120 sq km/46 sq miles; pop. 1300)

Ebro, River A river flowing across north-eastern SPAIN, from its source near the north coast to the MEDITERRANEAN SEA south of TARRAGONA. (Length 909 km/565 miles)

Ecuador A republic in north-western South AMERICA with a coast on the PACIFIC OCEAN. The Equator runs through the centre of the country (hence its name), and the ANDES cross it from north to south. To the west lie the coastal plains, and to the east tropical forests. Oil, coffee, bananas and other vegetable products are exported. Spanish is the principal language, and the capital is QUITO. (283 562 sq km/109 483 sq miles; pop. 9 120 000; cur. Sucre = 100 centavos)

Edinburgh The capital of SCOTLAND, a university city and commercial centre, on the Firth of Forth (the estuary of the Forth River). (Pop. 439 000)

Edmonton The capital of ALBERTA, CANADA. (Pop. 657 000)

Edo *see* Tokyo.

Edward (Rutanzige), Lake A lake in the GREAT RIFT VALLEY, on the border between UGANDA and ZAIRE. (2135 sq km/820 sq miles)

Egypt A republic in north-eastern AFRICA with coasts on the MEDITERRANEAN and RED SEAS. The Ancient Egyptians created one of the world's first major civilizations, dating back some 5000 years. Occupied by the British in 1882, Egypt became independent in 1922 and a republic in 1953. The country is almost entirely desert except for the fertile NILE valley and delta. Exports include cotton, vegetables and some oil, while the pyramids and other monuments built by the Ancient Egyptians form the basis of an active tourist industry. Arabic is the official language. The capital is CAIRO. (1 002 000 sq km/386 900 sq miles; pop. 49 560 000; cur. Egyptian pound = 100 piastres)

Eifel An upland area of western GERMANY between the MOSELLE River and the border with BELGIUM.

Eiger, The A mountain in southern central SWITZERLAND, renowned among climbers for its daunting north face. (3970 m/13025 ft)

Eilat *see* Elat.

Eindhoven An industrial city in the southern central part of the NETHERLANDS. (Pop. 194 600)

Eire *see* Ireland, Republic of.

Ekaterinburg An industrial city to the east of the URAL MOUNTAINS, RUSSIA. It was called Sverdlovsk from 1924 to 1992. (Pop. 1 288 000)

Ekaterinoslav *see* Dnepropetrovsk.

El Alamein A village on the Mediteranean coast of EGYPT, to the south-west of ALEXANDRIA, which gave its name to the battle fought between Allied troops under General Montgomery and German troops under General Rommel in 1942.

Elat (Eilat) A port and tourist resort in the very south of ISRAEL at the tip of the Gulf of AQABA, an arm of the RED SEA. (Pop. 18 800)

Elba An island lying about 10 km (6 miles) off the coast of TUSCANY, ITALY. (223 sq km/86 sq miles; pop. 28 400)

Elbe, River A largely navigable river flowing northwards from its source in CZECHOSLOVAKIA through GERMANY to HAMBURG, and then into the NORTH SEA. (Length 1160km/720 miles)

Elbrus, Mount The highest mountain in EUROPE, situated in the western CAUCASUS, GEORGIA. (5642 m/ 18 510 ft)

Elburz Mountains A range of mountains in northern IRAN, between TEHRAN and the CASPIAN SEA. The highest peak is the extinct volcano, DAMAVAND (5670 m/18 600 ft).

Eleuthera *see* Bahamas.

El Faiyum (Fayum) A large and fertile oasis to the west of the River NILE in EGYPT. (Pop. 167 080)

El Gezira A major irrigation scheme in SUDAN between the Blue NILE and the White Nile.

El Giza A sprawling suburb of CAIRO, EGYPT, at the edge of which stand the three most famous pyramids of the Ancient Egyptians. (Pop. 1 230 500)

Elisabethville *see* Lubumbashi.

El Mansura A city in the delta of the River NILE in northern EGYPT. (Pop. 323 000)

El Paso A city in western TEXAS, U.S.A., close to the border with MEXICO. (Pop. city 463 000/metropolitan area 526 500)

Elsinore (Helsingør) A town of medieval origins on the island of ZEALAND, DENMARK, to the north of COPENHAGEN. Kronborg Castle, which dominates the town, is the setting for Shakepeare's play *Hamlet*. (Pop. 65 200)

El Qahira *see* Cairo.

El Salvador A republic in Central AMERICA bordering the PACIFIC OCEAN. Coastal plains rise to a plateau in the centre. Continuing civil war has damaged the economy, but coffee, cotton, sugar and textiles are exported. Spanish is the main language. The capital is SAN SALVADOR. (21 041 sq km/8124 sq miles; pop. 5 220 000; cur. Colon = 100 centavos)

Emilia Romagna A region on the east coast of northern central ITALY; the capital is BOLOGNA. (22 123 sq km/ 8542 sq miles; pop. 3 943 000)

Emmenthal The valley of the River Emme, in SWITZERLAND, famous for its distinctive cheese.

Empty Quarter *see* Rub al-Khali.

Enewetak *see* Marshall Islands.

Engel's An industrial town on the River VOLGA, in RUSSIA. (Pop. 175 000)

England The country occupying the greater part of the island of GREAT BRITAIN, and the largest of the countries that make up the UNITED KINGDOM. SCOTLAND lies to the north and WALES to the west. The capital is LONDON. (130 357 sq km/50 331 sq miles; pop. 46 795 000)

English Channel The arm of the eastern ATLANTIC OCEAN which separates the south coast of ENGLAND from FRANCE.
Enschede An industrial town in the eastern part of the NETHERLANDS, close to the border with GERMANY. (Pop. 144 900)
Entebbe A town with an international airport on Lake VICTORIA, UGANDA. It was the capital until 1962. (Pop. 30 000)
Enugu A coal-mining centre in southern central NIGERIA, the capital of Biafra (IBOLAND) during the Civil War (1967–70). (Pop. 222 600)
Eolian (Lipari) Islands A group of small volcanic islands which lie between the north coast of SICILY and mainland ITALY. The main islands are Stromboli, Lipari, Salina, Panarea and Vulcano. (Pop. 12 500)
Ephesus The ruins of an ancient Greek city on the east coast of TURKEY, overlooking the AEGEAN SEA. Its Temple of Diana (or Artemis) was one of the Seven Wonders of Ancient World.
Eptanisos *see* Ionian Islands.
Equatorial Guinea A republic in West AFRICA lying just north of the Equator, comprising a region on the mainland (Rio Muni) and several islands (the most important being BIOKO) in the Gulf of GUINEA. It became independent of SPAIN in 1968. Rio Muni is thickly forested, but the fertile land on Bioko is cultivated. Cocoa and timber are the principal exports. Spanish is the official language. The capital, on Bioko, is MALABO. (28 051 sq km/10 828 sq miles; pop. 289 000; cur. CFA franc = 100 centimes)

Erfurt A historic town and tourist centre in central GERMANY. (Pop. 215 000)

Erie, Lake One of the five GREAT LAKES (the second smallest after Lake ONTARIO), on the border between CANADA and the U.S.A. (25 670 sq km/9910 sq miles)

Eritrea An autonomous province of northern ETHIOPIA, bordering the RED SEA. The capital is ASMARA. (117 400 sq km/ 45 316 sq miles; pop. 3 000 000)

Erzurum A market town in western TURKEY, and the name of the surrounding province. (Pop. town 252 700)

Escorial, El (San Lorenzo del Escorial) A small town 40 km (25 miles) north-west of Madrid famous for its splendid royal palace built (1563–84) for Philip II. (Pop. 9500)

Esfahan (Isfahan) A city in central IRAN noted for its magnificent blue-tiled mosques and other Islamic buildings. (Pop. 926 700)

Eskisehir A spa town in western TURKEY and the name of the surrounding province. (Pop. town 367 300)

Espiritu Santo *see* Vanuatu.

Esseg *see* Osijek.

Essen An industrial city in western GERMANY, and the largest of the RUHR region. (Pop. 635 200)

Essex A county in south-east ENGLAND; the county town is Chelmsford. (3674 sq km/1419 sq miles; pop. 1 492 000)

Estonia One of the three BALTIC republics which declared itself independent of the U.S.S.R. in 1991. The capital is TALLININ. (45 100 sq km/17 400 sq miles; pop. 1 518 000)

Ethiopia A republic in north-east AFRICA with a coast on the RED SEA. Formerly known as Abyssinia, it was ruled by an emperor until 1975, when the military took control. The centre of the country is mountainous, while much of the east is desert. Separatist wars waged in the provinces of ERITREA and TIGRAY and persistent drought have crippled the economy, which is dependent on foreign aid. Coffee is the principal export. Amharic and Arabic are the main langages. The capital is ADDIS ABABA. (221 900 sq km/471 800 sq miles; pop. 42 580 000; cur. Birr = 100 cents)

Etna, Mount The largest volcano in EUROPE, situated near the east coast of SICILY, ITALY, and still highly active. (3323 m/10 902 ft)

Euboea (Evvoia) A large island in the AEGEAN SEA lying close to the east coast of mainland GREECE and joined to the mainland by a bridge. (3655 sq km/1411 sq miles; pop. 188 400)

Euphrates, River (Al Furat) One of the great rivers of the Middle East, flowing from its source in eastern TURKEY, across SYRIA and central IRAQ to The GULF. (Length 2720 km/1690 miles)

Europe A continent that is divided from ASIA by a border that runs down the URAL Mountains to the CASPIAN SEA and then west to the BLACK SEA. For convenience it is commonly divided into two areas: Eastern Europe (the countries that have or had Communist governments since the Second World War) and Western Europe. (10 498 000 sq km/ 4 053 300 sq miles; pop. 682 000 000)

Everest, Mount The highest mountain in the world,

situated on the border between NEPAL and CHINA in the eastern HIMALAYAS. (8848 m/29 028 ft)

Everglades A vast area of subtropical swampland on the western side of southern FLORIDA, U.S.A.

Evvoia *see* Euboea.

Eyre, Lake A large salt lake in SOUTH AUSTRALIA. (8900 sq km/3400 sq miles)

F

Faeroe (Faroe) Islands A group of 18 islands in the North ATLANTIC OCEAN belonging to DENMARK, which lie approximately half way between NORWAY and SCOTLAND. (1399 sq km/540 sq miles; pop. 44 500)

Fair Isle A small island situated between the ORKNEY and SHETLAND ISLANDS to the north of SCOTLAND, famous for the distinctive, patterned sweaters made there. (37 sq km/ 23 miles; pop. 75)

Faisalabad (Lyallpur) An industrial city and agricultural centre in north-east PAKISTAN. (Pop. 1 092 000)

Faiyum *see* El Faiyum.

Falkland Islands (Islas Malvinas) A British Crown Colony consisting of two large islands and some 200 smaller ones lying about 650 km (410 km) east of southern ARGENTINA. The capital is PORT STANLEY. (12 173 sq km/4700 sq miles; pop. 1800)

Fao (Al Faw) A port and oil tanker terminal in IRAQ, at the mouth of the SHATT AL ARAB waterway.

Faro The capital of the ALGARVE province of PORTUGAL. (Pop. 28 200)

Faroe Islands *see* Faeroe Islands.

Fatehpur Sikri A magnificent deserted palace complex some 150 km (93 miles) south of DELHI, INDIA, built as a capital by the Moghul Emperor Akbar in 1580 but abandoned in 1605.

Fayum *see* El Faiyum.

Fermanagh A lakeland county in the south-west of NORTHERN IRELAND; the county town is Enniskillen. (1676 sq km/647 sq miles; pop. 51 400)

Fernando Póo *see* Bioko.

Ferrara A historic city in north-eastern ITALY in the PO plain. (Pop. 150 300)

Fès (Fez) A city in northern MOROCCO, the oldest of that country's four imperial cities. (Pop. 448 823)

Fife A region of eastern Scotland. The administrative centre is Glenrothes. (1308 sq km/505 sq miles; pop. 344 000)

Fiji A republic comprising some 800 islands in the south-west PACIFIC OCEAN. (The main islands are VITI LEVU and VANUA LEVU). Formerly a British colony, the country became independent in 1970. Much of the forest on the islands has been cleared for plantations. Exports include sugar, gold and ginger. English is the main language. The capital is SUVA, on Viti Levu. (18 376 sq km/7095 sq miles; pop. 715 000; cur. Fiji dollar = 100 cents)

Finistère The department of FRANCE occupying the tip of the BRITTANY peninsula. (Pop. 828 000)

Finisterre, Cape The north-west corner of SPAIN.

Finland A republic in northern EUROPE with coasts on the BALTIC SEA and the ARCTIC OCEAN. It is a flat country, half of it lying within the ARCTIC CIRCLE. There are some 50 000 lakes, and deep forests to the south. Exports include timber, paper, chemicals and ships. Finnish and Swedish are the main languages. The capital is HELSINKI. (338 142 sq km/130 557 sq miles; pop. 4 910 000; cur. Markka = 100 penni)

Finland, Gulf of The easternmost arm of the BALTIC SEA, with the southern coast of FINLAND to the north, ST PETERSBURG at its eastern end, and ESTONIA to the south.

Firenze *see* Florence.

Flanders (Vlaanderen, Flandre) A Flemish-speaking coastal region of northern BELGIUM, now divided into two provinces, East and West Flanders. (6115 sq km/ 2361 sq miles; pop. 2 400 000)

Flinders Range Mountains in the eastern part of SOUTH AUSTRALIA, stretching over 400 km (250 miles). St Mary Peak is the highest point. (1188 m/3898 ft)

Flintshire *see* Clwyd.

Florence (Firenze) One of the great Renaissance cities of ITALY, straddling the River ARNO, and the capital of the region of TUSCANY. (Pop. 453 300)

Flores A volcanic island in the SUNDA group in INDONESIA, lying in the chain which stretches due east of JAVA. (14 250 sq km/550 sq miles; pop. 803 000)

Flores Sea A stretch of the PACIFIC OCEAN between FLORES and SULAWESI.

Florida A state occupying the peninsula in the south-eastern corner of the U.S.A. The state capital is TALLAHASSEE. (151 670 sq km/58 560 sq miles; pop. 11 366 000)

Florida, Straits of The waterway which separates the southern tip of FLORIDA, U.S.A. from CUBA, some 145 km (90 miles) to the south.

Flushing (Vlissingen) A port on the south-west coast of the NETHERLANDS. (Pop. 46 400)

Fly, River A largely navigable river flowing from the central mountains in western PAPUA NEW GUINEA to its broad estuary on the Gulf of PAPUA to the south. (Length 1200 km/750 miles)

Foggia A city in the PUGLIA region of south-eastern ITALY. (Pop. 158 400)

Fontainebleau A town 55 km (35 miles) south-east of PARIS, FRANCE, with a 16th-century royal château and a famous forest. (Pop. 39 400)

Formosa *see* Taiwan.

Fortaleza A major port on the north-eastern coast of BRAZIL. (Pop. 1 309 000)

Fort-de-France A port and the capital of the island of MARTINIQUE. (Pop. 100 000)

Fort Knox A military reservation in KENTUCKY, U.S.A., 40 km (25 miles) south-west of LOUISVILLE; also the site of the principal depository of the country's gold bullion. (Pop. 37 600)

Fort Lamy *see* Ndjamena.

Fort Lauderdale A city and resort on the east coast of FLORIDA, U.S.A., 40 km (25 miles) north of MIAMI. (Pop. city 149 900/metropolitan area 1 093 300)

Fort Worth A city in north-east TEXAS, U.S.A., just to the west of DALLAS and part of a Dallas–Fort Worth conurbation (the Southwest Metroplex). (Pop. city 414 600/metropolitan area 1 144 400)

Foshan An industrial city in GUANGDONG province, CHINA. (Pop. 500 000)

France A republic in western EUROPE with coasts on the ENGLISH CHANNEL, the MEDITERRANEAN SEA and the ATLANTIC OCEAN. It is relatively flat to the north and west, with mountains to the south-west and the east, and the uplands of the MASSIF CENTRAL in the centre. A member of the European Community, it has many major industries, and exports foodstuffs, iron and steel, machinery and clothes. The capital is PARIS. (551 600 sq km/212 900 sq miles; pop. 55 300 000; cur. Franc = 100 centimes)

Frankfort The state capital of KENTUCKY, U.S.A. (Pop. 26 800)

Frankfurt (Frankfurt am Main) A city in central western GERMANY, on the River MAIN. (Pop. 614 700)

Frankfurt an der Oder A town on the River ODER in eastern GERMANY, on the border with POLAND. (Pop. 84 800)

Fraser, River A river flowing through southern BRITISH COLUMBIA, CANADA, from its source in the ROCKY MOUNTAINS to the Strait of GEORGIA by VANCOUVER. (Length 1370 km/850 miles)

Fredericton The capital of NEW BRUNSWICK, CANADA. (Pop. 43 750)

Freetown The main port and capital of SIERRA LEONE. (Pop. 316 300)

Freiburg (Freiburg im Breisgau) The largest city in the BLACK FOREST in south-west GERMANY, close to the border with FRANCE. (Pop. 175 000)

Freemantle *see* Perth (Australia).

French Guiana (Guyane) An overseas territory of FRANCE on the north-east coast of SOUTH AMERICA, with BRAZIL lying to the east and south and SURINAM to the west. The capital is CAYENNE. (89 941 sq km/ 34 726 sq miles; pop. 73 000)

French Polynesia A total of about 130 islands in the South PACIFIC OCEAN administered as overseas territories by FRANCE.

French Southern and Antarctic Territories A set of remote and widely scattered territories in ANTARCTICA and the ANTARCTIC OCEAN administered by FRANCE. They include the Crozet Islands and KERGUELEN.

Fresno A city in central eastern California. (Pop. city 267 400/metropolitan area 564 900)

Friesian (Frisian) Islands A string of sandy, low-lying islands that line the coasts in the south-eastern corner of the NORTH SEA. The West Friesians (including Terchelling and Texel) belong to the NETHERLANDS; the East Friesians (including Borkum and Norderney) belong to GERMANY; and the North Friesians are divided between Germany and DENMARK.

Frunze The capital of KIRGHIZIA. (Pop. 577 000)

Fuji, Mount (Fuji-yama) The highest peak in JAPAN, a distinctive volcanic cone 100 km (62 miles) to the south-west of TOKYO. (3776 m/12 389 ft)

Fujian (Fukien) A coastal province in south-east CHINA. The capital is FUZHOU. (120 000 sq km/46 350 sq miles; pop. 24 800 000)

Fukuoka A port and the largest city on the island of KYUSHU, JAPAN. (Pop. 1 160 400)

Funafuti The capital of TUVALU, and the name of the

atoll on which it is sited. (2.4 sq km/0.9 sq miles; pop. 2600)

Funchal The capital of MADEIRA. (Pop. 45 600)

Fundy, Bay of The bay between NOVA SCOTIA and NEW BRUNSWICK, CANADA. It has the world's largest tidal range – 15 m (50 ft) between low and high tide.

Fünen (Fyn) The second largest of the islands of DENMARK, in the centre of the country. (2976 sq km/ 1048 sq miles; pop. 433 800)

Fushun A mining city in LIAONING province, CHINA, situated on one of the largest coalfields in the world. (Pop. 1 800 000)

Fuzhou An important port and the capital of FUJIAN province, CHINA. (Pop. 1 050 000)

Fyn *see* Fünen

G

Gabès, Gulf of A branch of the MEDITERRANEAN SEA which, with the Gulf of SIRTE to the east, makes a deep indent in the coast of NORTH AFRICA.

Gabon A republic in west central AFRICA with a coast on the ATLANTIC. Formerly part of the French CONGO, it gained independence in 1960. Most of the land is forested and the main exports are oil, minerals and timber. The capital is LIBREVILLE. (267 667 sq km/ 103 346 sq miles; pop. 1 020 000; cur. CFA franc = 100 centimes)

Gaborone The capital of BOTSWANA, in the south-east of the country. (Pop. 79 000)

Galapagos Islands A group of 15 islands on the Equator administered by ECUADOR, but located some 1100 km (680 miles) to the west of that country. (7812 sq km/3016 sq miles; pop. 6200)
Galati An inland port on the River DANUBE in eastern ROMANIA, close to the border with the MOLDAVIA. (Pop. 261 000)
Galicia A region in the very north-west corner of SPAIN. (Pop. 2 754 000)
Galilee The most northerly region of ISRAEL, bordering LEBANON and SYRIA, with the Sea of Galilee (Lake TIBERIAS) on its eastern side.
Gallipoli The peninsula which marks the northern side of the DARDANELLES in TURKEY, and also the name of a port on the peninsula. In 1915 and 1916 Allied troops (particularly Australians and New Zealanders) landed here and suffered heavy losses in an unsuccessful attempt to take control of the Dardanelles.
Galloway *see* Dumfries and Galloway.
Galveston A port in TEXAS, U.S.A., sited on an island in the Gulf of MEXICO. (Pop. city 62 400/metropolitan area 215 400)
Galway A county in the central part of the west coast of IRELAND. The county town is also called Galway, or Galway City. (5940 sq km/2293 sq miles; pop. county 171 800/city 37 700)
Gambia, River A major river of West AFRICA, flowing into the ATLANTIC OCEAN from its source in GUINEA, through SENEGAL and then through The GAMBIA, for which it provides a central and vital focus. (Length 1130 km/700 miles)

Gambia, The A republic in West AFRICA occupying a narrow strip of land that is completely surrounded by SENEGAL, save a small coastline on the ATLANTIC. It was formerly a British colony and gained independence in 1965, becoming a member of the Commonwealth. It has few exports besides groundnuts; one of its primary sources of income is tourism. The capital is BANJUL. (11295 sq km/4361 sq miles; pop. 777 000; cur. Dalasi = 100 bututs)

Gand *see* Ghent.

Ganges, River The holy river of the Hindus, flowing from its source in the HIMALAYAS, across northern INDIA and forming a delta in BANGLADESH as it flows into the Bay of BENGAL. (Length 2525 km/1568 miles)

Gansu A mountainous province in northern central CHINA. The capital is LANZHOU. (450 000 sq km/ 170 000 sq miles; pop. 19 600 000)

Garonne, River A major river of south-western FRANCE, flowing north from its source in the central PYRENEES in SPAIN to BORDEAUX, where it contributes to the GIRONDE estuary. (Length 575 km/355 miles)

Gascony (Gascogne) The historic name of an area in the south-western corner of FRANCE bordering SPAIN.

Gaza Strip A finger of coastal land stretching from the Egyptian border to the MEDITERRANEAN port of Gaza, with borders with ISRAEL to its east and north. It was administered by Egypt after the creation of ISRAEL in 1948, and became home to numerous Palestinian refugees. It was taken over by Israel in the Six-Day War of 1967. (Pop. 510 000)

Gaziantep A town in southern central TURKEY, close to the border with SYRIA, and also the name of the surrounding province. (Pop. town 466 300)

Gdansk (Danzig) The main port of POLAND, on the BALTIC SEA. (Pop. 464 500)

Gdynia (Gdingen) A port on the BALTIC coast of POLAND 16 km (10 miles) north-west of GDANSK. (Pop. 240 200)

Geelong A port and the second largest city of VICTORIA, AUSTRALIA. (Pop. 142 000)

Gelsenkirchen An industrial and coal-mining town in the RUHR region of GERMANY. (Pop. 290 000)

Geneva (Genève; Genf) A city in the extreme south-west of SWITZERLAND, at the western end of Lake Geneva, and close to the border with FRANCE. It is also the name of the surrounding canton. (Pop. city 165 000)

Genoa (Genova) The major seaport of north-west ITALY, and the capital of LIGURIA. (Pop. 760 300)

Gent *see* Ghent.

George Town A port and the main city of PENANG island, MALAYSIA. (Pop. 250 600)

Georgetown The main port and capital of GUYANA. (Pop. 200 000)

Georgia 1 A state in the south-east of the U.S.A., named after George II by English colonists in 1733; the state capital is ATLANTA. (152 490 sq km/58 876 sq miles; pop. 5 837 000). **2** A former republic in the south-west of the U.S.S.R., situated in the CAUCASUS. It declared itself independent in 1991. The capital is TBILISI. (69 700 sq km/26 900 sq miles; pop. 5 976 000)

Georgia, Strait of The southern part of the stretch of water which separates VANCOUVER ISLAND from the coast of BRITISH COLUMBIA in CANADA.

Germany A country in central EUROPE which has northern coastlines on the NORTH SEA and the BALTIC SEA, and a southern border that runs through the ALPS. After its defeat in the Second World War, the country was effectively divided in two. West Germany had a democratic government while East Germany came under Communist rule and formed part of the 'Soviet bloc'. After the demise of the Communist government in East Germany, the two parts of the country were reunited into one nation in 1990. A member of the European Community, Germany is an industrialized nation with a thriving economy. The capital is BERLIN. (357 020 sq km/137 845 sq miles; pop. 77 709 700; cur. Deutsche Mark = 100 Pfennig)

Gezira *see* El Gezira.

Ghana A republic in West AFRICA with a coastline on the Gulf of GUINEA. It was created when two former British colonies, British Gold Coast and British Togoland, were united in 1957; the new country was granted independence within the Commonwealth in 1960. Cocoa, gold and diamonds are the major exports. The official language is English and the capital is ACCRA. (238 537 sq km/92 099 sq miles; pop. 13 590 000; cur. Cedi = 100 pesewas)

Ghats The two ranges of mountains that line the coasts of the DECCAN peninsula of INDIA: the Eastern Ghats (rising to about 600 m/2000 ft) and the Western Ghats (1500 m/5000 ft).

Ghent (Gent; Gand) A medieval city spanning the Rivers Lys and SCHELDE and the capital of the province of East FLANDERS, BELGIUM. (Pop. city 235 000/ metropolitan area 490 000)

Gibraltar A self-governing British Crown Colony on the south-western tip of SPAIN, where a limestone hill called the Rock of Gibraltar rises to 425 m (1394 ft). Its commanding view over the Strait of Gibraltar has made the territory strategically significant. SPAIN lays claim to Gibraltar, but the U.K. is reluctant to relinquish it. English is the official language, although Spanish is also spoken. The capital is Gibraltar Town. (6.5 sq km/2.5 sq miles; pop. 32 200; cur. Gibraltar pound = 100 pence)

Gibraltar, Strait of The narrow waterway, 13 km (8 miles) at its narrowest, which connects the MEDITERRANEAN SEA to the ATLANTIC OCEAN, with SPAIN to the north and MOROCCO to the south.

Gibson Desert A desert of sand and salt marshes in central western AUSTRALIA, with the GREAT SANDY DESERT to the north and the GREAT VICTORIA DESERT to the south.

Gifu A town in central HONSHU island, JAPAN. (Pop. 411 700)

Gijón A port and industrial town in ASTURIAS, in the centre of the north coast of SPAIN. (Pop.256 000)

Gilbert Islands *see* Kiribati.

Gilgit A mountain district in northern PAKISTAN, noted for its great beauty. The small town of Gilgit perches startlingly beneath a dramatic rockface.

Gironde The long, thin estuary stretching some 80 km

(50 miles) which connects the Rivers DORDOGNE and GARONNE to the ATLANTIC coast of south-west FRANCE.

Giuba, River *see* Jubba, River.

Giza *see* El Giza.

Glamorgan A former county of south WALES, which was divided into three administrative regions in the 1970s: MID GLAMORGAN, WEST GLAMORGAN and SOUTH GLAMORGAN.

Glasgow A port on the River CLYDE, a major industrial centre and the largest city in SCOTLAND. (Pop.751 000)

Gliwice (Gleiwitz) An industrial city in southern POLAND. (Pop. 211 000)

Gloucestershire A county in western ENGLAND; the county town is Gloucester. (2638 sq km/1019 sq miles; pop. 508 000)

Goa A territory on the west coast of INDIA, 400 km (250 miles) south of BOMBAY, which was captured by the Portuguese in 1510 and remained under the control of PORTUGAL until it was annexed by India in 1961. (3702 sq km/1429 sq miles; pop. 1 007 800)

Gobi Desert A vast expanse of arid land which occupies much of MONGOLIA and central northern CHINA. Temperatures range from very hot to extremely cold over the year. (1 295 000 sq km/500 000 sq miles)

Godavari, River A river which runs across the middle of the DECCAN peninsula of INDIA from its source in the Western GHATS near BOMBAY to its delta on the central east coast. (Length 1465 km/910 miles)

Godthåb (Nuuk) The capital of GREENLAND. (Pop. 10 500)

Godwin Austen *see* K2.

Golan Heights An area of high ground in south-west SYRIA on the border with northern ISRAEL. The Heights were captured by ISRAEL in the Arab–Israeli War of 1967 and annexed by Israel in 1981. (2225 m/ 7300 ft)

Gold Coast 1 The name given to a string of beach resorts on the east coast of QUEENSLAND, AUSTRALIA, to the south of BRISBANE. **2** *See* GHANA.

Golden Triangle The remote and mountainous region where the borders of THAILAND, BURMA and LAOS meet, noted in particular for its opium cultivation and as one of the world's main sources of the drug heroin.

Gomel An industrial city in south-eastern BELORUSSIA. (Pop. 452 000)

Gomera *see* Canary Islands.

Good Hope, Cape of The tip of the narrow Cape Peninsula which extends from the south-western corner of SOUTH AFRICA.

Gor'kiy (Gorky) An industrial city in central eastern RUSSIA on the River VOLGA, formerly known as Nizhni Novgorod. (Pop. 1 392 000)

Gothenburg (Göteborg) A major port on the KATTEGAT and the second largest city in SWEDEN. (Pop. 425 500)

Gotland An island in the BALTIC SEA which forms a county of SWEDEN. (3140 sq km/1210 sq miles; pop. 56 100)

Göttingen A university town in central GERMANY. (Pop. 138 000)

Gouda A historic town in eastern NETHERLANDS, famous for its cheese. (Pop. 59 200)

Gozo *see* Malta.

Grampian An administrative region of north-eastern SCOTLAND created in 1975 out of the former counties of Aberdeenshire, Kincardineshire, Banffshire and part of Morayshire. The capital is ABERDEEN. (8550 sq km/3301 sq miles; pop. 497 000)

Grampian Mountains A range of mountains that stretch across northern SCOTLAND to the south of Loch NESS. The mountains rise to their highest point at BEN NEVIS. (1344 m/4409 ft), the highest peak in the U.K.

Gran Canaria *see* Canary Islands.

Granada A city in the SIERRA NEVADA of central southern SPAIN, an administrative centre during the Moorish occupation of Spain, during which its famous Alhambra Palace was built (1248–1345). Granada is also the name of the surrounding province. (Pop. city 262 200)

Grand Bahama *see* Bahamas.

Grand Canyon The dramatic gorge of the COLORADO RIVER, in places over 1.5 km (1 mile) deep, in north-western ARIZONA.

Grand Rapids A city 40 km (14 miles) to the east of Lake Michigan in the state of MICHIGAN, U.S.A. (Pop. city 183 000/metropolitan area 626 500)

Graz The second largest city in AUSTRIA, in the south-east of the country. (Pop. 243 000)

Great Australian Bight The arm of the SOUTHERN OCEAN which forms the deep indentation in the centre of the southern coastline of AUSTRALIA.

Great Australian Desert The collective word for the deserts that occupy much of the centre of AUSTRALIA. (3 830 000 sq km/1 480 000 sq miles)

Great Barrier Reef The world's most extensive coral reef which lines the coast of QUEENSLAND, AUSTRALIA, stretching some 2000 km (1250 miles).

Great Bear Lake The fourth largest lake in NORTH AMERICA, in the remote north-west of CANADA. It drains into the MACKENZIE RIVER. (31 153 sq km/ 12 028 sq miles)

Great Britain The island shared by ENGLAND, SCOTLAND and WALES, and which forms the principal part of the UNITED KINGDOM of Great Britain and Northern Ireland.

Great Dividing Range A range of mountains which runs down the east coast of AUSTRALIA, from QUEENSLAND in the north, across NEW SOUTH WALES to VICTORIA in the south, some 3600 km (2250 miles) in all. The highest point is Mount KOSCIUSKO. (2230 m/7316 ft)

Greater Manchester *see* Manchester.

Greater Sunda Islands *see* Lesser Sunda Islands.

Great Lakes The largest group of freshwater lakes in the world, drained by the ST LAWRENCE RIVER. There are five lakes, four of which (Lakes HURON, SUPERIOR, ERIE and ONTARIO) are on the border of CANADA and the U.S.A.; the fifth (Lake MICHIGAN) is in the U.S.A.

Great Plains A huge plateau consisting mainly of grasslands which lies to the east of the ROCKY MOUNTAINS and stretches from the MACKENZIE MOUNTAINS in north-west CANADA to the state of TEXAS in the U.S.A.

Great Rift Valley A series of geological faults which has created a depression stretching 6400 km (4000 miles) from the the valley of the River JORDAN across the RED SEA and down East AFRICA to MOZAMBIQUE.

Great Salt Lake A salt lake in north-west UTAH, U.S.A., lying just to the north-west of SALT LAKE CITY. (5200 sq km/2000 sq miles)

Great Sandy Desert The desert region in the northern part of WESTERN AUSTRALIA.

Great Slave Lake A lake drained by the MACKENZIE RIVER in the southern part of the NORTHWEST TERRITORIES of CANADA. (28 570 sq km/11 030 sq miles)

Great Smoky Mountains Part of the APPALACHIAN MOUNTAINS, running along the border between TENNESSEE and NORTH CAROLINA. The highest point is Clingmans Dome (2025 m/6643 ft).

Great Victoria Desert A vast area of sand dunes straddling the border between WESTERN AUSTRALIA and SOUTH AUSTRALIA.

Greece A republic in south-east EUROPE consisting of the southern section of the BALKAN peninsula and more than 1400 islands in the IONIAN and AEGEAN SEAS. Europe's earliest civilizations were established in what is now modern Greece and many ancient monuments remain. A member of the European Community, exports include farm produce, textiles and chemicals; tourism also provides a lucrative income. The capital is ATHENS. (131 986 sq km/ 50 960 sq miles; pop. 10 000 000; cur. Drachma = 100 lepta)

Greenland A huge island to the north-east of North

AMERICA, most of which lies within the ARCTIC CIRCLE. A province of DENMARK, the island was granted home rule in 1979. The economy is heavily reliant on fishing and most of the population is Eskimo. The capital is GODHAB (Nuuk). (2 175 600 sq km/840 000 sq miles; pop. 54 600; cur. Danish Krone = 100 øre)

Greenwich A borough of east LONDON, ENGLAND, on the south bank of the River THAMES. It was the site of the Royal Observatory, and since 1884 has been accepted to be on 0° meridian from which all lines of longitude are measured. Greenwich Mean Time is the time at 0° longitude, against which all world time differences are measured.

Grenada An island state which gained independence from the U.K., while remaining within the Commonwealth, in 1974. It is the most southerly of the WINDWARD ISLANDS and is largely mountainous, except along the coastline. With its fine climate and beautiful scenery, it has a buoyant tourist industry. Its main exports are cocoa, bananas and spices. The capital is ST GEORGE'S. (344 sq km/133 sq miles; pop. 87 600; cur. East Caribbean dollar = 100 cents)

Grenadines A string of some 600 small islands that lie between ST VINCENT to the north and GRENADA to the south. Most of them belong to St Vincent, but the largest, Carriacou is divided between St Vincent and Grenada. Other islands include Union, Mustique and Bequia.

Grenoble A manufacturing city in south-east FRANCE, in the foothills of the ALPS. (Pop. 396 800)

Groningen The largest city in the north-east of the

NETHERLANDS, and also the name of the surrounding province. (Pop. city 206 600)

Guadalajara A major city of central western MEXICO. (Pop. 2 300 000)

Guadalcanal An island at the southern end of the archipelago where HONIARA, capital of the SOLOMON ISLANDS, is located. The bitterly contested battle in 1942/3 here between U.S. forces and the occupying Japanese marked a turning point in the U.S. Pacific campaign which eventually led to the defeat of the Japanese in 1945.

Guadeloupe A group of islands in the LEEWARD ISLANDS in the eastern CARIBBEAN which since 1946 has been an overseas department of FRANCE. The principal island is Guadeloupe (divided into two parts, Basse Terre and Grande Terre). The other islands include Marie Galante, La Désirade, Iles des Saintes, St Barthélémy and St Martin. The capital is BASSE TERRE. (1779 sq km/687 sq miles; pop. 328 400)

Guam The largest of the MARIANA ISLANDS in the western PACIFIC OCEAN. (549 sq km/212 sq miles; pop. 112 000)

Guangdong A province of south-east CHINA. The capital is GUANGZHOU (Canton). (210 000 sq km/ 81 000 sq miles; pop. 56 810 000)

Guangxi-Zhuang An autonomous region of southern CHINA on the border with VIETNAM. To the south of the city of Guilin, around the Gui Jiang River, is a famous landscape of towering rock hills which rise up from the watery plains. The regional capital is NANNING. (230 000 sq km/890 000 sq miles; pop. 34 700 000)

Guangzhou (Canton) A major port in south-east CHINA, the country's sixth largest city, and the capital of GUANGDONG province. (Pop. 5 350 000)

Guantanamo A city in the south-east of CUBA, and also the name of the surrounding province. The U.S.A. has a naval base at nearby Guantanamo Bay. (Pop. city 205 000)

Guatemala A republic in central AMERICA which has coastlines on both the ATLANTIC and PACIFIC OCEANS. The ancient Mayan civilization flourished here before being stamped out by the Spanish in the 16th century. Exports include bananas, coffee and chemicals. The official language is Spanish, although Indian languages are widely spoken. The capital is GUATEMALA CITY. (108 889 sq km/42 042 sq miles; pop. 8 600 000; cur. Quetzal = 100 centavos)

Guatemala City The capital of GUATEMALA, in the south-east of the country. (Pop. 1 329 600)

Guayaquil The main port and the largest city of ECUADOR. (Pop. 1 223 500)

Guernica A small town in the BASQUE country of north-east SPAIN where the Basque parliament used to assemble. In 1937, during the Spanish Civil War, it was heavy bombed from the air by German forces. (Pop. 17 836)

Guernsey One of the CHANNEL ISLANDS, lying in the centre of the group and some 50 km (30 miles) off the coast of FRANCE. The capital is St Peter Port. (78 sq km/30 sq miles; pop. 55 000)

Guinea A republic in tropical West AFRICA with a seaboard on the ATLANTIC. It was formerly a French colony (French Guinea) and gained independence in 1958. Its principal exports include minerals and diamonds, but it remains an impoverished nation. The official language is French. The capital is CONAKRY. (245 857 sq km/94 926 sq miles; pop. 5 890 000; cur. Guinean franc)

Guinea, Equatorial *see* Equatorial Guinea.

Guinea, Gulf of The arm of the South ATLANTIC OCEAN which creates the deep, right-angled indent in the west coast of AFRICA.

Guinea-Bissau A West-African republic which was a Portuguese territory (Portuguese Guinea) until it gained independence in 1974. Rising from the coast to a plateau of wooded savannah, it struggles to support itself and is one of AFRICA's poorest nations. The official language is Portuguese, but a number of local languages are also spoken. The capital is BISSAU. (36 125 sq km/13 984 sq miles; pop. 874 000; cur. Peso = 100 centavos)

Guiyang An industrial city in central southern CHINA, and capital of GUIZHOU province. (Pop. 1 260 000)

Guizhou A province of central southern CHINA. The capital is GUIYANG. (170 sq km/65 600 sq miles/pop. 27 310 000)

Gujarat A state lining the north-west coast of INDIA, on the border with PAKISTAN. The capital is Gandinagar. (196 024 sq km/75 665 sq miles; pop. 34 085 800)

Gujranwala A textile city in the province of PUNJAB, PAKISTAN, some 65 km (40 miles) north of LAHORE. (Pop. 34 085 800)

Gulf, The The huge inlet to the south of IRAN which is

connected to the ARABIAN SEA by the Strait of HORMUZ. It is often referred to as the Persian Gulf, or the Arabian Gulf

Guyana A republic in the north-east of South AMERICA with a seaboard on the ATLANTIC. It was a British colony, but gained independence in 1966 and joined the Commonwealth. Much of the country is covered with dense forest and the bulk of the population lives on the coast. The chief exports are bauxites. The official language is English, and the capital is GEORGETOWN. (215 00 sq km/83 000 sq miles; pop. 801 000; cur. Guyana dollar = 100 cents)

Guyane *see* French Guiana.

Gwalior A city in central INDIA 280 km (174 miles) south-east of DELHI. (Pop. 555 900)

Gwangju *see* Kwangju.

Gwent A county in south-east WALES, bordering the SEVERN estuary just to the east of CARDIFF. The county was created in 1974 and more or less coincides with the old county of Monmouthshire. The county town is Cwmbran. (1376 sq km/532 sq miles; pop. 440 000)

Gwynedd A county in north-west WALES which includes the island of ANGLESEY. It was created in 1974 out of the former county of Caernarfonshire, and parts of Denbighshire and Merionethshire. The administrative centre is Caernarfon. (3868 sq km/1493 sq miles; pop. 232 000)

H

Haarlem A city in central western NETHERLANDS, 18 km (11 miles) from AMSTERDAM. (Pop. 154 300)

Hagen A steel town in the industrial RUHR region of western GERMANY. (Pop. 210 000)

Hague, The (Den Haag; 's-Gravenhage) The administrative centre of the NETHERLANDS, on the west coast. (Pop. 449 300)

Haifa The main port of ISRAEL. (Pop. 224 700)

Hainan Island A large tropical island in the SOUTH CHINA SEA belonging to CHINA, and the southernmost extremity of that country. (33 670 sq km/13 000 sq miles ; pop. 5 400 000)

Haiphong A port in the north of VIETNAM, 90 km (55 miles) east of the capital, HANOI. It is Vietnam's second largest city after HO CHI MINH CITY. (Pop. 1 379 000)

Haiti A republic occupying the mountainous western west part of HISPANIOLA in the WEST INDIES. It is one of the poorest of nations, and since the demise of the Duvalier family, who ruled the country for 30 years (until 1986), it has struggled to achieve political stability. Coffee, sugar and minerals are among the principal exports. Roman Catholicism is the main religion, but voodoo is widely practised. The official language is French; the capital is PORT-AU-PRINCE. (27 750 sq km/10 7145 sq miles; pop. 5 900 000; cur. Gourde = 100 centimes)

Hakodate A port in on the southern tip of HOKKAIDO island, JAPAN. (Pop. 319 200)

Halicarnassus *see* Bodrum.

Halifax 1 The capital of NOVA SCOTIA, CANADA. (Pop. city 114 595/metropolitan area 278 000) **2** A town in West YORKSHIRE, ENGLAND. (Pop. 88 000)

Halle An industrial town and inland port served by the Saale River in central GERMANY. (Pop. 236 500)

Halmahera *see* Maluku.

Hamah An industrial city in eastern SYRIA, on the River ORONTES. (Pop. 514 750)

Hamamatsu A city in southern HONSHU island, JAPAN. (Pop. 514 100)

Hamburg The main port of GERMANY, situated on the River ELBE. (Pop. 1 617 800)

Hamelin (Hameln) A town in northern GERMANY. It is famous for its legendary Pied Piper, who in 1284 is said to have rid the town of a plague of rats by playing his pipe to them and luring them to their deaths in the River WESER. (Pop. 56 300)

Hamersley Range Part of the PILBARA RANGE in WESTERN AUSTRALIA. The highest peak is Mount BRUCE (1235 m/4052 ft)

Hamhung (Hamheung) A port and industrial city on the east coast of NORTH KOREA. (Pop. 420 000)

Hamilton 1 The capital of BERMUDA. (Pop. 3000) **2** A port and industrial city at the western end of Lake ONTARIO, CANADA. (Pop. city 306 430/metropolitan area 542 090). **3** A town in the north-western part of NORTH ISLAND, NEW ZEALAND. (Pop. 97 900). **4** A town in the STRATHCLYDE region of SCOTLAND, 17 km (10 miles) south-east of GLASGOW. (Pop. 51 700)

Hammerfest A town in the very north of NORWAY, and

one of the world's most northerly settlements. (Pop. 7400)

Hampshire A county of central southern ENGLAND; the county town is WINCHESTER. (3773 sq km/1456 sq miles, pop. 1 500 000)

Hangzhou (Hangchow) A port and industrial city on the east coast of central CHINA, at the head of an estuary called Hangzhou Wan. Hangzhou is at the southern end of the Grand Canal, which links it to BEIJING 1100 km (690 miles) to the north. (Pop. 1 105 000)

Hankow *see* Wuhan.

Hannover *see* Hanover.

Hanoi The capital of VIETNAM, in the north of the country. (Pop. 2 570 900)

Hanover (Hannover) A historic city in central northern GERMANY. (Pop. 514 000)

Haora (Howrah) An industrial city in WEST BENGAL, on the HUGLI River, facing CALCUTTA. (Pop. 744 4000)

Harare The capital of ZIMBABWE; it was formerly called Salisbury (until 1982). (Pop. 656 000)

Harbin The largest city of northern CHINA, situated in central DONGBEI (Manchuria), and capital of HEILONGJIANG province. (Pop. 2 100 000)

Hari Rud A river which flows westwards from central AFGHANISTAN, through the city of HERAT before turning north to form part of the border with IRAN, ending in TURKMENISTAN. (Length 1125 km/700 miles)

Harrisburg The state capital of PENNSYLVANIA, U.S.A. (Pop. city 52 100/metropolitan area 570 200)

Hartford The state capital of CONNECTICUT, U.S.A. (Pop. city 136 400/metropolitan area 1 030 400)

Haryana A state in northwest INDIA, formed in 1966. (44 212 sq km/17 066 sq miles; pop. 12 922 600)

Harz Mountains A range of mountains, noted for their forests, in central GERMANY. The highest peak is Mount Brocken (1142 m/3747 ft).

Hastings A historic port and resort on the south coast of ENGLAND, in the county of EAST SUSSEX. The Battle of Hastings of 1066, in which the English were defeated by the Normans, was fought nearby. (Pop. 77 000)

Hatteras, Cape The tip of a chain of islands lining the coast of NORTH CAROLINA, U.S.A., notorious for its violent weather.

Havana (La Habana) The capital of CUBA, a port on the north-west coast of the island. It is also the name of the surrounding province. (Pop. 1 925 000)

Hawaii A group of 122 islands just to the south of the Tropic of Cancer, some 3700 km (2300 miles) from the coast of CALIFORNIA. Since 1959 they have formed a state of the U.S.A. The main islands are OAHU, MAUI and Hawaii island, which at 10 488 sq km (4049 sq miles) is by far the largest. HONOLULU, the state capital, is on Oahu. (16 705 sq km/6450 sq miles; pop. 1 054 000)

Hebei A province in northern CHINA which surrounds (but does not include) BEIJING. The capital is SHIJIAZHUANG. (180 000 sq km/70 000 sq miles; pop. 51 046 400)

Hebrides *see* Western Isles.

Hefei An industrial city in central eastern CHINA, capital of ANHUI province. (Pop. 1 484 000)

Heidelberg A university town in south-west GERMANY on the NECKAR RIVER. (Pop. 130 000)

Heilongjiang A province of DONGBEI (Manchuria) in northern CHINA; the capital is HARBIN. (464 000sq km/ 179 000 sq miles; pop. 32 700 000)

Heilong Jiang, River *see* Amur, River.

Hejaz A mountainous region which lines the RED SEA, formerly an independent kingdom but since 1932 a part of SAUDI ARABIA.

Helena The state capital of MONTANA, U.S.A. (Pop. 24 600)

Heligoland (Helgoland) A small island and former naval base in the NORTH SEA off the coast of GERMANY. (2.1 sq km/0.5 sq miles; pop. 2000)

Hellespont *see* Dardanelles.

Helsingfors *see* Helsinki.

Helsingør *see* Elsinore.

Helsinki (Helsingfors) The capital and chief industrial centre and port of FINLAND. (Pop. 482 900)

Henan A province of central CHINA; the capital is ZHENGZHOU. (160 000 sq km/62 000 sq miles; pop. 71 890 000)

Heraklion (Iraklion) The capital and main port of the island of CRETE. (Pop. 111 000)

Herat A city in western AFGHANISTAN on the HARI RUD River. (Pop. 150 500)

Hercegovina *see* Bosnia Herzegovina.

Herculaneum (Ercolano) An excavated Graeco-Roman town on the Bay of NAPLES which was buried by the eruption of Mount VESUVIUS, along with POMPEII, in AD 79.

Herefordshire *see* Hereford and Worcester.

Hereford and Worcester A county in the west of ENGLAND, on the border with WALES, which was created in 1974 when the old counties of Herefordshire and Worcestershire were combined. The county town is Worcester. (3927 sq km/1516 sq miles; pop. 648 000)

Hertfordshire A county in south-east ENGLAND, to the north of LONDON. The county town is Hertford. (1634 sq km/631 sq miles; pop. 980 000)

Hermon, Mount A mountain in southern LEBANON near the borders with SYRIA and ISRAEL. It is the source of the River JORDAN. (2814 m/9332 ft)

Herzegovina *see* Bosnia Herzegovina.

Hessen A state in central western GERMANY. The capital is WIESBADEN. (21 112 sq km/8151 sq miles; pop. 5 500 000)

Highland Region An administrative region in northern SCOTLAND comprising the most northerly part of the mainland. It is the largest county in the U.K. It was created in 1975 out of the old counties of Caithness, Nairnshire, Sutherland, most of Inverness-shire, Ross and Cromarty and parts of Argyllshire and Morayshire. The capital is INVERNESS. (26 136 sq km/10 091 sq miles; pop. 196 000)

Highlands The rugged region of northern SCOTLAND, which includes the GRAMPIAN mountains and the North-west Highlands.

Himchal Pradesh A state in northern INDIA, in mountainous country bordering TIBET. (55 673 sq km/21 490 sq miles; pop. 4 280 000)

Himalayas The massive mountain range stretching some 2400 km (1500 miles) in a broad sweep from the northern tip of INDIA, across NEPAL, BHUTAN and southern TIBET to ASSAM in north-eastern India. The average height of the mountains is some 6100 m (20 000 ft), rising to the world's tallest peak, Mount EVEREST (8848 m/29 028 ft).

Himeji An industrial city and port in southern HONSHU island, JAPAN. (Pop. 452 900)

Hims *see* Homs.

Hindu Kush A range of mountains which stretches some 600 km (370 miles) at the western end of the HIMALAYAS, straddling the web of borders where AFGHANISTAN, the U.S.S.R., CHINA, INDIA and PAKISTAN meet. The highest peak is Tirich Mir (7690 m/ 25 229 ft) in Pakistan.

Hiroshima An industrial city in south-western HONSHU island, JAPAN. Three-quarters of the city was destroyed on 6 August 1945 when the world's first atomic bomb was dropped here, killing 78 000 people. (Pop. 899 400)

Hispaniola The name of the large CARIBBEAN island that is shared by HAITI and the DOMINICAN REPUBLIC. (76 200 sq km/29 400 sq miles)

Hitachi An industrial city on the east coast of HONSHU island, JAPAN. (Pop. 206 100)

Ho Chi Minh City (Saigon) The largest city in VIETNAM, and the former capital of independent South Vietnam. (Pop. 3 500 000)

Hobart A port and capital of the island of TASMANIA, AUSTRALIA, on the south-east coast. (Pop. 173 700)

Hoggar (Ahaggar) A remote mountain range rising from the desert landscape of southern ALGERIA, and noted for the weathered shapes of its rock formations. The highest peak is Mount Tahat (2918 m/9573 ft).

Hohe Tauern A part of eastern ALPS in southern AUSTRIA, rising to the highest point at Grossglockner (3797 m/12 460 ft), Austria's highest peak.

Hohhot An industrial city and the capital of the NEI MONGOL AUTONOMOUS REGION (Inner Mongolia), CHINA. (Pop. 1 130 000)

Hokkaido The most northerly of the main islands of JAPAN, and the second largest after HONSHU. The capital is SAPPORO. (78 509 sq km/30 312 sq miles; pop. 5 679 400)

Holland A name generally applied to the NETHERLANDS, but in fact the term really applies to the central coastal region which comprise the two provinces of Noord-Holland and Zuid-Holland.

Hollywood A suburb in the northern part of LOS ANGELES in CALIFORNIA, U.S.A. It has long served as the base for the U.S.A.'s powerful film industry.

Homs (Hims) An industrial city of ancient origins on the River ORONTES in SYRIA. (Pop. 414 401)

Honduras A mountainous republic in Central AMERICA with a long seaboard on the CARIBBEAN SEA and a small outlet on the PACIFIC OCEAN. Fruit, particularly bananas, is the main export. The official language is Spanish; Indian dialects are also spoken. The capital is TEGULCIGALPA. (112 088 sq km/43 266 sq miles; pop. 4 543 000; cur. Lempira (peso) = 100 centavos)

Hong Kong A British Crown colony on an island and

peninsula on the coast of south-eastern CHINA, due to be handed back to China in 1997. The colony consists of three territories: Hong Kong Island, KOWLOON and the NEW TERRITORIES. The capital is VICTORIA. (1067 sq km/412 sq miles; pop. 5 580 000; cur. Hong Kong dollar = 100 cents)

Honiara The capital of the SOLOMON ISLANDS, situated on GUADACANAL. (Pop. 23 500)

Honolulu The state capital of HAWAII, U.S.A., on the south coast of the island of OAHU. (Pop. city 373 000/ metropolitan area 805 300)

Honshu The central and largest of the islands of JAPAN. (230 988 sq km/89 185 sq miles; pop. 96 685 000)

Hooghly, River *see* Hugli, River.

Hormuz (Ormuz), Strait of The narrow strait at the mouth of the GULF between the horn-like protrusion of the MUSANDAM peninsula of OMAN to the south, and IRAN to the north.

Horn, Cape (Cabo de Hornos) The southern tip of SOUTH AMERICA, represented by a spattering of remote islands belonging to CHILE off TIERRA DEL FUEGO.

Houston The largest city in TEXAS, U.S.A. (Pop. city 1 705 700/metropolitan area 3 164 400)

Howrah *see* Haora.

Hrvatska *see* Croatia.

Huang He (Hwang Ho; Yellow River) The second longest river in CHINA after the CHANG JIANG (Yangtze), flowing from the central mountains across northern central China to the YELLOW SEA, to the south of BEIJING. (Length: 4670 km/2900 miles)

Huascaran A peak in the ANDES in central PERU, and that country's highest mountain. (6768 m/22 205 ft)
Hubei A landlocked province of central CHINA. (180 000 sq km/69 500 sq miles; pop. 46 320 000)
Hudson River A river flowing from its source in the ADIRONDACK MOUNTAINS in NEW YORK State, U.S.A., to the ATLANTIC OCEAN at NEW YORK City. The ERIE Canal joins the Hudson River to link New York to the GREAT LAKES. (Length 500 km/510 miles)
Hudson Bay A huge bay in north-eastern CANADA, hemmed in to the north by BAFFIN ISLAND, and connected to the ATLANTIC OCEAN by the Hudson Strait.
Hue The capital and powerbase of the rulers of VIETNAM from 200 BC to the 19th century, located in the central coastal region of the country. (Pop. 190 100)
Hugli (Hoogly) A major branch of the River GANGES which forms at its delta and flows through CALCUTTA and the surrounding industrial conurbations into the Bay of BENGAL. (Length 193 km/120 miles)
Hull *see* Kingston upon Hull.
Humber The estuary of the Rivers OUSE and TRENT which cuts deep into the east coast of ENGLAND to the north of the WASH. (Length 60 km/35 miles)
Humberside A county on the north-east coast of ENGLAND, centring upon the HUMBER estuary. It was created in 1974 out of parts of the East and West Ridings of YORKSHIRE and LINCOLNSHIRE. The county town is Beverley. (3512 sq km/1356 sq miles; pop. 854 000)

Hunan An inland province of south-east CHINA. The capital is CHANGSHA. (210 000 sq km/81 000 sq miles; pop. 52 320 000)

Hungary A landlocked republic in central EUROPE consisting of broad plains and mountains to the north. Formerly a part of the 'Soviet bloc' of Eastern Europe, Hungary broke free from Communist rule in 1989. The main exports are foodstuffs, chemicals, machinery and timber. Hungarian is the official language. The capital, BUDAPEST, straddles the River DANUBE, which crosses the middle of the country. (93 032 sq km/ 35 920 sq miles; pop. 10 620 000; cur. Forint = 100 filler)

Hunter Valley The valley of the Hunter River, lying 100 km (60 miles) north-west of SYDNEY, AUSTRALIA. It is particularly noted for its wine.

Huntingdonshire *see* Cambridgeshire.

Huron, Lake One of the GREAT LAKES, lying at the centre of the group on the border between CANADA and the state of MICHIGAN in the U.S.A. (59 570 sq km/ 23 000 sq miles)

Hwang Ho *see* Huang He.

Hyderabad 1 The capital of the state of ANDHRA PRADESH in eastern south INDIA. (Pop. 2 093 5000). **2** A city on the INDUS delta 160 km (100 miles) north-east of KARACHI, PAKISTAN. (Pop. 795 000)

Hydra (Idhra) A small island in the AEGEAN SEA, off the east coast of the PELOPONNESE, GREECE, noted as a haven for tourists where motor traffic is prohibited.

I

Iasi A historic city in north-eastern ROMANIA, near the border with the MOLDAVIA (Pop. 271 400)

Ibadan The second largest city in NIGERIA some 120 km (75 miles) north of the capital, LAGOS. It is a busy market town, and noted for its university. (Pop. 1 009 000)

Ibiza (Iviza) *see* Balearic Islands.

Iboland A densely populated region of south-eastern NIGERIA inhabited by the Ibo people. The attempt by the region to break away from Nigeria (1967–70) under the name of Biafra caused a civil war that led to a famine which killed over a million people. (Pop. 10 000 000)

Ica, River *see* Putumayo, River.

Içel *see* Mersin.

Iceland A European island state in the North ATLANTIC OCEAN which gained independence from Denmark in 1918 and became a republic in 1944. It is a volcanic island and has many hot springs. The national economy is heavily dependent on fishing. Icelandic is the official language and REYKJAVIK is the capital. (103 000 sq km/39 768 sq miles; pop. 243 000; cur. Krona = 100 aurar)

Idaho A inland state in the north-west of the U.S.A. The state capital is BOISE. (216 413 sq km/83 557 sq miles; pop. 1 005 000)

Idhra *see* Hydra.

Idlib A large commercial and agricultural centre in north-western SYRIA. (Pop. 428 000)

Ieper *see* Ypres.

IJsselmeer Formerly a large inlet of the NORTH SEA on the north-eastern coast of the NETHERLANDS, but after the creation of the dam called the Afsluitdijk across its mouth, it has filled with water from the River IJssel and is now a freshwater lake, bordered by fertile areas of reclaimed land (polders).

Ile de France A region and former province of FRANCE with PARIS at its centre, now consisting of eight separate departments. (12 012 sq km/4638 sq miles; pop. 10 073 000)

Illinois A state in the MIDWEST of the U.S.A., bordering Lake MICHIGAN to the north. The capital is SPRINGFIELD, but CHICAGO is its main city. (146 075 sq km/ 56 400 sq miles; pop. 11 535 000)

Imjin River A river which flows from its source in southern NORTH KOREA across the border into SOUTH KOREA and to the YELLOW SEA. In 1951, during the Korean War, it was the scene of a heroic stand by the British 1st Gloster Regiment. (Length 160 km/ 100 miles)

Inagua *see* Bahamas.

Inch'on (Incheon) A port and industrial city on the western (YELLOW SEA) coast of SOUTH KOREA, 39 km (24 miles) west of SEOUL. (Pop. 1 083 900)

India A republic in South ASIA which gained independence from British rule in 1950, while still remaining within the Commonwealth. It is the world's largest democracy. Agriculture is heavily dependent on the monsoon winds which bring rain from June to September. The terrain varies from the colossal mountains of the north to deserts, tropical jungles and fertile plains. The main exports are textiles and foodstuffs. Many different peoples live in India, each with their own language, but the official languages are Hindi and English. The capital is New DELHI. (3 166 829 sq km/ 1 261 816 sq miles; pop. 843 930 900; cur. Rupee = 100 paisa)

Indian Desert *see* Thar Desert.

Indian Ocean The third largest ocean, bounded by ASIA to the north, AFRICA to the west and AUSTRALIA to the east. The southern waters merge with the ANTARCTIC OCEAN.

Indiana A state in the MIDWEST of the U.S.A. to the south-east of Lake MICHIGAN. The state capital is INDIANAPOLIS. (93 994 sq km/36 291 sq miles; pop. 5 499 000)

Indianapolis The state capital of INDIANA. (Pop. city 710 300/metropolitan area 1 194 600)

Indonesia A republic in South-East ASIA, comprising over 13 000 islands, many of them volcanic. The main ones are SUMATRA, JAVA, FLORES, TIMOR, SULAWESI, BALI, the larger part of BORNEO (KALIMANTAN) and half of NEW GUINEA (IRIAN JAYA). Formerly known as the Dutch East Indies, it became independent in 1945 and a republic in 1950. The Equator runs through the northern part of the archipelago and the climate is tropical. Oil, timber, rubber, and metal ores are the main exports. The dominant religion is Islam, and the official language is Bahasa Indonesia. The capital is JAKARTA. (2 027 087 sq km/ 782 660 sq miles; pop. 176 740 000; cur. Rupiah = 100 sen)

Indore A textile-manufacturing city, and once the capital of the princely state of Indore, in western MADHYA PRADESH, central INDIA. (Pop. 829 300)

Indus, River One of the great rivers of ASIA, whose valleys supported some of the world's earliest civilizations, notably at MOHENJO DARO. It flows from its source in TIBET and across the northern tip of INDIA before turning south to run through the entire length of PAKISTAN to its estuary on the ARABIAN SEA, to the south of KARACHI. (Length 3059 km/1900 miles)

Inner Mongolia *see* Nei Mongol Autonomous Region.

Inverness A town in north-eastern SCOTLAND at the head of the MORAY FIRTH and at the eastern end of Loch NESS. (Pop. 40 000)

Iona A small island off the south-western tip of MULL in western SCOTLAND where the Irish monk St Columba founded a monastery in AD 563. (8 sq km/3 sq miles)

Ionian Islands (Eptanisos) The seven largest of the islands which lie scattered along the west coast of GREECE in the IONIAN SEA. They are CORFU, Paxoi, Cephalonia, Levkas, ITHACA, Zakinthos and Kithira. (Pop. 182 700)

Ionian Sea That part of the MEDITERRANEAN SEA which lies between southern ITALY and GREECE. It is named after Io, a mistress of the Ancient Greek god Zeus.

Ios (Nios) *see* Cyclades.

Iowa A state in the MIDWEST of the U.S.A. bounded on the east and west by the upper reaches of the MISSISSIPPI and MISSOURI rivers. The capital is DES MOINES. (145 791 sq km/56 290 sq miles; pop. 2 884 000)

Iran A republic in south-western ASIA, lying between the CASPIAN SEA and the GULF. Formerly known as Persia, the country was ruled by a monarch or Shah. However, the monarchy was overthrown in 1979 and Iran became an Islamic republic. Most of the land is a high desert plateau, with mountains around the peripheries where the watered valleys are fertile. The rim around the Caspian is semi-tropical. Oil, found in the south of the country, is the main source of revenue. Iranian (Farsi) is the official language, and the principal religion is Shia Islam. The capital is TEHRAN. (1 648 000 sq km/636 293 sq miles; pop. 46 500 000; cur. Rial = 100 dinar)

Iraq A republic in south-western ASIA, landlocked except where the SHATT AL ARAB waterway flows into the GULF. Rich in ancient history, IRAQ became a republic in 1958 and has had a troubled recent past under the dictatorship of Saddam Hussein. To the north stand the inhospitable mountains of KURDISTAN and to the west the bleak Syrian Desert. Most of the people live in the towns that dot the fertile valleys of the Rivers TIGRIS and EUPHRATES. Oil is the chief export. The dominant religion is Sunni Islam; the official language is Arabic. The capital is BAGHDAD. (434 925 sq km/167 925 sq miles; pop. 16 000 000; cur. Dinar = 20 dirhams = 1000 fils)

Ireland An island off the west coast of GREAT BRITAIN, almost five sixths of which is the independent Republic of IRELAND, while the remainder is NORTHERN IRELAND, which is a province of the U.K. (80 400 sq km/32 588 sq miles, pop. 5 202 000)

Ireland, Republic of (Eire) A state that occupies the greater part of the island of IRELAND. It was a Commonwealth country until 1949 when it finally severed its links with the U.K. and became a totally independent republic. Called the 'Emerald Isle' because of its lush countryside, Ireland's economy is largely based on agriculture, although machinery, textiles and chemicals number among its exports. It also has a busy tourist industry. It joined the European Community in 1973. There are two official languages, Irish (Gaelic) and English. The capital is DUBLIN. (70 283 sq km/27 136 sq miles; pop. 3 630 000; cur. Punt = 100 pennies)

Irian Jaya The western half of the island of NEW GUINEA, which has been part of INDONESIA since 1963. (410 660 sq km/158 556 sq miles; pop. 2 584 000)

Irish Sea The arm of the ATLANTIC that separates the islands of IRELAND and GREAT BRITAIN.

Irkutsk An industrial city on the Trans-Siberian Railway lying near the southern end of Lake BAIKAL in southern central RUSSIA. (Pop. 590 000)

Irrawaddy, River The central focus of BURMA, flowing from its two primary sources in the north of the country to MANDALAY and then south to its delta in the Bay of BENGAL. (Length 2000 km/1250 miles)

Irtysh, River A largely navigable river flowing northwards from its source near the border between northwest CHINA and MONGOLIA across the centre of KAZAKHSTAN and through OMSK to join the River OB' on its journey to the ARCTIC OCEAN. (Length 4440 km/2760 miles)

Ischia A beautiful volcanic island at the northern end of the Bay of NAPLES. (46 sq km/18 sq miles; pop. 43 900)

Isfahan *see* Esfahan.

Iskenderun A port of ancient origin in southern TURKEY, in the north-eastern corner of the MEDITERRANEAN SEA. (Pop. 173 600)

Islamabad The capital of PAKISTAN since 1967, in the north of the country. (Pop. 201 000)

Israel A republic in south-western ASIA with a seaboard on the MEDITERRANEAN and a small coast on the Gulf of AQABA. The country was created as a Jewish state, out of what was called Palestine, in 1948. Since then Israel has had numerous disputes with its Arab neighbours (JORDAN, SYRIA, LEBANON and EGYPT) and with Palestinians who claim the country to be their homeland. Two important pieces of disputed territory, the WEST BANK and the GAZA STRIP, where many Palestinian refugees live, have been occupied by Israel. The country has succeeded in becoming self-sufficient in food and now exports excess produce, especially citrus fruits, to gain much-needed revenue. Nevertheless, Israel relies heavily on aid from the U.S.A., especially in times of international tension. The official language is Hebrew, but Arabic and English are also widely used. The capital is JERUSALEM. (20 700 sq km/7992 miles (1949 boundaries); pop. 4 150 000; cur. Shekel = 100 agorot)

Issyk-Kul' A lake in southern central KAZAKHSTAN, set in the high mountains that line the border with CHINA. (6280 sq km/2424 sq miles)

Istanbul The largest city in TURKEY, built mainly on the western bank of the BOSPHORUS, with a commanding view of shipping entering the BLACK SEA. It was founded by the Greeks in 660 BC and was known as Byzantium; between AD 330 and 1930 it was called Constantinople. (Pop. 5 858 600)

Italy A republic in southern EUROPE comprising a long peninsula that thrusts into the MEDITERRANEAN SEA, and two large islands, SICILY to the south and SARDINIA to the west. It became a modern republic in 1946. Much of the country is mountainous, with the ALPS to the north and the APENNINES running down the middle of the peninsula. Italy is a thriving member of the European Community with important heavy and agricultural industries. It also maintains an active tourist industry throughout the year, thanks to its climate as well as to its outstanding monuments of Ancient Rome and the Renaissance. The capital is ROME. (301 225 sq km/116 304 sq miles; pop. 57 320 000; cur. Lira)

Ithaca (Ithaki) The smallest of the IONIAN ISLANDS, situated off the west coast of GREECE. Odysseus (Ulysses), the hero of Homer's Odyssey, was a son of the royal house of Ithaca. (93 sq km/36 sq miles; pop. 3650)

Ivanovo A textile-manufactiuring city in eastern RUSSIA, 240 km (150 miles) north-east of MOSCOW. (Pop. 476 000)

Iviza *see* Balearic Islands.

Ivory Coast *see* Côte d'Ivoire.

Iwo Jima The largest in the group of islands called the

Volcano Islands belonging to JAPAN, which lie some 1200 km (745 miles) south of TOKYO in the PACIFIC OCEAN. It was the scene of bitter fighting in 1945 at the end of the Second World War when U.S. troops took the island from the Japanese. (21 sq km/8 sq miles)

Ixtaccihuatl A volcanic peak south of MEXICO CITY, which is twinned with neighbouring POPOCATAPETL. (5286 m/17 342 ft)

Izhevsk *see* Ustinov.

Izmir (Smyrna) A port of ancient Greek origin on the AEGIAN coast of TURKEY, to the south of ISTANBUL. (Pop. 1 489 800)

Izmit (Kocaeli) A port and naval base on the Sea of MARMARA 90 km (55 miles) south-east of ISTANBUL. (Pop. 236 100)

J

Jackson The state capital of MISSISSIPPI. (Pop. city 208 800/metropolitan area 382 400)

Jacksonville A port on the northern east coast of FLORIDA, U.S.A. (Pop. city 578 000/metropolitan area 795 300)

Jaffna A port on the tip of the northern peninsula of SRI LANKA, and the main centre for the Tamil population of the island. (Pop. 118 200)

Jaipur The capital of the state of RAJASTHAN, INDIA. (Pop. 1 015 200)

Jakarta The capital of INDONESIA, a port on the north-western tip of JAVA. (Pop. 6 503 000)

Jamaica An island state in the CARIBBEAN SEA and the third largest of the WEST INDIES. It was a British colony until 1962, when it gained independence within the Commonwealth. Much of the island is mountainous, but suitable for growing coffee, bananas and sugar cane, which are among the main exports. Bauxite is also an important source of revenue. The official language is English, and the capital is KINGSTON. (10 991 sq km/4244 sq miles; pop. 2 470 000; cur. Jamaican dollar = 100 cents)

James Bay The southern arm of the HUDSON BAY, CANADA, which extends 440 km (273 miles) into ONTARIO and QUEBEC.

Jammu and Kashmir The state in the very north of INDIA, bordering CHINA and PAKISTAN. The total size of the state is 222 236 sq km (85 783 sq miles), but its borders are disputed and following wars with Pakistan (1947–49, 1967 and 1971) and annexation by China in the 1950s, India occupies only about a half of what it claims. (Pop. 5 987 400)

Jamshedpur An industrial city in north-east INDIA which grew up around steel foundries set up by Jamshedi Tata in 1907–11. (Pop. 669 600)

Jamuna, River The name given to the river formed by the BRAHMAPUTRA and the Tista as it flows through BANGLADESH to join the GANGES.

Japan An empire state in Eastern ASIA comprising four large islands (HONSHU, HOKKAIDO, KYUSHU, SHIKOKU) and the many smaller ones that separate the Sea of Japan from the PACIFIC OCEAN. After the Second World War, Japan embarked upon a course of economic growth that has made it one of the most successful industrial nations in the world. Most of the population live in the densely populated coastal towns and cities. Japan's exports include cars, ships, iron and steel and electronic goods. The main religions are Shintoism and Buddhism. Japanese is the language used, and the capital is TOKYO. (373 313 sq km/ 143 750 sq miles; pop. 121 400 000; cur. Yen = 100 sen)

Japan, Sea of A part of the PACIFIC OCEAN that lies between JAPAN and the Korean peninsula.

Java (Jawa) The central island in the southern chain of islands of INDONESIA. The capital is JAKARTA. (130 987 sq km/50 574 sq miles; pop. 91 269 600)

Java Sea An arm of the PACIFIC OCEAN that separates JAVA and BORNEO.

Jeddah (Jidda) A port on the RED SEA coast of SAUDI ARABIA, and one of the country's main centres of population. (Pop. 750 000)

Jefferson City The state capital of MISSOURI, U.S.A. (Pop. 35 000)

Jena A university town in southern central GERMANY, 80 km (50 miles) south-west of LEIPZIG. The Prussian army was defeated by the French under Napoleon here in 1806. (Pop. 107 700)

Jerba (Djerba) An island in the Gulf of GABES belonging to TUNISIA. It has become a popular tourist resort in recent years. (67 sq km/42 sq miles; pop. 92 300)

Jerez de la Frontera (Jerez) A town in south-west SPAIN, just inland from CADIZ, famous for the sweet wine to which it has given its name: sherry. (Pop. 176 200)

Jericho A town in the WEST BANK area occupied by ISRAEL since 1967, on the site of a city that dates back to about 7000 BC. (Pop. 15 000)

Jersey The largest of the British CHANNEL ISLANDS. The capital is St Helier. (117 sq km/45 sq miles; pop. 77 000)

Jerusalem The capital of ISRAEL, and an historic city considered holy by Muslims, Christians and Jews. (Pop. 446 500)

Jaingsu A heavily populated but highly productive province on the central east coast of CHINA. The capital is NANJING. (100 000 sq km/38 600 sq miles; pop. 60 521 000)

Jiangxi An inland province of south-eastern CHINA. Its capital is NANCHANG. (160 000 sq km/39 000 sq miles; pop. 32 290 000)

Jilin (Kirin) A province of central DONGBEI (Manchuria) in northern CHINA. The capital is CHANGCHUN. (180 000 sq km/69 500 sq miles; pop. 22 502 000)

Jinan The capital of SHANDONG province, situated close to the HUANG HE River, 360 km (225 miles) to the south of BEIJING. (Pop. 3 200 000)

Jodhpur A city in central RAJASTHAN, INDIA, on the perimeter of the THAR DESERT. The city has given its name to the riding britches that first became popular here. (Pop. 506 300)

Jogjakarta *see* Yogyakarta.

Johannesburg The centre of the old gold-mining area of SOUTH AFRICA and now that country's largest town. (Pop. 1 536 500)

John o'Groats The village traditionally held to be on

the most northerly point of SCOTLAND and of mainland GREAT BRITAIN.

Johor Bahru (Johore) A port and growing city in MALAYSIA situated on the southern tip of the MALAY PENINSULA opposite SINGAPORE, to which it is connected by a causeway. It is also the capital of the state of Johor. (Pop. city 246 400)

Jordan A kingdom in south-western ASIA which did not become fully independent of British protection until 1946. The country is landlocked except for a small opening on the Gulf of AQABA. Much of the land is desert, but wherever fertile land is available it is farmed intensively. The western border is with ISRAEL (the WEST BANK, theoretically Jordanian territory, has been occupied by Israel). About half the population of Jordan is made up of Palestinian refugees, who live in United Nations camps. Jordan has no oil, but it does refine and export it; it also exports chemicals and agricultural produce. With its history of stable government and well-placed capital, AMMAN, Jordan has come to play a crucial role in MIDDLE EAST politics. The dominant religion is Sunni Islam, and the official language is Arabic. (97 740sq km/37 730 sq miles, (including West Bank); pop. 29 960 000 (including West Bank); cur. Dinar = 1000 fils)

Jordan, River A river flowing southwards from Mount HERMON in southern LEBANON, through northern ISRAEL to Lake TIBERIAS (Sea of Galilee) and then on through JORDAN into the DEAD SEA, where it evaporates. The WEST BANK to the north of the Dead Sea is disputed Jordanian territory which has been occupied by Israelis since the Six Day War in 1967. (Length 256 km/159 miles)

Juan de Fuca Strait The channel to the south of VANCOUVER ISLAND on the border between CANADA and the U.S.A., through which ships from VICTORIA, VANCOUVER and SEATTLE can pass to reach the PACIFIC OCEAN.

Juan Fernández Islands A group of three remote islands in the PACIFIC OCEAN belonging to CHILE and some 650 km (400 miles) due west of SANTIAGO. (181 sq km/62 sq miles; pop. 550)

Judaea The southern part of PALESTINE, occupying the area between the MEDITERRANEAN coast to the west and the DEAD SEA and River JORDAN to the east.

Jumna, River *see* Yamuna, River.

Juneau The state capital of ALASKA. (Pop. 23 800)

Jungfrau A famous peak in the Bernese Oberland range in the Swiss ALPS, popular with climbers but now also ascended by cable car. (4158 m/13 642 ft)

Jura A large upland band of limestone in eastern central FRANCE which lines the border with SWITZERLAND, giving its name to a department in France and a canton in Switzerland. A further extension continues across southern GERMANY as far as NUREMBURG (the Swabian and Franconian Jura).

Jutland A large peninsula stretching some 400 km (250 miles) northwards from GERMANY to separate the NORTH SEA from the BALTIC SEA. Most of it is occupied by the mainland part of DENMARK, which calls it Jylland, while the southern part belongs to the German state of SCHLESWIG-HOLSTEIN.

K

K2 (Godwin Austen) The second highest mountain in the world after Mount EVEREST, situated in the KARAKORAM mountain range on the border between PAKISTAN and CHINA. (8611 m/28 250 ft)

Kabul The capital and main city of AFGHANISTAN, in the north-east of the country on the Kabul River. (Pop. 1 036 400)

Kachchh *see* Kutch.

Kagoshima A port on the south coast of KYUSHU island, JAPAN. (Pop. 530 500)

Kaifeng A city of ancient origins in HENAN province, CHINA. (Pop. 500 000)

Kairouan A city in northern TUNISIA, to Muslims the most holy city of the MAGHREB. (Pop. 72 300)

Kalahari A region of semi-desert occupying much of southern BOTSWANA and straddling the border with SOUTH AFRICA and NAMIBIA.

Kalgoorlie A town in southern WESTERN AUSTRALIA which has grown up around its gold and nickel reserves. (Pop. 19 800)

Kalimantan The greater part of BORNEO, which is governed by INDONESIA. (538 718 sq km/208 000 sq miles; pop. 6 724 000)

Kalimnos (Calino) *see* Dodecanese.

Kalinin An industrial city on the navigable part of the River VOLGA, RUSSIA, 160 km (100 miles) north-west of MOSCOW. Founded in 1181, it was called Tver until renamed in 1932 after Mikhail Kalinin, the Soviet President 1937–46. (Pop. 437 000)

Kaliningrad (Königsberg) A port and industrial city on the BALTIC coast belonging to RUSSIA, in an enclave between LITHUANIA and POLAND. Founded in the 13th century, it was called Königsberg and was the capital of East PRUSSIA, but was ceded to the U.S.S.R. in 1945 and renamed after Mikhail Kalinin, the Soviet President 1937–46. (Pop. 380 000)

Kalmyk (Kalmuck) Republic An autonomous republic of the RUSSIAN FEDERATION, lying to the north-west of the CASPIAN SEA. (75 900 sq km/29 300 sq miles; pop. 315 000)

Kamchatka A peninsula, some 1200 km (750 miles) long, which drops south from eastern SIBERIA, RUSSIA, into the north PACIFIC OCEAN. (Pop. 422 000)

Kampala The capital and main city of UGANDA, situated on Lake VICTORIA. (Pop. 500 000)

Kampuchea *see* Cambodia.

Kananga A city in central southern ZAIRE, founded in 1894 as Luluabourg. (Pop. 704 000)

Kanazawa A historic port on the central northern coast of HONSHU island, JAPAN. (Pop. 430 500)

Kandahar The second largest city in AFGHANISTAN, situated in the south-eastern part of the country, near the border with PAKISTAN. (Pop. 191 400)

Kandy A town in the central mountains of SRI LANKA which was once the capital of the Sinhalese kings, and is sacred to Buddhists. (Pop. 101 300)

Kangchenjunga The world's third highest mountain (after Mount EVEREST and K2), situated in the eastern HIMALAYAS, on the borders between NEPAL, CHINA and the Indian state of SIKKIM. (8585 m/28 165 ft)

KaNgwane A small state, formerly a Bantu homeland, in east TRANSVAAL, SOUTH AFRICA, bordering SWAZILAND. (3910 sq km/1510 sq miles; pop. 458 000)
Kano A historic trading city of the Hausa people of northern NIGERIA, the third largest city in NIGERIA after LAGOS and IBADAN. (Pop. city 475 000)
Kanpur (Cawnpore) An industrial city in northern central INDIA. (Pop. 1 639 100)
Kansas A state in the GREAT PLAINS of the U.S.A. The state capital is TOPEKA. (213 064 sq km/82 264 sq miles; pop. 2 450 000)
Kansas City An industrial city on the MISSOURI RIVER which straddles the border between the states of MISSOURI and KANSAS. (Pop. city 603 600/metropolitan area 1 476 700)
Kao-hsiung The second largest city in TAIWAN and a major port, situated in the south-west of the island. (Pop. 1 269 000)
Kara Kum (Karakumy) A sand desert in southern TURKMENISTAN, to the east of the CASPIAN SEA, and on the borders with IRAN and AFGHANISTAN.
Kara Sea A branch of the ARCTIC OCEAN off the central northern coast of the RUSSIA.
Karachi A port and industrial city, and the largest city in PAKISTAN. (Pop. 5 103 000)
Karaganda An industrial city in the mining region of KAZAKHSTAN. (Pop. 608 000)
Karakoram A range of mountains at the western end of the HIMALAYAS on the borders between PAKISTAN, CHINA, and INDIA.
Karbala A town in central IRAQ, 90 km (55 miles)

south of BAGHDAD. As the site of the tomb of Hussein bin Ali and his brother Abbas, grandsons of the prophet Muhammad, it is held sacred by the Shia Muslims. (Pop. 107 500)

Karelia A region which straddles the border between FINLAND and the RUSSIA.

Kariba A hydroelectric dam on the River ZAMBEZI on the border between ZAMBIA and ZIMBABWE.

Karl-Marx-Stadt *see* Chemnitz.

Karlovy Vary (Carlsbad; Karlsbad) A spa town in CZECHOSLOVAKIA. (Pop. 59 200)

Karlsruhe (Carlsruhe) An industrial city in the valley of the River RHINE, in south-western GERMANY. (Pop. 275 000)

Karnak The site of the extensive ruins of a temple complex dating from about 1560–1090 BC on the eastern bank of the River NILE in central EGYPT.

Karnataka A state in south-west INDIA. The capital is BANGALORE. (191 791 sq km/74 031 sq miles; pop. 37 135 700)

Kärnten *see* Carinthia.

Karoo (Karroo) Two separate regions of semi-desert, the Great Karoo and the Little Karoo, lying between the mountain ranges of southern CAPE PROVINCE, SOUTH AFRICA.

Kasai (Cassai), River A major river of ZAIRE. (Length 2150 km/1350 miles)

Kashmir A mountainous region straddling the border between INDIA and PAKISTAN and subject to dispute since the partition of India and Pakistan in 1947. About half of the former princely state of JAMMU AND

KASHMIR is now ruled by Pakistan and is known as Azad (Free) Kashmir.

Kassel (Cassel) An industrial city in central GERMANY. (Pop. 190 400)

Kasvin *see* Qazvin.

Kathmandu (Katmandu) The capital and principal city of NEPAL. (Pop. 195 260)

Katowice (Kattowitz) An industrial city in central southern POLAND. (Pop. 361 300)

Kattegat (Cattegat) The strait, 34 km (21 miles) at its narrowest, at the entrance to the BALTIC SEA which separates SWEDEN from the JUTLAND peninsula of DENMARK.

Kaunas (Kovno) An industrial city in LITHUANIA, formerly (1920–40) the capital of independent Lithuania. (Pop. 400 000)

Kavango (Cubango), River A river, known formerly as the Okavango, which flows south-east from central ANGOLA to form the border with NAMIBIA before petering out in the swampy inland Okavango Delta in northern BOTSWANA. (Length 1600 km/1000 miles)

Kaveri (Caveri, Cauvery), River A holy river of southern INDIA, flowing south-east from the DECCAN plateau to the coast on the Bay of BENGAL. (Length 800 km/ 497 miles)

Kavkaz *see* Caucasus.

Kawasaki An industrial city on the east coast of HONSHU island, JAPAN, forming part of the TOKYO–YOKOHAMA conurbation. (Pop. 1 088 600)

Kazakhstan A former republic of the U.S.S.R., lying in the central southern region between the CASPIAN

SEA and CHINA. It declared sovereignty in 1990. The capital is ALMA-ATA. (2 717 000 sq km/1 050 000 sq miles; pop. 15 654 000)

Kazan' An industrial city and capital of the TATAR REPUBLIC in central RUSSIA. (Pop. 1 039 000)

Keeling Islands *see* Cocos Islands.

Kefallinia *see* Ionian Islands.

Kells A market town in County MEATH, IRELAND. It was the site of a monastery founded in the 6th century by St Columba, which was the source of the illuminated *Book of Kells*.

Kelsty *see* Kielce.

Kemerovo An industrial city in the coal-mining region of southern SIBERIA. (Pop. 505 000)

Kennedy, Cape *see* Canaveral, Cape.

Kent A county in the extreme south-east of ENGLAND. The county town is Maidstone. (3732 sq km/1441 sq miles; pop. 1 494 000)

Kentucky A state in east central U.S.A. The state capital is FRANKFORT. (104 623 sq km/40 395 sq miles; pop. 3 726 000)

Kenya A republic in East AFRICA with a coast on the INDIAN OCEAN. It was a British colony until 1963, when it gained independence within the Commonwealth. The Equator runs through the middle of the country and the climate is tropical on the coast, but more temperate inland. Coffee, tea and tourism are the principal sources of revenue. The official languages are Swahili and English. The capital is NAIROBI. (582 646 sq km/224 960 sq miles; pop. 21 040 000; cur. Kenya shilling = 100 cents)

Kenya, Mount A towering extinct volcano in central KENYA, the second highest mountain in AFRICA after Mount KILIMANJARO. (5200 m/17 058 ft)

Kerala A state occupying the western coast of the southern tip of INDIA. The capital is TRIVANDRUM. (38 863 sq km/15 005 sq miles; pop. 25 453 000)

Kerguelen The largest in a remote group of some 300 islands in the southern INDIAN OCEAN forming part of the FRENCH SOUTHERN AND ANTARCTIC TERRITORIES, now occupied only by the staff of a scientific base. (3414 sq km/1318 sq miles)

Kérkira *see* Corfu.

Kermanshah *see* Bakhtaran.

Kerry A county in the south-west of the Republic IRELAND, noted for the rugged beauty of its peninsulas and its green dairy pastures. The county town is Tralee. (4701 sq km/1815 sq miles; pop. 122 800)

Key West A port and resort at the southern end of Florida Keys, a chain of coral islands off the southern tip of FLORIDA, U.S.A. (Pop. 24 900)

Khabarovsk A major industrial city in south-eastern SIBERIA, lying just 35 km (22 miles) north of the border with CHINA. (Pop. 569 000)

Khajuraho A town in northern MADYA PRADESH, INDIA, noted in particular for its Hindu and Jain temples which are famed for their intricate and erotic sculpture.

Kharg Island A small island in the northern GULF where IRAN has constructed a major oil terminal.

Khar'kov A major industrial and commercial centre of the UKRAINE. (Pop. 1 536 000)

Khartoum The capital of SUDAN, situated at the confluence of the Blue NILE and White Nile. (Pop. 561 000)

Khios *see* Chios.

Khone Falls A massive set of waterfalls on the MEKONG RIVER in southern Laos, which effectively prevent the Mekong from being navigable beyond this point. With a maximum width of 10.8 km (6.7 miles), these are the widest falls in the world.

Khorasan The north-eastern province of IRAN, bordering AFGHANISTAN and TURKMENISTAN. The capital is MASHHAD. (Pop. 3 267 000)

Khulna A port and district in south-west BANGLADESH. (Pop. town 646 400)

Khuzestan (Khuzistan) A province in south-western IRAN, and the country's main oil-producing area. The capital is AHVAZ. (Pop. 2 177 000)

Khyber Pass A high pass (1072 m/3518 ft), over the Safed Koh mountains connecting PESHAWAR in PAKISTAN with KABUL in AFGHISTAN. It has been of great strategic importance throughout history.

Kiel A port and shipbuilding city on the BALTIC coast of northern GERMANY. It stands at the mouth of the Kiel Ship Canal which permits ocean-going ships to cross the JUTLAND peninsula from the BALTIC to HAMBURG and the NORTH SEA. (Pop. 248 400)

Kielce (Kelsty) An industrial city in central southern POLAND. (Pop. 197 000)

Kiev The capital of the UKRAINE, situated on the DNIEPER River. Founded in the 6th century, it is now a major industrial city. (Pop. 2 411 000)

Kigali The capital of Rwanda. (Pop. 170 000)
Kikládhes *see* Cyclades.
Kildare A county in the south-east of the Republic of IRELAND, famous for its racehorses and the racecourse, The Curragh. The county town is Naas. (1694 sq km/654 sq miles; pop. 104 100)
Kilimanjaro, Mount Africa's highest mountain, in north-eastern TANZANIA. (5895 m/19 340 ft)
Kilkenny A county in the south-east of the Republic of IRELAND, and also the name of its capital city. (2062 sq km/769 sq miles; pop. county 70 800/city 10 100)
Killarney A market town in county KERRY, in the Republic of IRELAND, which is at the centre of a landscape of lakes and mountains much admired and visited for its beauty. (Pop. 7700)
Kimberley A town in the north of CAPE PROVINCE, SOUTH AFRICA, which is at the centre of South Africa's diamond mining industry. (Pop. 153 900)
Kimberleys, The A vast plateau of hills and gorges in the north of WESTERN AUSTRALIA. (420 000 sq km/ 162 000 sq miles)
Kincardineshire *see* Grampian.
Kingston The capital and main port of JAMAICA. (Pop. 700 000)
Kingston upon Hull (Hull) A port in the county of HUMBERSIDE in eastern ENGLAND, situated on the north side of the HUMBER estuary. (Pop. 270 000)
Kingstown The capital of ST VINCENT and a port, famed for its botanical gardens. (Pop. 22 800)
Kinshasa The capital of ZAIRE, on the banks of the

River ZAIRE. It is the largest city in Central AFRICA. (Pop. 2 444 000)

Kirghizia (Kirghiz Republic) A former republic of south central U.S.S.R. on the border with CHINA. It declared itself independent in 1990. The capital is FRUNZE. (198 500 sq km/76 600 sq miles; pop. 3 886 000)

Kirin *see* Jilin.

Kiribati A republic comprising a group of 33 islands scattered over some 3 000 000 sq km (1 160 000 sq miles) in the southern PACIFIC. Formerly known as the Gilbert Islands they were granted independence from the U.K. in 1979, while still remaining within the Commonwealth. The country is heavily dependent on aid, but copra and fish are exported. The official languages are Gilbertese and English, and the capital is TARAWA. (717 sq km/277 sq miles; pop. 63 000; cur. Australian dollar = 100 cents)

Kiritimati *see* Christmas Island.

Kircudbrightshire *see* Dumfries and Galloway.

Kirkuk An industrial city and regional capital in the Kurdish north of IRAQ. (Pop. 650 000)

Kirov An industrial city in east central RUSSIA, founded in the 12th century. (Pop. 407 000)

Kisangani A commercial centre and regional capital in northern ZAIRE, on the River ZAIRE. It was originally called Stanleyville. (Pop. 339 000)

Kishinev (Chişinău) The capital of MOLDAVIA. (Pop. 605 000)

Kistna, River *see* Krishna, River.

Kita-Kyushu A major industrial city situated in the north of KYUSHU island, JAPAN. (Pop. 1 056 400)

Kitchener-Waterloo Two towns in southern ONTARIO, CANADA, which have become twin cities, 100 km (62 miles) west of TORONTO. (Pop. 288 000)
Kithira (Cerigo) *see* Ionian Islands.
Kivu, Lake A lake in the GREAT RIFT VALLEY on the border between RWANDA and ZAIRE. (2850 sq km/ 1100 sq miles)
Kizil Irmak, River The longest river in TURKEY, flowing westwards from the centre of the country near SIVAS, before curling north to the BLACK SEA. (Length 1130 km/700 miles)
Klaipeda A major port and shipbuilding centre on the BALTIC coast of LITHUANIA. (Pop. 181 000)
Klondike, River A short river flowing through YUKON TERRITORY in north-western CANADA to meet the Yukon River at Dawson. Gold was discovered in the region in 1896 causing the subsequent goldrush. (Length 160 km/100 miles)
Knock A village in County MAYO, in the west of the Republic of Ireland, where group of villagers witnessed a vision of the Virgin Mary and other saints in 1879. It has now become a Marian shrine of world importance. (Pop. 1400)
Knossos The site of an excavated royal palace of the Minoan civilization, 5 km (3 miles) south-east of HERAKLION, the capital of CRETE. The palace was built in about 1950 BC and destroyed in 1380 BC.
Knoxville An industrial city in eastern TENNESSEE, U.S.A., and a port on the TENNESSEE RIVER. (Pop. city 174 000/metropolitan area 589 400)
Kobe A major container port and shipbuilding centre

at the southern end of HONSHU island, JAPAN. (Pop. 1 410 800)

Kobenhavn *see* Copenhagen.

Koblenz (Coblenz) A city at the confluence of the Rivers RHINE and MOSELLE in western GERMANY, and a centre for the German wine-making industry. (Pop. 113 000)

Kola Peninsula A bulging peninsula in the BARENTS SEA in the extreme north-west of RUSSIA, to the east of MURMANSK.

Köln *see* Cologne.

Kolonia The capital of the Federated States of MICRONESIA, on the island of Ponape. (Pop. 22 000).

Kolyma, River A river in north-eastern SIBERIA, flowing north from the gold-rich Kolyma mountains into the East Siberian Sea. (Length 2600 km/1600 miles)

Komi Republic An autonomous republic in the north of the RUSSIAN FEDERATION, which produces timber, coal, oil and natural gas. (415 900 sq km/160 600 sq miles; pop. 1 197 000)

Komodo A small island of INDONESIA in the Lesser SUNDA group, between SUMBAWA and FLORES, noted above all as the home of the giant monitor lizard, the Komodo Dragon. (520 sq km/200 sq miles)

Königsberg *see* Kaliningrad.

Konya A carpet-making town and capital of the province of the same name in central southern TURKEY, 235 km (145 miles) south of ANKARA. (Pop. town 438 900)

Korcula *see* Dalmatia.

Korea, North A Communist republic occupying the

northern part of the Korean peninsula that divides the YELLOW SEA from the Sea of JAPAN in north-eastern ASIA. The country was created in 1948 and sparked off the Korean War (1950–3) when it invaded its neighbour to the south. The invasion was repulsed by United Nations forces and a Demilitarized Zone currently separates South Korea from North Korea. It is a mountainous country and only a small percentage is cultivated. Minerals and chemicals are among the main exports. Korean is the principal language, and the capital is PYONGYANG. (122 098 sq km/47 142 sq miles; pop. 20 540 000; cur. North Korean won = 100 chon)

Korea, South A republic occupying the lower part of the Korean peninsula and some 3000 small islands. Like North Korea, it was created in 1948, but unlike its neighbour it has succeeded in becoming a successful industrial nation, exporting ships, cars, steel, electronic goods, clothes, food and chemicals. The principal language is Korean, and the capital is SEOUL. (98 992 sq km/38 221 sq miles; pop. 43 280 000; cur. South Korean won = 100 chon)

Korea Strait The stretch of water, 64 km (40 miles) at its narrowest) which separates the southern tip of South KOREA from JAPAN. It is also sometimes known as the Tsushima Strait, after the island of that name.

Korinthos *see* Corinth.

Koror The capital of BELAU. (Pop. 8000)

Kos (Cos) One of the DODECANESE ISLANDS, belonging to Greece, in the AEGIAN SEA, noted as the birthplace (*c*.460 BC) of Hippocrates, the father of medicine. (290 sq km/112 sq miles; pop. 20 300)

Kosciusko, Mount The highest mountain in AUSTRALIA, a peak in the SNOWY MOUNTAIN range in southern NEW SOUTH WALES. (2230 m/7316 ft)

Kosice A rapidly growing industrial city and in eastern CZECHOSLOVAKIA, and the regional capital of eastern SLOVAKIA. (Pop. 214 300)

Kosovo An autonomous province in the south-west of SERBIA, YUGOSLAVIA. About 75 per cent of the population are ethnic Albanians. The capital is PRISTINA. (10 887 sq km/4202 sq miles; pop. 1 584 000)

Kovno *see* Kaunas.

Kowloon A mainland territory of HONG KONG, lying opposite and to the north of Hong Kong Island. (Pop. 800 000)

Kra, Isthmus of The narrow neck of land, only some 50 km (30 miles) wide and shared by BURMA and THAILAND, which joins peninsula MALAYSIA to the mainland of South-East ASIA.

Krakatau (Krakatoa) A volcano which erupted out the sea between JAVA and SUMATRA in INDONESIA in 1883 in a explosion that was heard 5000 km (3100 miles) away, and which killed 36 000 people. Today is the site is marked by a more recent volcano called Anak Krakatau (Son of Krakatau).

Krakow *see* Cracow.

Krasnodar An agricultural centre and industrial city in the central CAUCASUS. (Pop. 604 000)

Krasnoyarsk A mining city on the Trans-Siberian Railway in central southern SIBERIA. (Pop. 860 000)

Krefeld A textile town specializing in silk in western GERMANY, near the border with the NETHERLANDS. (Pop. 224 000)

Krishna (Kistna), River A river that flows through southern INDIA from its source in the Western GHATS to the Bay of BENGAL. (Length 1401 km/871 miles)

Kristiania *see* Oslo.

Krivoy Rog A city in the DONETS BASIN mining region of the UKRAINE. (Pop. 680 000)

Krk (Veglia) An richly fertile island belonging to CROATIA, YUGOSLAVIA, in the northern ADRIATIC SEA. (408 sq km/158 sq miles; pop. 1500)

Krung Thep *see* Bangkok.

Kuala Lumpur The capital of MALAYSIA, sited on the banks of the Kelang and Gombak Rivers. (Pop. 937 900)

Kuanza, River *see* Cuanza, River.

Kumamoto A city in the west of KYUSHU island, JAPAN, noted for its electronics industries. (Pop. 555 700)

Kumasi A town in central southern GHANA, and the capital of the Ashanti people. (Pop. 415 300)

Kunming An industrial and trading city, and capital of YUNNAN province in southern, central CHINA. (Pop. 1 930 000)

Kurashiki A city in south-western HONSHU island, JAPAN. Although now a major industrial centre, it still preserves much of its medieval heritage. (Pop. 411 400)

Kurdistan A region of the MIDDLE EAST occupied by the Kurdish people spanning the borders of IRAQ, IRAN and TURKEY. Although proposals for an independent

Kurdistan were agreed in 1920 between the First World War Allies and Turkey, this plan has never been realized. Greater autonomy was in principle granted to the Kurdish people in Iraq after the Gulf War of 1991.

Kuril (Kurile) Islands A long chain of some 56 volcanic islands stretching between the southern coast of the KAMCHATKA peninsula in eastern RUSSIA and HOKKAIDO island, northern JAPAN. The archipelago was taken from Japan by the U.S.S.R. in 1945; this remains an issue of contention between Russia and Japan. (15 600 sq km/6020 sq miles)

Kursk A major industrial city in central western RUSSIA, 450 km (280 miles) south of MOSCOW. It was the scene of a devastating tank battle in 1943 which left the city in ruins. (Pop. 423 000)

Kurukshetra A sacred Hindu city in northern INDIA, 140 km (87 miles) north of DELHI. (Pop. 186 100)

Kutch (Kachchh) An inhospitable coastal region on the border between PAKISTAN and INDIA, which floods in the monsoon and then dries out into a baking, salty desert. (44 185 sq km/17 060 sq miles)

Kuwait A sovereign state that became independent of British protection in 1961. It is situated on the north-west coast of the GULF and the terrain is largely flat desert. Although a small country, it is one of the world's largest oil producers, providing its citizens with a very high *per capita* income. In 1990 the country was invaded and vandalized by IRAQ, its neighbour to the north, but the Iraqis were repulsed by an international force of the United Nations led by the U.S.A.

The main language is Arabic. The capital is Kuwait City. (17 818 sq km/6879 sq miles; pop. 1 900 000; cur. Dinar = 1000 fils)

Kuybyshev A major industrial city and port on the River VOLGA in eastern central RUSSIA. Founded in 1586, it was known as Samara until 1935, when it was renamed after the Revolutionary leader Valerian Kuybyshev (1888–1933). (Pop. 1 251 000)

Kuznetsk *see* Novokuznetsk.

Kwai, River Two tributaries of the Mae Khlong River in western THAILAND, the Kwai Yai (Big Kwai) and the Kwai Noi (Little Kwai). During the Second World War Allied prisoners of war were forced by their Japanese captors to build a railway line and a bridge over the Kwai Yai at the cost of some 110 000 lives.

Kwajalein One of the largest atolls in the world, with a lagoon covering some 2800 sq km (1100 sq miles). The island forms part of the MARSHALL ISLANDS in the PACIFIC OCEAN, and is leased to the U.S.A. as a missile target.

KwaNdebele A semi-autonomus black homeland in central TRANSVAAL province, north-eastern SOUTH AFRICA. (3410 sq km/1317 sq miles)

Kwangju (Gwangju; Chonnam) An industrial city and regional capital in the south-western corner of South KOREA. (Pop. 727 600)

Kwango (Cuango), River A river which rises in northern ANGOLA and flows northwards to join the River KASAI in ZAIRE. (Length 110 km/680 miles)

KwaZulu A self-governing black homeland consisting

of 10 separate territories in NATAL, SOUTH AFRICA. (32 390 sq km/12 503 sq miles; pop. 4 186 000)

Kyongju A ancient city in the south-east of South KOREA which was the capital of the Silla kingdom from 57 BC to AD 935. (Pop. 108 000)

Kyoto Situated in central southern HONSHU island, this was the old imperial capital of JAPAN from AD 794 to 1868. (Pop. 1 479 100)

Kyushu The most southerly of JAPAN's main islands, and the third largest after HONSHU and HOKKAIDO. (43 065 sq km/16 627 sq miles; pop. 13 276 000)

L

Laatokka, Lake *see* Ladogo, Lake.

Labrador The mainland part of the province of NEWFOUNDLAND, on the east coast of CANADA. (295 800 sq km/112 826 sq miles)

Laccadive Islands *see* Lakshadweep.

Ladakh A remote and mountainous district in the north-eastern part of the state of JAMMU AND KASHMIR, INDIA, noted for its numerous monasteries which preserve the traditions of Tibetan-style Buddhism. The capital is LEH. (Pop. 70 000)

Ladoga (Ladozhskoye; Laatokka), Lake Europe's largest lake, in western RUSSIA, to the north-east of ST PETERSBURG. (18 390 sq km/7100 sq miles)

Lagos The principal port and former capital (until 1992) of NIGERIA, situated on the Bight of BENIN. (Pop. 1 477 000)

Lahore A city in eastern central PAKISTAN, close to the border with INDIA. (Pop. 2 922 000)

Lake District A region of lakes and mountains in the county of CUMBRIA, in north-west ENGLAND. It includes England's highest peak, Scafell Pike (978 m/3208 ft), and a series of lakes famed for their beauty, notably Windermere, Coniston and Ullswater.

Lake of the Woods A lake spattered with some 17 000 islands in south-western ONTARIO, CANADA, on the border with the U.S.A. (4390 sq km/1695 sq miles)

Lakshadweep A territory of INDIA consisting of 27 small islands (the Amindivi Islands, Laccadive Islands and Minicoy) lying 300 km (186 miles) off the south-west coast of mainland INDIA. (32 sq km/12 sq miles; pop. 40 250)

La Mancha A high, arid plateau in central SPAIN, some 160 km (100 miles) south of MADRID, the setting for *Don Quixote* (1605–15) by Miguel de Cervantes.

Lambaréné A provincial capital in eastern central GABON, famous as the site of the hospital founded by Albert Schweitzer (1875–1965). (Pop. 28 000)

Lanarkshire *see* Strathclyde.

Lancashire A county of north-west ENGLAND, once the heart of Industrial Britain. The county town is Preston. (3043 sq km/1175 sq miles; pop. 1 378 000)

Landes A department of the AQUITAINE region on the coast of south-west FRANCE. (Pop. 297 400)

Land's End The tip of the peninsula formed by CORNWALL in south-west ENGLAND, and the most westerly point of mainland England.

Languedoc-Rousillon A region of FRANCE which lines

the MEDITERRANEAN coast from the River RHONE to the border with SPAIN. (27 376 sq km/10 567 sq miles; pop. 1 927 000)

Lansing The state capital of MICHIGAN, U.S.A. (Pop. city 128 000/metropolitan area 416 200)

Lantau The largest of the islands which form part of the New Territories of HONG KONG. (150 sq km/ 58 sq miles; pop. 17 000)

Lanzarote *see* Canary Islands.

Lanzhou A major industrial city and the capital of GANSU province, central CHINA. (Pop. 2 260 000)

Laois A county in the centre of the Republic of IRELAND. The county town is Portlaoise. (1718 sq km/ 664 sq miles; pop. 51 200)

Laos A landlocked republic in South-East ASIA. It was formerly a part of French Indochina, but gained independence in 1949. After a bitter civil war, a Communist regime took control and declared a new republic in 1975. Most of the country is forested and mountainous and a large proportion of the population live in the MEKONG valley, which forms a natural boundary with THAILAND to the west. Laos has almost no industry; the main exports are timber and coffee. The official language is Lao; the capital is VIENTIANE. (236 800 sq km/91 400 sq miles; pop. 3 820 700; cur. Kip = 100 at)

La Paz A city set high in the ANDES of BOLIVIA, and the capital and seat of government. (Pop. 900 000)

La Plata A port on the estuary of the River PLATE (Rio de la Plata) in north-eastern ARGENTINA, 56 km (35 miles) south-east of BUENOS AIRES. (Pop. 455 000)

Lappland The region of northern SCANDINAVIA and the adjoining territory of RUSSIA, traditionally inhabited by the nomadic Lapp people; also a province of northern FINLAND, called Lappi.

Laptev Sea Part of the ARCTIC OCEAN bordering central northern SIBERIA.

Larnaca A port, with an international airport, on the south-east coast of CYPRUS. (Pop. 48 400)

Lascaux A set of caves in the DORDOGNE department of south-west FRANCE where (in 1940) wall paintings by Paleolithic people dating back to about 15 000 BC were discovered.

Las Palmas de Gran Canaria The main port and largest city of the CANARY ISLANDS, on the island of Gran Canaria. (Pop. 366 500)

Las Vegas A city in the south-east of the state of NEVADA, U.S.A. This state's liberal gaming laws has allowed Las Vegas to develop as an internationally famous centre for gambling and entertainment. (Pop. city 183 200/metropolitan area 536 500)

Latakia (Al Ladhiqiyah) A city on the MEDITERRANEAN coast of SYRIA, founded by the Romans, and now that country's main port. (Pop. 204 000)

Latium *see* Lazio.

Latvia One of the three so-called BALTIC republics which declared itself independent of the USSR in 1991. The capital is RIGA. (63 700 sq km/24 600 sq miles; pop. 2 589 000)

Lausanne A city on the north shore of Lake GENEVA, and capital of the French-speaking canton of Vaud. (Pop. 140 000)

Laval A city in QUEBEC province of CANADA which effectively forms a northern surburb of MONTREAL. (Pop. 238 300)

Lazio (Latium) A region occupying the central western coast of ITALY around ROME, the regional capital. (17 203 sq km/6642 sq miles; pop. 3 076 000)

Lebanon A republic in western ASIA with a coast on the MEDITERRANEAN SEA. The home of the Phoenicians in ancient times, it was controlled by the French after the demise of the Ottoman Empire and became an independent republic in 1941. Once one of the MIDDLE EAST's most flourishing centres of commerce, since 1975 the Lebanon has been ravaged by civil wars between the many rival Arab and Christian factions. The once beautiful capital, BEIRUT, was effectively divided in two and partially destroyed, but peace brought about by the intervention of SYRIA has afforded a measure of political stability. Arabic is the official language. (10 400 sq km/4015 sq miles; pop. 2 600 000; cur. Lebanese pound = 100 piastres)

Lebowa A self-governing homeland created for the North Sotho people, made up of several unconnected areas, in the north of the province of TRANSVAAL, SOUTH AFRICA. (Pop. 2 246 000)

Lecce A historic city in the PUGLIA region of ITALY. (Pop. 97 200)

Leeds An important industrial town on the River Aire in WEST YORKSHIRE, in northern ENGLAND. (Pop. 450 000)

Leeward and Windward Islands 1 The Lesser ANTILLES in the southern CARIBBEAN are divided into two groups. The northern islands in the chain, from the VIRGIN ISLANDS to GUADELOUPE are the Leeward Islands; the islands further south, from DOMINICA to GRENADA form the Windward islands. **2** The SOCIETY ISLANDS of FRENCH POLYNESIA are also divided into Leeward and Windward Islands.

Leghorn *see* Livorno.

Le Havre The largest port on the north coast of FRANCE. (Pop. 255 900)

Leicester A historic cathedral city, and the county town of LEICESTERSHIRE. (Pop. 280 000)

Leicestershire A county in central ENGLAND. Since 1974 it has also incorporated the former county of Rutland. The county town is LEICESTER. (2553 sq km/ 986 sq miles; pop. 864 000)

Leiden (Leyden) A university city in western NETHERLANDS on the River Oude Rijn. (Pop. 103 800)

Leinster One of the four ancient provinces into which IRELAND was divided, covering the south-eastern quarter of the country.

Leipzig An industrial city and important cultural centre in south-eastern GERMANY. (Pop. 559 000)

Leitrim A county in the north-west of the Republic of IRELAND, with a small strip of coast and a northern border with FERMANAGH in NORTHERN IRELAND. The county town is Carrick-on-Shannon. (1525 sq km/ 589 sq miles; pop. 27 600)

Léman, Lake Another name for Lake GENEVA.

Le Mans A university city in north western FRANCE, famous for the 24-hour car race held annually at a circuit nearby. (Pop. 194 000)

Lemberg *see* L'vov.

Lena, River A river, navigable for much of its length, which flows across eastern SIBERIA, from its source close to Lake BAIKAL to the LAPTEV SEA in the north. (Length 4270 km/2650 miles)

Leningrad *see* St Petersburg.

Lens A sprawling industrial city in the coal-mining region of northern FRANCE. (Pop. 327 400)

Léon 1 A major manufacturing city in central MEXICO. (Pop. 675 000) **2** A historic city, founded by the Romans, in north-west SPAIN, and capital of the province of the same name. (Pop. city 131 200)

Léopoldville *see* Kinshasa.

Leptis Magna The well-preserved ruins of an ancient Roman port on the MEDITERRANEAN coast of LIBYA.

Lesbos A large, fertile island in the eastern AEGIAN SEA, belonging to GREECE, but only 10 km (6 miles) from the coast of TURKEY. It was the birthplace of the poetess Sappho (*c*.612–580 BC) whose love for other women gave rise to the term lesbian. (1 630 sq km/ 630 sq miles; pop. 41 900)

Lesotho A kingdom completely surrounded by SOUTH AFRICA. Formerly a British protectorate, it gained independence in 1966, and became a member of the Commonwealth. It is a poor, mountainous country, almost totally dependent on South Africa. Its revenue is derived mainly from the export of labour, wool, and diamonds, and from tourism. Sesotho and English are the main languages, and the capital is MASERU. (30 355 sq km/11 720 sq miles; pop. 1 550 000; cur. Loti = 100 lisente)

Lesser Sunda Islands (Nusa Tenggara) A chain of islands to the east of JAVA, INDONESIA, stretching from BALI to TIMOR. (The Greater Sunda Islands comprise Borneo, Sumatra, Java and Sulawesi.)

Levkas *see* Ionian Islands

Lexington A city in central KENTUCKY, U.S.A., named after the Battle of Lexington in MASSACHUSETTS (1775) which marked the beginning of the American War of Independence. (Pop. city 210 200/metropolitan area 327 200)

Leyden *see* Leiden

Leyte An island of the VISAYAN group in the central PHILIPPINES. The main town is Tacloban. (7213 sq km/2785 sq miles; pop. 1 480 000)

Lhasa The capital of TIBET. It lies 3606 m (11 830 ft) above sea level. (Pop. 120 000)

Liaoning A coastal province of DONGBEI (Manchuria), north-east CHINA, bordering North KOREA. The capital is SHENYANG. (140 000 sq km/540 sq miles; pop. 34 426 000)

Liberia A republic in West AFRICA with a coast on the ATLANTIC. It was established in 1822 as a country for freed slaves from the U.S.A. Rubber, minerals and timber are the main exports, but the economy of the country has been badly disrupted in recent years by civil strife. The official language is English, and the capital is MONROVIA. (111 370 sq km/43 000 sq miles; pop. 2 300 000; cur. Liberian dollar = 100 cents)

Libreville The capital and main port of GABON. It is so-called ('Freetown') because it was originally a settlement for freed slaves. (Pop. 308 000)

Libya A republic in North AFRICA with a coast on the MEDITERRANEAN. It became independent of French and British occupation in 1951; the monarchy was overthrown by a military coup in 1969. The country is almost entirely desert, although ambitious irrigation schemes have created areas of fertile land. Oil is by far the biggest export, but the country is becoming more industrialized along the coast, and chemicals are also exported. Arabic is the official language, and TRIPOLI is the capital. (1 760 000 sq km/680 000 sq miles; pop. 4 260 000; cur. Dinar = 100 dirhams)

Liechtenstein A tiny principality in the ALPS, sandwiched between SWITZERLAND and AUSTRIA. It has lenient tax laws which make it attractive to businessmen, and tourism is a major source of revenue. The principal language is German, and the capital is VADUZ. (160 sq km/61 sq miles; pop. 28 500; cur. Swiss franc = 100 centimes)

Liège (Luik) A historic city in eastern BELGIUM, and capital of the province of Liège, built on the confluence of the Rivers MEUSE and Ourthe. (Pop. city 203 000/metropolitan area 609 000)

Liffey, River The river upon which DUBLIN, the capital of the Republic of IRELAND, is set. (Length 80 km/ 49 miles)

Liguria The region of north-western ITALY which fronts the Gulf of GENOA; it has a border with FRANCE. (5415 sq km/2091 sq miles; pop. 1 772 000)

Ligurian Sea The northern arm of the MEDITERRANEAN SEA to the west of ITALY, which includes the Gulf of GENOA.

Lille-Roubaix-Tourcoing A conurbation of industrial towns in north-eastern FRANCE. (Pop. 945 600)

Lilongwe The capital of MALAWI, and the second largest city in the country after BLANTYRE. (Pop. 172 000)

Lima The capital of PERU, situated on the banks of the River Rimac, 13 km (8 miles) from the coast. (Pop. 5 500 000)

Limassol The main port of CYPRUS in the southern part of the island. (Pop. 107 200)

Limerick A city and port on the River SHANNON, and the county town of the county of Limerick, in the south-west of the Republic of IRELAND. (County 26 86 sq km/ 1037 sq miles; pop. county 161 700; pop. city 60 700)

Limoges A city in eastern central FRANCE, famous for its richly decorated porcelain. It is the capital of the LIMOUSIN region. (Pop. 144 100)

Limousin A region of east-central FRANCE in the foothills of the MASSIF CENTRAL, famous in particular for its Limousin cattle. (Pop. 737 000)

Limpopo, River A river which flows northwards from its source in the TRANSVAAL to form part of the border between SOUTH AFRICA and BOTSWANA before crossing southern MOZAMBIQUE to reach the INDIAN OCEAN. (Length 1610 km/1000 miles)

Lincoln 1 A historic city, with a fine cathedral dating from the 11th century, and the county town of LINCOLNSHIRE, ENGLAND. (Pop. 77 000). **2** The state capital of NEBRASKA, U.S.A. (Pop. city 180 400/metropolitan area 203 000)

Lincolnshire A county on the east coast of central ENGLAND. The county town is LINCOLN. (5885 sq km/ 2272 sq miles; pop. 558 000)

Lindisfarne A small island, also known as Holy Island, just off the east coast of NORTHUMBERLAND in north-east ENGLAND. It has an 11th-century priory built on the site of a monastery founded in the 7th century.

Linz A city and port on the River DANUBE in northern AUSTRIA. (Pop. 201 500)

Lion, Golfe de (Gulf of Lions) The arm of the MEDITERRANEAN SEA which forms a deep indent in the southern coast of FRANCE, stretching from the border with SPAIN to TOULON, and centring on the delta of the River RHONE.

Lipari The largest of the volcanic EOLIAN ISLANDS that lie off the north coast of SICILY, ITALY. (38 sq km/ 15 sq miles; pop. 10 700)

Lisbon (Lisboa) The capital and principal port of PORTUGAL, situated on the broad River TAGUS, approximately 15 km (9 miles) from the ATLANTIC coast. (Pop. 817 600)

Lithuania The largest of the three so-called BALTIC republics which first declared itself independent of the U.S.S.R. in 1990, but this was not recognized until 1991. The capital is VILNIUS. (65 200 sq km/25 200 sq miles; pop. 3 539 000)

Little Rock The state capital of ARKANSAS, U.S.A. (Pop. city 170 100/metropolitan area 492 700)

Liverpool A major port on the estuary of the River MERSEY in north-west ENGLAND; it is the administrative centre of MERSEYSIDE. (Pop. 497 000)

Livorno (Leghorn) A port and industrial city on the coast of TUSCANY, northern ITALY. (Pop. 175 300)
Ljubljana An industrial city on the River Sava, and the capital of SLOVENIA. (Pop. 305 200)
Loch Ness *see* Ness, Loch.
Lodz An industrial city and the second largest city in POLAND, located in the centre of the country. It was rebuilt after being destroyed in the Second World War. (Pop. 848 500)
Logan, Mount The highest mountain in CANADA, and the second highest in North AMERICA after Mount McKINLEY. It is situated in south-west YUKON, on the border with ALASKA. (5951 m/19 524 ft)
Loire, River The longest river in FRANCE, flowing northwards from the south-eastern MASSIF CENTRAL and then to the west to meet the ATLANTIC OCEAN just to the west of NANTES. Its middle reaches are famous for their spectacular châteaux, and for the fertile valley which produces fine white wines. (Length: 1020 km/635 miles)
Lombardy (Lombardia) The central northern region of ITALY, which drops down from the ALPS to the plain of the River PO, one of the country's most productive areas in both agriculture and industry. MILAN is the regional capital. (23 854 sq km/9210 sq miles; pop. 898 700)
Lombok An island of the LESSER SUNDA group, east of BALI. (5435 sq km/2098 sq miles; pop. 1 300 200)
Lomé The capital and main port of TOGO, situated close the border with GHANA. (Pop. 283 000)
London 1 The capital of the UNITED KINGDOM, which

straddles both banks of the River THAMES near its estuary. It consists of 33 boroughs, including the City, an international centre for trade and commerce. (Pop. 6 755 000). **2** An industrial city in south-western ONTARIO, CANADA. (Pop. 284 000)

Londonderry (Derry) The second largest city in NORTHERN IRELAND after BELFAST, and the county town of the county of Londonderry. (County 2076 sq km/ 801 sq miles; pop. county 84 000; pop. city 62 000)

Long Island An island off the coast of NEW YORK State, stretching some 190 km (118 miles) to the north-east away from the city of NEW YORK. Its western end forms part of the city of New York (the boroughs of Brooklyn and Queens) but the rest is a mixture of residential suburbs, farmland and resort beaches. (3685 sq km/1423 sq miles)

Longford A county in the centre of the Republic of IRELAND, with a county town of the same name. (1044 sq km/403 sq miles; pop. 31 100)

Lord Howe Island A small island lying some 600 km (375 miles) to the east of the coast of NEW SOUTH WALES, AUSTRALIA, now a popular resort. (16 sq km/ 6 sq miles; pop. 300)

Lorraine A region of north-east FRANCE, with a border shared by BELGIUM, LUXEMBOURG and GERMANY. The regional capital is METZ. (Pop. 2 320 000)

Los Angeles A vast, sprawling city on the PACIFIC OCEAN in southern CALIFORNIA, U.S.A., the second largest city in the U.S.A. after NEW YORK. (Pop. city 3 096 700/conurbation 12 372 600)

Lothian A local government region in south-east

central SCOTLAND, with EDINBURGH as its administrative centre. It was created in 1975 out of the former counties of Midlothian, and East and West Lothian. (1756 sq km/678 sq miles; pop. 745 000)

Louisiana A state in central southern U.S.A., on the lower reaches of the MISSISSIPPI River, and with a coastline on the Gulf of MEXICO. The state capital is BATON ROUGE. (125 675 sq km/48 523 sq miles; pop. 4 481 000)

Louisville A city and commercial centre, in northern KENTUCKY, U.S.A., on the OHIO River. (Pop. city 289 800/metropolitan area 962 600)

Lourdes One of the world's most important Marian shrines, in the foothills of the central PYRENEES, FRANCE. It became a place of miraculous healing after a series of visions of the Virgin Mary witnessed by Bernadette Soubirous in 1858. (Pop. 17 600)

Lourenço Marques *see* Maputo.

Louth A county on the east coast of the Republic of IRELAND, bordering NORTHERN IRELAND. The county town is Dundalk. (823 sq km/318 sq miles; pop. 88 500)

Lualaba, River A river that flows northwards across the eastern part of ZAIRE from the border with ZAMBIA before joining the River LOMANI to form the River ZAIRE. (Length 1800 km/1120 miles)

Luanda The capital of ANGOLA, and a major port on the ATLANTIC OCEAN. (Pop. 700 000)

Lübeck A BALTIC port in northern GERMANY, lying some 20 km (12 miles) from the coast on the River Trave. (Pop. 80 000)

Lublin (Lyublin) A city and agricultural centre in south-eastern POLAND. (Pop. 320 000)
Lubumbashi The principal mining town of ZAIRE, and the capital of the Shaba region in the south-east of the country. It was founded in 1910 and known as Elisabethville until 1966. (Pop. 600 000)
Lucca A town in north-western TUSCANY, ITALY, Surrounded by impressive 16th century fortifications, its medieval streetplan incorporates the site of Roman amphitheatre. (Pop. 89 100)
Lucerne (Luzern) A city set on the beautiful Lake Lucerne in central SWITZERLAND, retaining much of its medieval past; also the name of the surrounding canton. (Pop. city 67 500)
Lucknow The capital of the state of UTTAR PRADESH in central northern INDIA. (Pop. 1 007 600)
Luda (Dalian) An industrial city and port in LIAONING province, north-eastern CHINA. (Pop. 4 000 000)
Ludhiana A town in central PUNJAB, INDIA, home of the respected Punjab Agricultural University. (Pop. 607 000)
Ludwigshafen A town, industrial centre and river port on the River RHINE in south-western GERMANY. (Pop. 163 000)
Lugansk *see* Voroshilovgrad.
Luik *see* Liège.
Luluabourg *see* Kananga.
Lumbini The birthplace of Buddha (Prince Siddhartha Gautama, *c*.563–488 BC), part of the village of Rummindei in central southern NEPAL.
Luoyang A city of ancient origins, founded in about

2100 BC, in HENAN province in eastern central CHINA. As a principal centre of the Shang dynasty (18th–12th centuries BC), the area is rich in archaeological remains. (Pop. 500 000)

Lusaka The capital of ZAMBIA, situated in the south-east of the country. (Pop. 538 500)

Luton An industrial town in BEDFORDSHIRE, ENGLAND, 50 km (30 miles) north of LONDON. It is a centre of the British car-manufacturing industry, and also has a busy international airport. (Pop. 165 000)

Luxembourg 1 A landlocked grand duchy in western EUROPE which has borders with BELGIUM, GERMANY and FRANCE. It is a member of the European Community, and is an important financial centre. Iron and steel are among the main exports. Languages spoken include French, Letzeburghish (a German dialect) and German. The capital, also called Luxembourg, stands on the River Alzette. (2586 sq km/998 sq miles; pop. country 367 400/city 78 000; cur. Luxembourg franc/Belgian franc). **2** The province of BELGIUM adjoining the Grand Duchy of Luxembourg.

Luxor A town that has grown up around one of the great archaeological sites of ancient EGYPT, on the east bank of the River NILE in the centre of the country, just south of the ancient capital THEBES and 3 km (2 miles) from KARNAK. (Pop. 78 000)

Luzern *see* Lucerne.

Luzon The largest island of the PHILIPPINES, in the north of the group, with the nation's capital, MANILA, at its centre. (104 688 sq km/40 420 sq miles; pop. 29 400 000)

L'vov (Lemberg) A major industial city of medieval origins in the western UKRAINE. (Pop. 688 000)
Lyallpur *see* Faisalabad.
Lyons (Lyon) The second largest city in FRANCE after PARIS, situated at the confluence of the Rivers RHONE and SAONE in the south-east of the country. (Pop. 1 236 100)
Lyublin *see* Lublin.

M

Maas, River *see* Meuse.
Macáu (Macao) A tiny Portuguese province on the coast of south CHINA, opposite HONG KONG. Occupied by the Portuguese since 1557, the territory will be handed over to China in 1999. The vast majority of the population is Chinese, and the dominant language is Cantonese. Tourism and the handling of trade destined for China are major sources of income. The capital is Macau City. (15.5 sq km/ 6 sq miles; pop. 406 000; cur. Pataca = 100 avos)
Macdonnell Ranges The parallel ranges of mountains of central AUSTRALIA, in the southern part of the NORTHERN TERRITORIES, near to ALICE SPRINGS. The highest peak is Mount Ziel (1510 m/4954 ft)
Maceió A port on the central east coast of BRAZIL. (Pop. 401 000)
Macedonia 1 The largest region of GREECE, occupying most of the northern part of the mainland, and with northern borders with ALBANIA, YUGOSLAVIA and

BULGARIA. (Pop. 2 122 000). **2** (Makedonija) The most southerly of the republics of YUGOSLAVIA, with SKOPJE as its capital. (25 713 sq km/9928 sq miles; pop. 1 912 200)

Macgillicuddy's Reeks A range of mountains in the south-west of the Republic of IRELAND which includes the country's highest peak at Carrauntoohil. (1040 m/ 3414 ft)

Machu Picchu The ruins of a great Inca city, set spectacularly on a mountain ridge high in the ANDES near CUZCO, in south central PERU. It was abandoned in the 16th century and only rediscovered in 1911.

Mackenzie, River A river flowing northwards through the western part of the NORTHERN TERRITORIES of CANADA from the GREAT SLAVE LAKE to the ARCTIC OCEAN. (Length 1800 km/1120 miles)

McKinley, Mount The highest mountain in North AMERICA, located in the Denali National Park in southern ALASKA, U.S.A. (6194 m/20 320 ft)

MacMurdo Sound An arm of the ROSS SEA on the International Date Line. The American MacMurdo Base on Ross Island is the largest scientific research station in ANTARCTICA.

Madagascar An island republic off the south-east coast of AFRICA. It gained full independence from FRANCE in 1960 and was known as the Malagasy Republic from 1958 to 1975. The island is partially covered with tropical forests, which contain a number of rare species of flora and fauna. It has huge mineral resources, but these have yet to be exploited and it remains one of the world's poorest nations. The chief exports include coffee, vanilla, fish and sugar. The official language is Malagasy, and ANTANANARIVO is the capital. (587 041 sq km/226 657 sq miles; pop. 10 200 000; cur. Madagascar franc = 100 centimes)

Madeira The main island in a small group in the eastern ATLANTIC OCEAN which have belonged to PORTUGAL since the the 16th century, lying some 1000 km (620 miles) due west of CASABLANCA in MOROCCO. The capital is FUNCHAL. (740 sq km/286 sq miles; pop. 248 500)

Madhya Pradesh The largest state in INDIA, in the centre of the country. The capital is BHOPAL. (443 446 sq km/171 170 sq miles; pop. 52 178 800)

Madinah, Al *see* Medina.

Madison The state capital of WISCONSIN, U.S.A. (Pop. city 170 700/metropolitan area 333 000)

Madras The main port on the east coast of INDIA, and the capital of the state of TAMIL NADU. (Pop. 4 289 300)

Madrid The capital of SPAIN, situated in the middle of the country, and also the name of the surrounding province. (Pop. city 3 188 300/province 4 727 000)

Madura An island off the north-eastern coast of JAVA. (5290 sq km/2042 sq miles; pop. 1 860 000)

Madurai A textile city in TAMIL NADU, in the southern tip of INDIA. (Pop. 907 700)

Mae Nam Khong, River *see* Salween, River.

Mafikeng (Mafeking) A town in the black state of BOPHUTHATSWANA, SOUTH AFRICA, scene of the Relief of Mafeking in 1890, ending an eight-month siege of British troops by the Boers. (Pop. 29 400)

Magdalena, River A river which flows northwards through western COLOMBIA and into the CARIBBEAN at BARRANQUILA. (Length 1550 km/965 miles)

Magdeburg A city and inland port on the River ELBE in eastern GERMANY, 120 km (75 miles) south-west of BERLIN. (Pop. 289 000)

Magellan, Strait of The waterway, 3 km (2 miles) across at its narrowest, which separates the island of TIERRA DEL FUEGO from the southern tip of mainland South AMERICA. It was discovered by the Portuguese navigator Ferdinand Magellan (?1480–1521) in 1520.

Maghreb (Maghrib) The name by which the countries of north-west AFRICA – MOROCCO, ALGERIA and TUNISIA – are often called collectively.

Magnitogorsk An industrial city specializing in iron and steel, founded in the southern URAL MOUNTAINS in the RUSSIA in 1930. (Pop. 421 000)

Maharashtra A state in the centre of the west coast of INDIA, with BOMBAY as its capital. (307 690 sq km/ 118 768 sq miles; pop. 62 784 200)

Mahore *see* Mayotte.

Main, River A river that snakes its way westwards from its source near BAYREUTH in central GERMANY, passing through FRANKFURT AM MAIN before joining the River RHINE at MAINZ. (Length 524 km/325 miles)

Maine A state in the north-eastern corner of the U.S.A., bordering CANADA. The state capital is AUGUSTA. (86 027 sq km/33 215 sq miles; pop. 1 164 000)

Mainz A city and inland port on the confluence of the Rivers RHINE and MAIN in western central GERMANY. (Pop. 185 000)

Majorca (Mallorca) The largest of the BALEARIC ISLANDS, in the western MEDITERRANEAN. The capital is PALMA. (3639 sq km/1405 sq miles; pop. 460 000)

Majuro An atoll of three islands (Dalap, Uliga and Darrit) which together form the capital of the MARSHALL ISLANDS. (Pop. 8700)

Makassar *see* Ujung Padang.

Makassar Strait The broad stretch of water, 130 km (81 miles) across at its narrowest, which separates the islands of BORNEO and SULAWESI in INDONESIA.

Makedonija *see* Macedonia.

Makeyevka An industrial city in the DONETS BASIN in the southern UKRAINE. (Pop. 448 000)

Makhachkala A port and industrial city on the west coast of the CASPIAN SEA, and the capital of the republic of DAGESTAN. (Pop. 269 000)

Makkah *see* Mecca.

Malabar Coast The name given to the coastal region of the state of KERALA in south-western INDIA.

Malabo A port and the capital of EQUATORIAL GUINEA, situated on the north coast of BIOKO island. (Pop. 37 200)

Malacca *see* Melaka.

Malacca, Strait of The busy waterway, just 50 km (31 miles) wide at its narrowest, which separates the island of SUMATRA in INDONESIA from the southern tip of MALAYSIA, with SINGAPORE at its eastern end.

Malaga A port, manufacturing city, and tourist resort on the MEDITERRANEAN coast of ANDALUCIA, southern SPAIN. Also the name of the province of which it is the capital. (Pop. town 503 300)

Malagasy Republic *see* Madagascar.

Malawi Formerly called Nyasaland, Malawi is a landlocked republic in east central AFRICA. It gained independence from the U.K. in 1964 and became a republic, within the Commonwealth, in 1966. Lake Malawi runs along the eastern flank of the country and is much admired by tourists for its beauty. The countryside is primarily grassland and wooded highlands. Agriculture is the main industry and tea, sugar and tobacco are exported. English and a number of local languages are spoken. The capital is LILONGWE. (118 484 sq km/45 747 sq miles; pop. 7 290 000; cur. Kwacha = 100 tambala)

Malawi (Nyasa), Lake A long, narrow lake which runs down most of the eastern side of MALAWI and forms Malawi's border with TANZANIA and MOZAMBIQUE. (23 300 sq km/9000 sq miles)

Malaysia A federation of states in South-East ASIA comprising the states on the Malay peninsula and SARAWAK and SABAH in the north of BORNEO. When the country was created in 1963 it included SINGAPORE, but Singapore seceded in 1965. Malaysia is a member of the Commonwealth. Most of the states are covered with tropical jungle. Exports include oil, rubber, timber and tin, as well as manufactured goods such as electronic equipment. Many languages are spoken, including Malay, English, Tamil and Chinese. The main religion is Islam. The capital is KUALA LUMPUR. (330 434 sq km/127 581 sq miles; pop. 16 010 000; cur. Ringgit (Malaysian dollar) = 100 sen)

Maldives A republic consisting of an archipelago of

over 1200 islands in the INDIAN OCEAN south-west of SRI LANKA. It became independent of the U.K. in 1965, and a republic in 1968, and joined the Commonwealth in 1982. Fish is the main export, but tourism also provides an important source of revenue. The main languages are Divehi and English. The capital is MALÉ. (298 sq km/115 sq miles; pop. 183 000; cur. Rufiyaa = 100 laari)

Malé The main atoll of the MALDIVES, and the town which is the country's capital. (2.6 sq km/1 sq mile; pop. 29 000)

Mali A landlocked republic in West AFRICA which was part of French West Africa before becoming independent in 1960. To the north lies the SAHARA DESERT, but the south is more fertile, particularly along the banks of the SENEGAL and NIGER Rivers. Mali is a poor country and exports mainly agricultural products. French is the official language. The capital is BAMAKO. (1 240 000 sq km/478 767 sq miles; pop. 7 910 000; cur. CFA franc = 100 centimes)

Malmö A port in south-west SWEDEN, on the narrow channel which separates Sweden from COPENHAGEN in DENMARK. (Pop. 229 900)

Malta A republic consisting of three islands – Malta, Gozo and Comino – situated to the south of SICILY in the MEDITERRANEAN SEA. It became independent of the U.K. in 1964, and a republic in 1974. It is a member of the Commonwealth. Malta has been of strategic importance for centuries, but never more so than during the Second World War. Today tourism is a major source of revenue. English and Maltese are both spoken, and the capital is VALLETTA. (316 sq km/ 122 sq miles; pop. 355 000; cur. Maltese lira (pound) = 100 cents = 1000 mils)

Maluku (Moluccas) A group of some 1000 islands in eastern INDONESIA. They are known as the Spice Islands, for they were once the only source of cloves and nutmegs in the world. The principal islands are Halmahera, Seram and Buru. The capital is AMBON. (74 505 sq km/28 766 sq miles; pop. 1 411 000)

Man, Isle of An island of the BRITISH ISLES, in the IRISH SEA, half way between ENGLAND and IRELAND. It is British Crown possession, not a part of the U.K., and has its own parliament, the Court of Tynwald. The capital is Douglas. (585 sq km/226 sq miles; pop. 66 000)

Managua The capital of NICARAGUA, situated on the edge of Lake Managua. (Pop. 630 000)

Manaus A major port on the River AMAZON in BRAZIL, lying 1600 km (1000 miles) from the sea. (Pop. 635 000)

Manchester A major industrial and commercial city in north-west ENGLAND, and the administrative centre for the metropolitan county of Greater Manchester. It is connected to the estuary of the River MERSEY by the Manchester Ship Canal. (County 1286 sq km/497 sq miles; pop. city 448 000/county 2 594 778)

Manchuria *see* Dongbei.

Mandalay The principal city of central BURMA, and a port on the River IRRAWADDY. (Pop. 417 300)

Manila The capital of the PHILIPPINES. The city is an important port and commercial centre, and is sited on

LUZON island. The surrounding urban area is known as Metro Manila (Pop. city 6 000 000/Metro Manila 8 000 000)

Manipur A small state of INDIA in the far north east, on the border with BURMA. The capital is Imphal. (22 327 sq km/8618 sq miles; pop. 1 421 000)

Manitoba The most easterly of the prairie provinces of CANADA. The capital is WINNIPEG. (650 087 sq km/ 250 998 sq miles; pop. 1 026 000)

Mannheim An inland port and industrial city on the confluence of the Rivers RHINE and NECKAR. (Pop. 300 000)

Mansura *see* El Mansura.

Mantua (Mantova) A city in the valley of the River PO, in the LOMBARDY region of ITALY, retaining much of its medieval heritage. (Pop. 60 400)

Maputo The capital and main port of MOZAMBIQUE. It was formerly known as Lourenço Marques. (Pop. 785 500)

Mar del Plata A coastal city and beach resort on the north-east coast of ARGENTINA, 400 km (250 miles) south of BUENOS AIRES. (Pop. 424 000)

Maracaibo The second largest city in VENEZUELA, in the north-west. (Pop. 1 100 000)

Maracaibo, Lake A shallow lake in north-west VENEZUELA, linked to the CARIBBEAN SEA by a channel. It contains one of the richest oil fields in the world. (13 280 sq km/5127 sq miles)

Marbella A popular resort on the MEDITERRANEAN coast of southern SPAIN, in the province of MALAGA. (Pop. 67 900)

Marburg *see* Maribor.

Marche (Marches) A region of central eastern ITALY, lining the ADRIATIC coast. The capital is ANCONA. (9694 sq km/3743 sq miles; pop. 1 424 000)

Margarita An island belonging to VENEZUELA, lying just off its north-eastern coast, rapidly becoming a popular tourist destination. (929 sq km/355 sq miles; pop. 38 000)

Marianske Lazne (Marienbad) A spa town in western CZECHOSLOVAKIA. (Pop. 18 400)

Maribor (Marburg) An industrial city in SLOVENIA, northern YUGOSLAVIA. (Pop. 185 700)

Marie Galante *see* Guadeloupe.

Marienbad *see* Marianske Lazne.

Marigot *see* St Martin.

Marmara, Sea of A small sea lying between the AEGIAN SEA and the BOSPHORUS, providing a vital link in the route between the MEDITERRANEAN SEA and the BLACK SEA. The surrounding coasts all belong the TURKEY.

Marmolada, Mount *see* Dolomites.

Marquesas Islands A group of a dozen or so fertile, volcanic islands in the north-eastern sector of FRENCH POLYNESIA, lying about 1400 km (875 miles) north-east of TAHITI. (1189 sq km/459 sq miles; pop. 6500)

Marrakech (Marrakesh) A historic oasis city in central western MOROCCO, founded in the 11th century and formerly the country's capital. (Pop. 440 000)

Marseilles (Marseille) The largest port in FRANCE, on the MEDITERRANEAN coast, and France's third largest city after PARIS and LYONS. (Pop. 1 110 500)

Marshall Islands A scattered group of some 1250 islands in MICRONESIA, in the western PACIFIC OCEAN. They form a self-governing republic which remains in free association with the U.S.A. Copra is the main export. The principal languages are Marshallese and English, and the capital is MAJURO. (181 sq km/ 70 sq miles; pop. 37 000; cur. US dollar = 100 cents)

Martinique One of the larger of the islands in the WINDWARD ISLAND group in the southern CARIBBEAN, lying between DOMINICA and ST LUCIA. It is administered as a department of FRANCE. FORT-DE-FRANCE is the capital. (1079 sq km/417 sq miles; pop. 330 000)

Maryland A state on the central east coast of the U.S.A., virtually divided in two by CHESAPEAKE BAY. The state capital is ANNAPOLIS. (27 394 sq km/10 577 sq miles; pop. 4 392 000)

Masbate *see* Visayan Islands.

Maseru The capital of LESOTHO. (Pop. 45 000)

Mashhad (Meshed) A major trading centre and the capital of KHORASAN province in north-eastern IRAN. (Pop. 1 120 000)

Mason-Dixon Line The state boundary between PENNSYLVANIA and MARYLAND to its south, surveyed 1763–7 by Charles Mason and Jeremiah Dixon. It is considered to be the traditional border between the North and the South of the U.S.A.

Massachusetts One of the NEW ENGLAND states on the north-eastern coast of the U.S.A. The capital is BOSTON. (21 386 sq km/8257 sq miles; pop. 5 822 000)

Massif Central The rugged upland region which occupies much of southern central FRANCE to the west of the

River RHONE. The highest point is at Puy de Sancy (1885 m/6184 ft)

Matsuyama A port and industrial city on the north coast of SHIKOKU island, JAPAN. (Pop. 426 600)

Matterhorn (Monte Cervino) A distinctive, pyramid-shaped peak on the border between ITALY and SWITZERLAND, 5 km (3 miles) south of ZERMATT. (4477 m/14 688 ft)

Maui The second largest island of HAWAII, U.S.A. (1885 sq km/727 sq miles; pop. 63 000)

Mauna Kea A dormant volcano in the north of the island of HAWAII, U.S.A. (4205 m/13 796 ft)

Mauna Loa An active volcano in the centre of the island of HAWAII. (4169 m/13 677 ft)

Mauritania A republic in north-western AFRICA with a coast on the ATLANTIC. It was formerly a French colony, but gained its independence in 1960. With the SAHARA DESERT covering most of the country, it is sparsely populated. Iron ore is the most profitable export. French is the official language, but Arabic and African languages are also spoken. NOUAKCHOTT is the capital. (1 030 700 sq km/397 953 sq miles; pop. 1 690 000; cur. Ouguiya = 5 khoums)

Mauritius An island state to the east of MADAGASCAR in the INDIAN OCEAN. It was seized from French control by the British in 1810, but became independent in 1968, while remaining within the Commonwealth. The beauty of the island attracts tourists, but the main source of revenue is sugar. English, French and Creole are spoken; the principal religions are Hinduism and Christianity. The capital is PORT LOUIS.

(1865 sq km/720 miles; pop. 1 020 000; cur. Mauritius rupee = 100 cents)

Mawsil *see* Mosul.

Mayo A county on the west coast of the Republic of IRELAND, noted for its rugged splendour. The county town is Castlebar. (4831 sq km/1865 sq miles; pop. 114 700)

Mayotte (Mahore) Part of the COMOROS ISLAND group, lying between MADAGASCAR and the mainland of AFRICA. Unlike the other three islands in the group, Mayotte voted to remain under the administration of FRANCE when the Comoros Islands became independent in 1974. (373 sq km/144 sq miles; pop. 60 000)

Mbabane The capital of SWAZILAND. (Pop. 36 000)

Meath A county on the east coast of the Republic of IRELAND, to the north of DUBLIN. The county town is Navan. (2336 sq km/902 sq miles; pop. 95 400)

Mecca (Makkah) A city in central western SAUDI ARABIA, 64 km (40 miles) east of the RED SEA port of JEDDAH. An important trading city on caravan routes in ancient times, it was the birthplace of the Prophet Muhammad, and as such is the holiest city of Islam. (Pop. 375 000)

Medan A major city in northern SUMATRA, INDONESIA. (Pop. 2 378 000)

Medellín The second largest city in COLOMBIA after the capital BOGOTA, situated in the centre of the country, 240 km (150 miles) north-west of the capital. (Pop. 1 998 000)

Medina (Al Madinah) The second holiest city of Islam after MECCA. The Prophet Muhammad fled from

Mecca to Medina, 350 km (217 miles) to the north, to escape persecution in AD 622 (year 0 in the Islamic lunar calendar). (Pop. 210 000)

Mediterranean Sea A large sea bounded by southern EUROPE, North AFRICA and south-west ASIA. It is connected to the ATLANTIC OCEAN by the Strait of GIBRALTAR.

Médoc One of the prime wine-producing regions of FRANCE, a flat, triangular-shaped piece of land between the GIRONDE estuary and the ATLANTIC OCEAN.

Meerut An industrial town of northern INDIA, 60 km (40 miles) north-east of DELHI. The Indian Mutiny began here in 1857. (Pop. 536 600)

Meghalaya A predominantly rural state in the hills of north-eastern INDIA, with BANGLADESH to the south. (22 429 sq km/8658 sq miles; pop. 1 335 800)

Meissen A historic town on the River ELBE, 20 km (12 miles) to the north-west of DRESDEN, in south-eastern GERMANY. It is famous above all for its fine porcelain, produced here since 1710. (Pop. 38 200)

Meknès A former capital, with a fine 17th century royal palace, in northern MOROCCO. (Pop. 320 000)

Mekong, River The great river of South-East ASIA, flowing from TIBET, through southern CHINA, LAOS and CAMBODIA before forming a massive and highly fertile delta in southern VIETNAM and flowing into the SOUTH CHINA SEA. (Length 4184 km/2562 miles)

Melaka (Malacca) A port on the south-west coast of MALAYSIA, overlooking the Straits of MALACCA, once a key port in Far Eastern trade. (Pop. 87 500)

Melanesia The central and southern group of islands in the South PACIFIC OCEAN, including the SOLOMON ISLANDS, VANUATU, FIJI and NEW CALEDONIA.

Melbourne The second largest city in AUSTRALIA after SYDNEY and the capital of the state of VICTORIA. (Pop. 2 700 000)

Melos *see* Cyclades.

Memel *see* Klaipeda.

Memphis A city on the River MISSISSIPPI in the south-west corner of TENNESSEE, U.S.A., on the border with – and extending into – ARKANSAS. (Pop. city 648 000/ metropolitan area 934 600)

Menai Strait The narrow strait, 180 m (590 ft) across at its narrowest, separating mainland WALES from the island of ANGLESEY, spanned by road and rail bridges.

Mendoza A trading, processing and wine-producing centre in the foothills of the ANDES, in western ARGENTINA. (Pop. 600 000)

Merida The historic capital of the YUCATAN province of eastern MEXICO. (Pop. 424 500)

Merionethshire *see* Gwynedd.

Mersey, River A river in north-west ENGLAND. It forms an estuary to the west of LIVERPOOL which is deep and wide enough to permit access for ocean-going ships to Liverpool and MANCHESTER (via the Manchester Ship Canal. (Length 110 km/70 miles)

Merseyside A metropolitan county created in 1974 out of parts of LANCASHIRE and CHESHIRE, centring on River MERSEY, with LIVERPOOL as its administrative centre. (652 sq km/252 sq miles; pop. 1 501 000)

Mersin (Içel) The principal MEDITERRANEAN port of

TURKEY, in the central south of the country, to the north of CYPRUS. (Pop. 314 100)

Meshed *see* Mashhad.

Mesolóngion (Missolonghi) A small town in south-western GREECE, on the north coast of the Gulf of PATRAS. It is remembered for its heroic role in the Greek struggle for independence from TURKEY, when it held out against three sieges 1824–6. (Pop. 10 200)

Mesopotamia The 'Fertile Crescent' of land lying between the Rivers TIGRIS and EUPHRATES, mainly in modern IRAQ, where some of the world's earliest civilizations arose (Sumer, ASSYRIA and BABYLON). The name means 'land between the rivers'.

Messina A historic port, founded in the 8th century BC, in north-east SICILY, overlooking the narrow Strait of Messina (6 km/4miles wide at its narrowest) which separates Sicily from mainland ITALY. (Pop. 266 300)

Metz The capital of the industrial LORRAINE region in eastern FRANCE, situated on the River MOSELLE, close to the border with GERMANY. (Pop. 194 800)

Meuse (Maas), River A river which flows north-west from its source in the LORRAINE region of FRANCE, across central BELGIUM and into the NETHERLANDS, where it joins part of the delta of the River RHINE before entering the NORTH SEA. (Length 935 km/ 580 miles)

Mexico A republic in North AMERICA, with the PACIFIC OCEAN to the west and the Gulf of MEXICO to the east. Early civilizations (Maya, Toltec and Aztec) flourished here before being stamped out by the Spanish in the 16th century; Mexico became independent of

Spanish rule in 1821. It is a mountainous country, with ranges (Sierra Madre) to the west, east and south; the central area is a high plateau. Compared to its wealthy neighbour to the north, the U.S.A., Mexico is a poor country. Exports include oil, minerals and agricultural produce. Spanish is the main language, but Indian languages are also spoken. The capital is MEXICO CITY. (1 972 547 sq km/762 600 sq miles; pop. 81 650 000; cur. Peso = 100 centavos)

Mexico, Gulf of An arm of the ATLANTIC OCEAN, bounded by the FLORIDA peninsula in the south-east U.S.A. and the YUCATAN peninsula in MEXICO, with the island of CUBA placed in the middle of its entrance.

Mexico City The capital of MEXICO, and the most populous city in the world. It lies to the south of the country on a high plateau 2200 m (7350 ft) above sea-level. (Pop. 17 000 000)

Miami A major city and resort on the ATLANTIC coast of south-east FLORIDA, U.S.A. (Pop. city 372 6000/ metro-politan area 1 706 000)

Michigan A state in north central U.S.A., formed out of two peninsulas between the GREAT LAKES, with Lake MICHIGAN in the middle. The capital is LANSING. (150 780 sq km/58216 sq miles; pop. 9 088 000)

Michigan, Lake One of the GREAT LAKES, and the only one to lie entirely within the U.S.A. (57 750 sq km/ 22 300 sq miles)

Micronesia One of the three main groupings of islands of the PACIFIC OCEAN, lying to the north-west of the other two main groupings MELANESIA and POLYNESIA. They stretch from BELAU to KIRIBATI.

Micronesia, Federated States of A group of some 600 tropical islands in the west PACIFIC which became a self-governing republic in 1982, while remaining in free association with the U.S.A., which considers it strategically important. Heavily dependent on U.S. aid, the country exports copra and fish. The principal language is English, and the capital is KOLONIA. (701 sq km/ 271 sq miles; pop. 89 000; cur. U.S. dollar = 100 cents)

Middle East A non-specific term used to describe an area of south-west ASIA, which is mainly Islamic and/or Arabic-speaking. Countries included are: TURKEY, IRAN, IRAQ, SYRIA, JORDAN, ISRAEL, SAUDI ARABIA, LEBANON, YEMEN, OMAN, The UNITED ARAB EMIRATES, QATAR, BAHRAIN and KUWAIT.

Middlesborough The county town of CLEVELAND, ENGLAND. (Pop. 149 800)

Middle West *see* Midwest.

Mid Glamorgan A county in central southern WALES, which was formed in 1974 out of part of the former counties of Breconshire, Glamorgan and Monmouthshire. The administrative centre is in Cardiff. (1000 sq km/393 sq miles; pop. 538 000)

Midlands, The A term used to describe the central industrial counties of ENGLAND: DERBYSHIRE, NORTHAMPTONSHIRE, NOTTINGHAMSHIRE, STAFFORDSHIRE, WARWICKSHIRE, LEICESTERSHIRE, and WEST MIDLANDS.

Midlothian *see* Lothian.

Midway Islands Two atolls in the north PACIFIC OCEAN, some 2000 km (1242 miles) north-west of HAWAII. They have been possessions of the U.S.A. since 1867, and were the scene of a decisive U.S. naval victory against the Japanese in 1942. (3 sq km/2 sq miles; pop. 2200)

Midwest (Middle West) A term used to describe the fertile north-central part of the U.S.A. States in the Midwest include OHIO, MICHIGAN, INDIANA, ILLINOIS, WISCONSIN, MINNESOTA, IOWA and MISSOURI, but others, such as KANSAS are also often included.

Mien Bac The northern region of VIETNAM, called Tonkin (Tongking) when a part of French Indochina.

Mien Trung The central region of VIETNAM, called Annam when a part of French Indochina.

Mikinai *see* Mycenae.

Mikinos *see* Cyclades.

Milan (Milano) The major industrial and commercial centre of northern ITALY, and the country's second largest city after ROME, situated in central LOMBARDY. (Pop. 1 605 000)

Milos *see* Cyclades.

Milwaukee A port on the west side of Lake MICHIGAN, and the main industrial centre of WISCONSIN, U.S.A. (Pop. city 620 800/metropolitan area 1 393 800)

Minch, The The broad channel separating north-west Scotland from the Outer HEBRIDES.

Mindanao The second largest island of the PHILIPPINES. (94 631 sq km/36 537 sq miles; pop. 11 100 000)

Mindoro An island in the western central PHILIPPINES. (9736 sq km/3759 sq miles)

Minicoy Islands *see* Lakshadweep.

Minneapolis A major agricultural and commercial centre in south-east MINNESOTA, U.S.A., on the River

MISSISSIPPI, and adjoining ST PAUL. (Pop. city 258 300/ metropolitan area 2 230 900)

Minnesota A state in north, central U.S.A. The state capital is ST PAUL. (217 736 sq km/84 068 sq miles; pop. 4 193 000)

Minorca (Menorca) The second largest of the BALEARIC ISLANDS (after MAJORCA). The capital is Mahon. (702 sq km/271 sq miles; pop. 50 200)

Minsk A major industrial city, and the capital of BELORUSSIA. (Pop. 1 442 000)

Miquelon *see* St Pierre and Miquelon.

Miskolc A city in the north-east of HUNGARY, and the country's second largest city after BUDAPEST. (Pop. 210 000)

Mississippi A state in central southern U.S.A. with a small coastline on the Gulf of MEXICO. The state capital is JACKSON. (123 585 sq km/47 716 sq miles; pop. 2 613 000)

Mississippi, River The second longest river in the U.S.A. after the MISSOURI. It rises in MINNESOTA and runs south the length of the country to the Gulf of MEXICO. (Length 3779 km/2348 miles)

Missolonghi *see* Mesolóngion.

Missouri A state in the MIDWEST of the U.S.A. The state capital is JEFFERSON CITY. (180 487 sq km/69 686 sq miles; pop. 5 029 000)

Missouri, River The main tributary of the MISSISSIPPI and the longest river in North AMERICA. It rises in MONTANA, flows north, east and south-east to join the Mississippi at ST LOUIS. (Length 3969 km/2466 miles)

Mitchell, Mount *see* Appalachian Mountains.

Mizoram A union territory of INDIA, in the hilly north-east, on the border with BURMA. The capital is Aijal. (21 081 sq km/8137 sq miles; pop. 493 800)
Mobile A port on the coast of ALABAMA, U.S.A., on the Gulf of MEXICO. (Pop. city 204 900/metropolitan area 465 700)
Mobutu Sese Seko, Lake *see* Albert, Lake.
Modena A industrial city retaining many vestiges of its medieval past, in north-eastern ITALY. (Pop. 178 300)
Mogadishu (Mogadiscio) The capital and main port of of SOMALIA. (Pop. 400 000)
Mohave Desert *see* Mojave Desert.
Mohenjo Daro An ancient city in the valley of the River INDUS, in southern PAKISTAN. It was inhabited for about 1000 years from 2500 BC.
Mojave (Mohave) Desert A desert in southern CALIFORNIA, stretching from DEATH VALLEY to LOS ANGELES. (38 850 sq km/15 000 sq miles)
Moldavia (Moldova) **1** A republic which declared its independence from the U.S.S.R. in 1991. It lies between ROMANIA and the UKRAINE. The capital is KISHINEV. (26 200 sq km/10 100 sq miles; pop. 971 000). **2** The neighbouring region of north-west Romania.
Molise A region of eastern ITALY, on the ADRIATIC coast, between ABRUZZI and PUGLIA. (4438 sq km/ 1714 sq miles; pop. 332 900)
Molotov *see* Perm'.
Moluccas *see* Maluku.
Mombasa The second city of KENYA and an important port on the INDIAN OCEAN. (Pop. 500 000)
Monaco A tiny principality forming an enclave in the

south-eastern corner of FRANCE on the MEDITERRANEAN SEA. Gambling (notably at MONTE CARLO) and tourism are major sources of income. French and Monégasque are spoken; MONACO VILLE is the capital. (1.9 sq km/0.73 sq miles; pop. 28 000; cur. Monégasque and French francs = 100 centimes)

Monaco-Ville The capital of MONACO, sited on a rocky headland that sticks out into the MEDITERRANEAN SEA. (Pop. 1250)

Monaghan A county in the central north of the Republic of IRELAND, with a county town of the same name. (1291 sq km/498 sq miles; pop. county 51 200)

Mönchengladbach An industrial city in the south-west of the RUHR region of western GERMANY, 25 km (16 miles) west of DUSSELDORF. (Pop. 257 000)

Mongolia An isolated republic in east central ASIA which came into being in 1924. The GOBI DESERT lies to the south and there are high mountains to the north. Mongolia has an extremely cold and harsh climate, and the majority of the population lives in towns to the north. Minerals and animal products are the main exports. The official language is Mongolian, and the capital is ULAN BATOR. (1 565 000 sq km/604 247 sq miles; pop. 1 960 000; cur. Tugrik or togrog = 100 mongo)

Monmouthshire *see* Gwent.

Monrovia The capital and principal port of LIBERIA. (Pop. 425 000)

Mons (Bergen) A town in south-west BELGIUM. (Pop. 94 000)

Montana A state in the north-west of the U.S.A., on the

border with CANADA. The state capital is HELENA. (381 087 sq km/147 138 sq miles; pop. 826 000)

Monte Carlo An elegant coastal town and resort in MONACO, famed in particular for its casinos. (Pop. 13 200)

Montenegro (Crna Gora) The smallest of the republics of YUGOSLAVIA, in the south-west on the ADRIATIC SEA and bordering ALBANIA. The capital is TITOGRAD. (13 812 sq km/5331 sq miles; pop. 584 300)

Monterey A resort town on the PACIFIC coast of central CALIFORNIA, U.S.A., 135 km (85 miles) south-east of SAN FRANCISCO. It is well known for its annual jazz festival. (Pop. 28 700)

Monterrey An industrial city in north-east MEXICO, the country's third largest city after MEXICO CITY and GUADALJARA. (Pop. 1 916 500)

Montevideo The capital of URUGUAY, and an important port on the River PLATE estuary. (Pop. 1 500 000)

Montgomery The state capital of ALABAMA, U.S.A. (Pop. city 185 000/metropolitan area 284 800)

Montgomeryshire *see* Powys.

Montpelier The state capital of VERMONT, U.S.A. (Pop. 8200)

Montpellier An university and trading city in central southern FRANCE, the capital of the LANGUEDOC-ROUSSILLON region. (Pop. 225 300)

Montreal The second largest city in CANADA after TORONTO, on the ST LAWRENCE RIVER, in the south of the province of QUEBEC. Two-thirds of the population are French-speaking Québecois. (Pop. 2 828 250)

Montserrat A British Crown colony in the LEEWARD

ISLANDS, in the south-eastern CARIBBEAN. The capital is called Plymouth. (102 sq km/39 sq miles)

Monza A city in northern ITALY, 12 km (8 miles) north-east of MILAN. (Pop. 122 500)

Moravia A historical region of central CZECHOSLOVAKIA, with POLAND to the north and AUSTRIA to the south.

Moray Firth The narrow inlet of the NORTH SEA cutting some 56 km (35 miles) into the eastern coast of north-east SCOTLAND, with INVERNESS at its head.

Morayshire *see* Grampian.

Morocco A kingdom in north-west AFRICA with coastlines on the MEDITERRANEAN SEA and ATLANTIC OCEAN. It was a French protectorate, but became independent in 1956. The SAHARA DESERT lies to the south-east and the ATLAS MOUNTAINS run through the middle of the country. Phosphates are the main export. The dominant religion is Sunni Islam, and Arabic is the official language. The capital is RABAT. (458 730 sq km/177 116 sq miles; pop. 24 950 000; cur. Dirham = 100 centimes)

Moroni The capital of the COMOROS islands. (Pop. 20 000)

Moscow (Moskva) The capital of the RUSSIAN FEDERATION, sited on the Moskva River. It is an ancient city with a rich heritage, and is the political, industrial and cultural focus of the country. (Pop. 8 600 000)

Moselle (Mosel), River A river which flows northwards from the south-eastern LORRAINE region of eastern FRANCE to form part of the border between LUXEMBOURG and GERMANY before flowing eastwards to meet the River RHINE at KOBLENZ. (Length 550 km/ 340 miles)

Mosul (Al Mawsil) A historic trading city on the banks of the River TIGRIS in north-west IRAQ, and an important centre for the surrounding oil-producing region. (Pop. 1 500 000)

Mourne Mountains A mountain range of noted scenic beauty in the south of County DOWN, Northern IRELAND. The highest point is Slieve Donard. (852 m (2795 ft).

Mozambique A republic in south-east AFRICA with a coast on the MOZAMBIQUE CHANNEL. It was an overseas province of PORTUGAL until 1975, when it gained independence. The climate is generally hot and humid. Tropical diseases, natural disasters and continuing civil strife have combined to blunt the economy, which is largely dependent on cash crops such as cashew nuts and cotton. Portuguese is the official language, and the capital is MAPUTO. (799 380 sq km/ 308 642 sq miles; pop. 14 160 000; cur. Metical = 100 centavos)

Mozambique Channel The broad strait, some 400 km (250 miles) across at its narrowest, which separates the island of MADAGASCAR from mainland AFRICA.

Mühlheim an der Ruhr An industrial city and port on the River RUHR, in the RUHR region of western GERMANY. (Pop. 174 000)

Mulhouse An industrial city in the ALSACE region of eastern FRANCE. (Pop. 222 700)

Mull An island just off the central western coast of SCOTLAND. (925 sq km/357 sq miles)

Multan An industrial city in PUNJAB province in eastern central PAKISTAN. (Pop. 730 000)

Munich (München) A historic and industrial city in southern GERMANY, and capital of BAVARIA. (Pop. 1 300 000)

Munster One of the four historic provinces of IRELAND, covering the south-west quarter of the country.

Münster An inland port and industrial centre on the DORTMUND–Ems canal in north-western GERMANY. (Pop. 260 000)

Murcia A trading and manufacturing city in south-eastern SPAIN, and capital of the province of the same name. (Pop. city 288 600)

Murmansk The largest city north of the ARCTIC CIRCLE, a major port and industrial centre on the KOLA PENINSULA in the far north-western corner of the RUSSIA. (Pop. 412 000)

Murray, River A major river of south-east AUSTRALIA, which flows westwards from its source in the SNOWY MOUNTAINS to form much of the boundary between the states of NEW SOUTH WALES and VICTORIA. It is joined by the River DARLING before flowing across the south-eastern corner of SOUTH AUSTRALIA and into the INDIAN OCEAN. (Length 2570 km/1600 miles)

Mururoa An atoll in the south-eastern sector of FRENCH POLYNESIA, used by FRANCE since 1966 as a testing ground for nuclear weapons.

Musandam A rocky, horn-shaped peninsula which juts out into the GULF to form the southern side of the Strait of HORMUZ. It belongs to OMAN, but is separated from it by part of the UNITED ARAB EMIRATES.

Muscat The historic capital of OMAN. The neighbouring port of Muttrah has developed rapidly in recent decades to form the commercial centre of Muscat. (Pop. (with Muttrah) 80 000)

Muscovy A principality of RUSSIA from the 13th to 16th century, with MOSCOW as the capital.

Mustique A privately owned island in the GRENADINES, to the south of ST VINCENT, in the south-eastern CARIBBEAN. (Pop. 200)

Muttrah *see* Muscat.

Myanmar *see* Burma.

Mycenae (Mikinai) An ancient city in the north-east of the PELOPONNESE, GREECE, inhabited from 1580 to 1100 BC.

Mysore An industrial city in the state of KARNATAKA, southern INDIA. (Pop. 470 000)

N

Naberezhnyye Chelny *see* Brezhnev.

Nablus The largest town on the WEST BANK of Israeli-occupied JORDAN. (Pop. 44 000)

Nagaland A primarily agricultural state in the hilly far north-eastern corner of INDIA, bordering BURMA. (16 579 sq km/6399 sq miles; pop. 774 900)

Nagasaki A port and industrial city on the west coast of KYUSHU island, JAPAN. Three days after the first atomic bomb destroyed HIROSHIMA, a second was dropped on Nagasaki (9 August 1945), killing 40 000 people. (Pop. 446 300)

Nagorny Karabakh A disputed autonomous enclave in AZERBAIDZHAN, which is claimed by ARMENIA. Three-quarters of the population are Armenian.
Nagoya A port and industrial centre on the south-eastern coast of HONSHU, JAPAN. (Pop. 2 065 800)
Nagpur A commercial centre and textile manufacturing city on the DECCAN plateau of MAHARASHTRA state, central INDIA. (Pop. 1 302 100)
Nairobi The capital of KENYA and a commercial centre, in the south-west highland region. (Pop. 1 250 000)
Nakhichevan An autonomous republic, enclaved by ARMENIA, but a part of AZERBAIDZHAN. The capital is also called Nakhichevan. (5500 sq km/2120 sq miles; pop. republic 252 000/capital 37 000)
Namib Desert A sand desert lining the coast of NAMIBIA in south-western AFRICA.
Namibia A republic in south-west AFRICA which fought a bitter struggle to oust South African occupation, becoming independent in 1990. One of the world's driest nations, much of the land is deserted of people, but it is rich in diamonds and valuable ores, which are exported. There are also rich fishing grounds off the ATLANTIC coast. The dominant languages are English, Afrikaans and German, and the capital is WINDHOEK. (823 172 sq km/317 827 sq miles; pop. 1 140 000; cur. South African rand = 100 cents)
Nanchang An industrial city and commercial centre in central south-eastern CHINA, and the capital of JIANGXI province. (Pop. 2 390 000)
Nancy A manufacturing city in north-east FRANCE, and former capital of LORRAINE. (Pop. 314 200)

Nanjing (Nanking) A major industrial and trading city built on the lower reaches of the CHANG JIANG (Yangtze) river, and the capital of JIANGSU province, central eastern CHINA. (Pop. 3 551 000)
Nanning The capital of the GUANGXI-ZHUANG autonomous region in the extreme south-east of CHINA. (Pop. 607 000)
Nansei-shoto *see* Ryukyu Islands.
Nantes A port and commercial centre in north-western FRANCE and capital of the Loire Atlantique department. (Pop. 474 100)
Naples (Napoli) The third largest city in ITALY after ROME and MILAN, a port situated on the spectacular Bay of Naples. (Pop. 1 203 900)
Nara A historic city in south HONSHU island, JAPAN, the the capital of Japan in the 8th century. (Pop. 327 000)
Nashville The state capital of TENNESSEE, U.S.A., an industrial city famous as the traditional home of Country and Western music. (Pop. city 462 500/ metropolitan area 890 300)
Nassau The capital of the BAHAMAS, on the north side of New Providence Island. (Pop. 120 000)
Nasser, Lake A massive artificial lake on the River NILE in southern EGYPT created when the ASWAN High Dam was completed in 1971. It was named after the former president (1956–70) of Egypt, Gamal Abdel Nasser (1918–70). (5000 sq km/1930 sq miles)
Natal A port city on the north-east tip of BRAZIL, and capital of the state of Rio Grande do Norte. (Pop. 417 000)
Natal A province on the eastern coast of SOUTH

AFRICA. The capital is Pietermaritzburg, but the main city is DURBAN. (86 976 sq km/33 573 sq miles; pop. 2 841 700)

Nauru An island republic in the south-west PACIFIC, just south of the Equator. It was jointly administered by the U.K., AUSTRALIA and NEW ZEALAND before gaining independence within the Commonwealth in 1968. The export of colossal phospate reserves has made the world's smallest republic rich. Nauruan and English are the main languages, and the capital is YAREN. (21 sq km/8 sq miles; pop. 8100; cur. Australian dollar = 100 cents)

Navarra (Navarre) A province in the mountainous north-eastern part of SPAIN. The capital is PAMPLONA. (10 420 sq km/4023 sq miles; pop. 507 400)

Naxos A fertile island in the southern AEGEAN SEA, the largest of the CYCLADES. (428 sq km/165 sq miles)

Nazareth A town in northern ISRAEL, and the childhood home of Jesus. (Pop. 46 300)

Ndjamena (N'Djamena) The capital of CHAD, in the south-east of the country. It was founded by the French in 1900 and named Fort Lamy. (Pop. 303 000)

Neagh, Lough The largest freshwater lake in the BRITISH ISLES, in the east of NORTHERN IRELAND. (381 sq km/147 sq miles)

Nebraska A state in the MIDWEST of the U.S.A., in the very centre of the country. The capital is LINCOLN. (200 018 sq km/77 227 sq miles; pop. 1 606 000)

Neckar, River A tributary of the River RHINE, rising in the BLACK FOREST in the south-west of GERMANY (365 km/227 miles)

Negev A desert in southern ISRAEL.
Negros The fourth largest island of the PHILIPPINES. (12 704 sq km/4905 sq miles; pop. 2 750 000)
Nei Mongol Autonomous Region (Inner Mongolia) A region of north-eastern CHINA, bordering MONGOLIA. The capital is HOHHOT. (1 200 000 sq km/460 000 sq miles; pop. 18 510 000)
Neisse, River A tributary of the ODER, which flows north from its source in CZECHOSLOVAKIA to form part of the border between GERMANY and POLAND. (Length 256 km/159 miles)
Nepal A landlocked kingdom in southern ASIA to the north-east of INDIA. The southern part of the country is mainly jungle-covered hills, but these rise up to the HIMALAYAS, which run across the north. The national economy is largely based on agricultural produce. The chief religion is Hinduism, and the official language is Nepali. The capital is KATHMANDU. (145 391 sq km/ 56 136 sq miles; pop. 17 420 000; cur. Rupee = 100 paisa)
Netherlands A kingdom in north-west EUROPE with a coast on the NORTH SEA. The land is generally flat and much of it lies below sea-level, with the water held back by dykes. It is a member of the European Community, and is a major exporter of petroleum products, farm products and steel. Dutch is the principal language, and the capital is AMSTERDAM (although the seat of government is The HAGUE). (41 548 sq km/33 930 sq miles; pop. 14 520 000; cur. Guilder or Florin = 100 cents)
Netherlands Antilles An overseas division of the

NETHERLANDS, spread over the southern CARIBBEAN. The principal islands are: CURACAO, ST MARTIN, ST EUSTATIUS, and BONAIRE. ARUBA was part of the group until 1986.

Neusatz *see* Novi Sad.

Neva, River The river which flows through ST PETERSBURG. (Length: 74 km/45 miles)

Nevada A state in the west of the U.S.A., consisting mostly of desert. The state capital is CARSON CITY. (286 298 sq km/110 540 sq miles; pop. 936 000)

Nevis *see* St Kitts and Nevis.

Newark A major port city in NEW JERSEY. (Pop. 314 400/metropolitan area 1 875 300)

New Britain The largest off-shore island belonging to PAPUA NEW GUINEA, in the BISMARCK Archipelago. (36 500 sq km/11 125 sq miles; pop. 237 000)

New Brunswick A state on the coast in south-east CANADA, bordering the U.S.A.. The state capital is FREDERICTON. (73 436 sq km/28 354 sq miles; pop. 696 000)

New Caledonia The main island of a group called by the same name in the South PACIFIC, which form an overseas territory of FRANCE The capital is NOUMEA. (19 103 sq km/7376 sq miles; pop. 155 000)

Newcastle A port and industrial city in NEW SOUTH WALES, AUSTRALIA. (Pop. 259 000)

Newcastle upon Tyne A historic and industrial city in the county of TYNE AND WEAR, north-east ENGLAND. (Pop. 280 000)

Newcastle-under-Lyme A town in the Potteries region of STAFFORDSHIRE, central ENGLAND. (Pop. 74 600)

New Delhi *see* Delhi

New England The name given to north-eastern states of the U.S.A.: MAINE, VERMONT, NEW HAMPSHIRE, CONNECTICUT, MASSACHUSETTS and RHODE ISLAND.

Newfoundland The province in the extreme east of CANADA. The capital is ST JOHN'S. (372 000 sq km/ 143 634 sq miles; pop. 568 000)

New Guinea One of the world's largest islands, divided into two parts: independent PAPUA NEW GUINEA in the east and IRIAN JAYA, a state of INDONESIA, in the west.

New Hampshire A state of NEW ENGLAND, in the north-west of the U.S.A. The state capital is CONCORD. (24 097 sq km/9304 sq miles; pop. 998 000)

New Haven A port in CONNECTICUT, U.S.A.. (Pop. city 124 200/metropolitan area 506 000)

New Hebrides *see* Vanuatu.

New Jersey A state on the ATLANTIC coast in the north-east of the U.S.A. The state capital is TRENTON. (20 295 sq km/7836 sq miles; pop. 7 562 000)

New Mexico A state is the south-west of the U.S.A., bordering MEXICO. The state capital is SANTA FE. (315 115 sq km/121 666 sq miles; pop. 1 450 000)

New Orleans An important and historic port in southern LOUISIANA, on the MISSISSIPPI delta. (Pop. city 559 100/metropolitan area 1 318 800)

Newport A port and naval base on RHODE ISLAND, U.S.A.. (Pop. 29 900)

Newport News A major eastern seaboard port in VIRGINIA, U.S.A.. (Pop. city 154 600/metropolitan area (with NORFOLK) 1 261 200)

New Providence *see* Bahamas.

New South Wales The most populous of the states of AUSTRALIA, situated in the south-east of the country. The capital is SYDNEY. (801 430 sq km/309 433 sq miles; pop. 5 379 000)

New Territories *see* Hong Kong.

New York (City) The most populous city in the U.S.A., its most important port, and a major financial centre. It is sited on the mouth of the HUDSON River, and comprises five boroughs: Manhattan, the Bronx, Queens, Brooklyn and Richmond. (Pop. city 7 322 600/metropolitan area 8 376 900)

New York (State) A state in the north-east of the U.S.A., on the ATLANTIC coast. The state capital is ALBANY (128 402 sq km/49 576 sq miles; pop. 17 783 000)

New Zealand An independent dominion within the Commonwealth in the south PACIFIC OCEAN, comprising two main islands (South Island and North Island). The bulk of the population lives on the more temperate North Island. Farming is the main industry, and New Zealand is a major producer of meat, wool and dairy products. English is the principal language, and the capital is WELLINGTON. (268 046 sq km/103 493 sq miles; pop. 3 300 000; cur. New Zealand dollar = 100 cents)

Ngaliema, Mount *see* Ruwenzori.

Niagara Falls Spectacular waterfalls on the Niagara River, situated on the CANADA–U.S.A. border between Lakes ERIE and ONTARIO.

Niamey The capital of NIGER. (Pop. 400 000)

Niassa, Lake *see* Malawi, Lake

Nicaragua A republic in Central AMERICA with coasts

on the CARIBBEAN SEA and PACIFIC OCEAN. It became a republic in 1838 after Mexican rule. Fertile lowlands lie to the east; to the west lie mountains and Lake NICARAGUA. Chemicals and agricultural produce, particularly coffee, are the main exports. Spanish is the principal language, and the capital is MANAGUA. (130 000 sq km/ 50 200 sq miles; pop. 3 140 000; cur. Cordoba = 100 centavos)

Nicaragua, Lake A large lake in the south-west of NICARAGUA. (8264 sq km/3191 sq miles)

Nice A city, harbour and famous resort town of the COTE D'AZUR, south-eastern FRANCE. (Pop. 451 500)

Nicosia The capital of CYPRUS, situated in the centre of the island. (Pop. 161 100)

Niger A landlocked republic in West AFRICA which became independent of French rule in 1960. The country has been crippled by the advance of the SAHARA DESERT, which covers most of the country. Uranium and groundnuts are the chief exports. French is the official language; the capital is NIAMEY. (1 267 000 sq km/489 191 sq miles; pop. 6 700 000; cur. CFA franc = 100 centimes)

Niger, River A river in West AFRICA flowing through GUINEA, MALI, NIGER and NIGERIA to the Gulf of GUINEA. (Length 4170 km/2590 miles)

Nigeria A republic in West AFRICA with a coastline on the Gulf of GUINEA. It was formerly a British colony, but gained independence in 1960. Tropical rainforests lie to the south, while the north is mainly semi-desert. Oil, cocoa and tin are among the main exports. English is the official language, and the capital is

ABUJA (since 1992). (923 768 sq km/356 669 sq miles; pop. 88 500 000) cur. Naira = 100 kobo)

Nijmegen A city of eastern central NETHERLANDS, close to the border with GERMANY. (Pop. 234 000)

Nikolayev A port and industrial city on the north coast of the BLACK SEA, in the UKRAINE. (Pop. 480 000)

Nile, River A river in AFRICA and, with the AMAZON, one of the longest rivers in the world. It rises in BURUNDI, flows into Lake VICTORIA and then flows northwards through UGANDA, SUDAN and EGYPT to its delta on the MEDITERRANEAN. The river is called the White Nile until it reaches KHARTOUM, where it is joined by its main tributary, the Blue Nile, which rises in ETHIOPIA. (Length 6695 km/4160 miles)

Nîmes A city in southern FRANCE, overlooking the River RHONE. (Pop. 138 000)

Nineveh The excavated remains of the ancient capital of ASSYRIA, near MOSUL in northern IRAQ.

Ningbo A port and industrial city in ZHEJIANG province, in central eastern CHINA. (Pop. 900 000)

Ningxia-Hui Autonomous Region A region of central northern CHINA, south of Inner Mongolia. The capital is YINCHUAN. (60 000 sq km/23 000 sq miles; pop. 3 640 000)

Nis (Nish) A historic city in the east of SERBIA, YUGOSLAVIA. (Pop. 230 000)

Nizhni Novgorod *see* Gor'kiy.

Nizhniy Tagil An industrial city in the central URAL MOUNTAINS, RUSSIA. (Pop. 415 000)

Nordkapp *see* North Cape.

Norfolk A county of EAST ANGLIA, ENGLAND. The

county town is NORWICH. (5355 sq km/2068 sq miles; pop. 714 000)

Norfolk A port and naval base in the state of VIRGINIA, U.S.A.. (Pop. city 279 700/metropolitan area (with NEWPORT NEWS) 1 261 200)

Normandy An area of central northern FRANCE, now divided into two regions, Haute Normandie and Basse Normandie. (Pop. 3 006 000)

Northampton The county town of NORTHAMPTONSHIRE. (Pop. 164 000)

Northamptonshire A county in central ENGLAND. The county town is NORTHAMPTON. (2367 sq km/914 sq miles; pop. 547 000)

North Cape (Nordkapp) A point in the very north of NORWAY.

North Carolina A state on the south-eastern coast of the U.S.A. The state capital is RALEIGH. (136 198 sq km/ 52 586 sq miles; pop. 6 255 000)

North Dakota A state in the west of the U.S.A. The state capital is BISMARCK. (183 022 sq km/70 665 sq miles; pop. 685 000)

Northern Ireland A province of the U.K., occupying most of the northern part of the island of IRELAND. It is divided into six counties. The capital is BELFAST. (14 121 sq km/5452 sq miles; pop. 1 572 000)

Northern Marianas A group of 14 islands in the western PACIFIC which in 1978 became a commonwealth of the U.S.A.. The capital is SUSUPE, on the island of SAIPAN.

Northern Territory A territory of northern AUSTRALIA. The capital is DARWIN. (1 346 2000 sq km/519 770 sq miles; pop. 136 800)

North Island *see* New Zealand.

North Pole The northernmost point on the earth's axis.

North Sea A comparatively shallow branch of the ATLANTIC OCEAN that separates the BRITISH ISLES from the European mainland.

Northumberland A county in north-eastern ENGLAND. The county town is Morpeth. (5033 sq km/1943 sq miles; pop. 302 000)

Northwest Territories A vast area of northern CANADA, occupying almost a third of the country's whole land area. The capital is YELLOWKNIFE. (3 246 000 sq km/ 1 253 400 sq miles; pop. 45 740)

Norway A kingdom in north-west EUROPE occupying the western part of the Scandinavian penisula with a jagged coastline on the NORWEGIAN SEA. It is a mountainous country and the northern part lies within the ARCTIC CIRCLE. Fishing and forestry are traditional industries, but the country is also a significant producer of oil and minerals. The capital is OSLO. (324 219 sq km/125 180 sq miles; pop. 4 170 000; cur. Krone = 100 øre)

Norwegian Sea A sea lying between NORWAY, GREENLAND and ICELAND; to the north it joins the ARCTIC OCEAN, and to the south, the ATLANTIC.

Norwich The county town of NORFOLK, in eastern ENGLAND. (Pop. 122 000)

Nottingham The historic county town of NOTTINGHAMSHIRE, situated on the River TRENT. (Pop. 277 000)

Nottinghamshire A county in the MIDLANDS of ENGLAND. The county town is NOTTINGHAM. (2164 sq km/ 836 sq miles; pop. 1 000 000)

Nouakchott The capital city of MAURITANIA, near the ATLANTIC coast. (Pop. 135 000)

Nouméa The capital and chief port of NEW CALEDONIA. (Pop. 85 000)

Nova Scotia A province on the eastern coast of CANADA. The capital is HALIFAX. (52 841 sq km/ 20 401 sq miles; pop. 847 000)

Novi Sad (Ujvidek, Neusatz) A city on the River DANUBE in YUGOSLAVIA, and the capital of Vojvodina, an autonomous province of SERBIA. (Pop. 257 700)

Novokuznetsk An industrial city in central southern SIBERIA. (Pop. 572 000)

Novosibirsk A major industrial city in central RUSSIA. (Pop. 1 386 000)

Nuku'alofa The capital and main port of TONGA. (Pop. 21 000)

Nullarbor Plain A huge, dry and treeless (the name is from the Latin for no trees) plain which borders the GREAT AUSTRALIAN BIGHT, in WESTERN and SOUTHERN AUSTRALIA.

Nuremberg (Nürnberg) A city in BAVARIA, central southern GERMANY. (Pop. 486 000)

Nürnberg *see* Nuremberg.

Nusa Tenggara *see* Lesser Sunda Islands.

Nuuk *see* Godthåb.

Nyasa, Lake *see* Malawi, Lake.

Nyasaland *see* Malawi.

O

Oahu The third largest of the islands of HAWAII, where the state capital, HONOLULU, and PEARL HARBOR are located. (1549 sq km/598 sq miles; pop. 797 400)

Oakland A port on the bay of SAN FRANCISCO in central western CALIFORNIA, U.S.A. (Pop. city 351 900/metropolitan area 1 871 400)

Ob', River A river in RUSSIA which rises near the border with MONGOLIA and flows northwards to the KARA SEA. (Length 5570 km/3460 miles)

Oberammergau A village in BAVARIA in south-west GERMANY, famed for the Passion play which it puts on every ten years. (Pop. 4800)

Oceania A general term used to describe the central and southern islands of the PACIFIC OCEAN.

Oder, River A river in central EUROPE rising in CZECHOSLOVAKIA and flowing north and west to the BALTIC SEA; it forms part of the border between GERMANY and POLAND. (Length 912 km/567 miles)

Odessa A major BLACK SEA port in the UKRAINE. (Pop. 1 113 000)

Offaly A county in the centre of the Republic of IRELAND. The county town is Tullamore. (1998 sq km/771 sq miles; pop. 58 300)

Ogaden A desert region of south-eastern ETHIOPIA, claimed by SOMALIA.

Ohio A MIDWEST state of the U.S.A., with a shoreline on Lake ERIE. The capital is COLUMBUS. (106 765 sq km/41 22 sq miles; pop. 10 744 00)

Ohio River A river in the eastern U.S.A., formed at the

confluence of the Allegheny and Monongahela Rivers. It flows west and south and joins the MISSISSIPPI at Cairo, ILLINOIS. (Length 1575 km/980 miles)

Okavango, River *see* Kavango (Cubango), River.

Okayama A commercial city in south-west HONSHU island, JAPAN. (Pop. 572 400)

Okhotsk, Sea of A part of the north-western PACIFIC OCEAN bounded by the KAMCHATKA peninsula, the KURILE islands, and the east coast of SIBERIA.

Oklahoma A state in the south-west of the U.S.A. The state capital is OKLAHOMA CITY. (173 320 sq km/ 66 919 sq miles; pop. 3 301 000)

Oklahoma City The state capital of OKLAHOMA. (Pop. city 443 200/metropolitan area 962 600)

Olympia 1 The original site of the Olympic Games, centring upon a temple to Zeus, on the PELOPONNESE in south-western GREECE. **2** A port and the state capital of WASHINGTON, on the west coast of the U.S.A. (Pop. city 29 200/metropolitan area 138 300)

Olympus, Mount A group of mountains in cental mainland GREECE, the home of the ancient Greek gods. The highest peak is Mytikas (2917 m/9570 ft)

Omaha A city in eastern NEBRASKA, U.S.A. (Pop. city 334 000/metropolitan area 607 400)

Oman A sultanate occupying the south-eastern corner of the Arabian peninsula, a mixture of rugged mountains, fertile valleys and sand desert. The country is divided in two by the UNITED ARAB EMIRATES: the tip of the MUSANDAM peninsula, overlooking the strategic Strait of HORMUZ, belongs to Oman, but the greater bulk if the country is to the south, on the shores of the

Gulf of OMAN and the ARABIAN SEA. Oil is the most important export. Arabic is the official language, and the capital is MUSCAT. (300 000 sq km/116 000 sq miles; pop. 1 276 000; cur. Omani rial = 1000 baiza)

Oman, Gulf of A branch of the ARABIAN SEA leading to the Strait of HORMUZ.

Omdurman A city situated across the River NILE from KHARTOUM, the capital of SUDAN. (Pop. 526 300)

Omsk An industrial city in central western SIBERIA, on the Trans-Siberian Railway. (Pop. 1 094 000)

Ontario A province of central CANADA. The capital is TORONTO. (1 068 582 sq km/412 580 sq miles; pop. 8 625 000)

Ontario, Lake The smallest and most easterly of the GREAT LAKES; it drains into the ST LAWRENCE River. (19 550 sq km/7550 sq miles)

Oporto (Porto) A port in north-west PORTUGAL, and the country's second largest city after LISBON. (Pop. 330 200)

Oran (Wahran) A MEDITERRANEAN port and the second largest city of ALGERIA. (Pop. 670 000)

Orange, River The longest river in southern AFRICA, rising is LESOTHO and flowing west to the ATLANTIC. (Length 2090 km/1299 miles)

Orange Free State A landlocked province in central SOUTH AFRICA, with its capital at BLOEMFONTEIN. (127 993 sq km/49 405 sq miles; pop. 2 080 000)

Oranjestad **1** The capital of ARUBA, and an important port. (Pop. 10 100) **2** The capital of ST EUSTATIUS, and a port. (Pop. 1200)

Oregon A state in the north-west of the U.S.A., on the

PACIFIC. The state capital is SALEM. (251 180 sq km/ 96 981 sq miles; pop. 2 687 000)

Orinoco, River A river in northern South AMERICA. It rises in southern VENEZUELA and flows west, then north and finally east to its delta on the ATLANTIC. It forms part of the border between COLOMBIA and Venezuela. (Length 2200 km/1370 miles)

Orissa An eastern state of INDIA. The capital is Bhubaneswar. (155 707 sq km/60 103 sq miles; pop. 26 370 300)

Orkney Islands A group of some 90 islands off the north-east coast of SCOTLAND. The capital is Kirkwall. (976 sq km/377 sq miles; pop. 19 000)

Orlando A city in central FLORIDA, and the focus for visitors to Disney World and Cape CANAVERAL. (Pop. city 137 100/metropolitan area 824 100)

Orléans A city in north central FRANCE, on the River LOIRE. (Pop. 225 000)

Orontes, River The river flowing through HOMS and HAMAH in SYRIA. (Length 384 km/238 miles)

Osaka A port on south HONSHU island, and the third largest city in Japan after TOKYO and YOKOHAMA. (Pop. 2 636 300)

Osijek A city in eastern CROATIA, on the DRAVA River. It was formerly called Esseg. (Pop. 158 800)

Oslo The capital of NORWAY, and its main port, in the south-east of the country. From 1624 to 1925 it was called Christiania (or Kristiania). (Pop. city 448 800/ metropolitan area 566 500)

Otranto, Strait of The waterway separating the heel of ITALY from ALBANIA.

Ottawa The capital of CANADA, in eastern ONTARIO, on the OTTAWA River. (Pop. 718 000)
Ottawa, River A river of central CANADA which flows into the ST LAWRENCE at MONTREAL. (Length 1271 km/ 790 miles)
Ouagadougou The capital of BURKINA, situated in the centre of the country. (Pop. 286 500)
Oviedo A steel-making city in northern SPAIN, capital of the province of ASTURIAS. (Pop. 190 100)
Oxford An old university city, and county town of OXFORDSHIRE, ENGLAND. (Pop. 117 000)
Oxfordshire A county in southern central ENGLAND. The county town is OXFORD. (2611 sq km/1008 sq miles; pop. 558 000)
Oxus, River *see* Amudar'ya, River.

P

Pacific Ocean The largest and deepest ocean on Earth, situated between ASIA and AUSTRALIA to the west and the AMERICAS to the east.
Padang A port and the capital of West SUMATRA, INDONESIA, on the west coast. (Pop. 480 900)
Padua A historic city in VENETO, north-east of ITALY. (Pop. 228 700)
Pagan The ruined 11th-century capital of BURMA, 160 km (100 miles) south-west of MANDALAY.
Painted Desert A desert of colourful rocks in northern ARIZONA, U.S.A. (19 400 sq km/7500 sq miles)
Pakistan A republic in southern ASIA with a coast on

the ARABIAN SEA. It was formerly West Pakistan until East Pakistan (BANGLADESH) seceded. The country was created out of British INDIA in 1947 as a homeland for India's Muslim people. It includes the fertile INDUS valley, high mountains to the north and desert to the west. The national economy is based on agriculture and manufacturing, and cotton is the main export. Urdu is the principal language, and the capital is ISLAMABAD. (803 943 sq km/310 402 sq miles; pop. 89 831 000; cur. Pakistani rupee)

Palau *see* Belau.

Palembang A port and the capital of South SUMATRA, on the south-east coast. (Pop. 787 200)

Palenque The ruins of one of the great Mayan cities in southern MEXICO.

Palermo The capital of SICILY, ITALY, on the north-west coast. (Pop. 718 900)

Palestine An area of the MIDDLE EAST which encompassed the modern countries of ISRAEL and parts of JORDAN and EGYPT.

Palm Beach A resort on a island off the east coast of FLORIDA, U.S.A., with the manufacturing centre of West Palm Beach on the mainland opposite. (Pop. Palm Beach 10 700/metropolitan area 692 200)

Palma (Palma de Mallorca) The capital of MAJORCA and of the BALEARIC ISLANDS. (Pop. 304 400)

Palma, La *see* Canary Islands.

Palmyra (Tadmor) An ancient ruined city in SYRIA.

Pamir A region of high plateaux in central ASIA which straddles the borders of TADZHIKISTAN, AFGHANISTAN and CHINA.

Pampas The flat grasslands of central ARGENTINA.
Pamplona A city in north-eastern SPAIN, famous for its bull-running festival in July. (Pop. 183 100)
Panama A republic in Central AMERICA on the isthmus of Panama which joins North and South America. It has shorelines on the CARIBBEAN SEA and the PACIFIC OCEAN which are linked by the PANAMA CANAL. The country became an independent state in 1903. Panama is humid and thickly forested; tropical diseases have been a serious problem in the recent past. The country's economy is heavily dependent on the canal, but exports include bananas and sugar. Spanish is the official language and the capital is PANAMA CITY. (78 046 sq km/30 134 sq miles; pop. 2 074 700; cur. Balboa = 100 centésimos)
Panama Canal A canal 64 km (40 miles) long that runs through the centre of PANAMA, linking the CARIBBEAN to the PACIFIC. It was completed in 1914.
Panama City The capital of PANAMA, situated at the PACIFIC end of the PANAMA CANAL. (Pop. 502 000)
Panay *see* Visayan Islands.
Papeete The capital of FRENCH POLYNESIA, on the north-west coast of TAHITI. (Pop. 62 700)
Papua New Guinea An independent state comprising the eastern half of the island of NEW GUINEA and a number of islands, including BOUGAINVILLE, NEW BRITAIN and New Ireland. Until 1975 it was administered by AUSTRALIA, when it became independent within the Commonwealth. Thickly forested and mountainous, the country is home to a number of rare species of flora and fauna. Exports include gold,

timber and cocoa. English and Pidgin are widely spoken. The capital is PORT MORESBY. (461 691 sq km/ 178 260 sq miles; pop. 3 396 000)

Paracel Islands A group of islands lying some 300 km (185 miles) to the east of VIETNAM, owned by CHINA, but claimed by Vietnam.

Paraguay A landlocked republic in South AMERICA which gained independence from SPAIN in 1871. The most fertile part of the country is in the centre, along the PARAGUAY River, where there are rich grasslands and forests. Exports include meat and other animal products. Spanish and Guarani are the main languages, and the capital is ASUNCION. (406 752 sq km/ 157 047 sq miles; pop. 3 820 000; cur. Guarani = 100 céntimos)

Paraguay, River A major river of South AMERICA. It rises in BRAZIL and flows south through PARAGUAY to join the PARANA River. (Length 1920 km/1190 miles)

Paramaribo The capital, principal city and main port of SURINAM. (Pop. 180 000)

Parana, River The second largest river in South AMERICA after the AMAZON. It rises in BRAZIL and flows south to join the River PLATE. (Length 4200 km/ 2610 miles)

Paris The capital of FRANCE, in the north of the country, on the River SEINE. (Pop. city 2 188 900/ Greater Paris 8 761 700)

Parma A historic city in northern ITALY, in EMILIA-ROMAGNA. (Pop. 176 800)

Páros An island in the CYCLADES group, GREECE. (194 sq km/75 sq miles; pop. 7400)

Pasadena A city in south-west CALIFORNIA, U.S.A. (Pop. 125 000)

Pascua, Isla de *see* Easter Island.

Patagonia A cold desert in southern ARGENTINA and CHILE.

Patna The capital of the state of BIHAR, in north-east INDIA, on the River GANGES. (Pop. 918 900)

Patras A port and the main city of the PELOPONNESE, GREECE. (Pop. 154 000)

Peace River A river in western CANADA, a tributary of the Slave River, rising in BRITISH COLUMBIA. (Length 1923 km/1195 miles)

Pearl Harbor A harbour and naval base on OAHU, HAWAII; the Japanese attack on the U.S. fleet in 1941, drew the U.S.A. into the Second World War.

Pécs The main city of south-west HUNGARY. (Pop. 174 500)

Peeblesshire *see* Borders.

Peking *see* Beijing.

Pelée, Mount An active volcano on MARTINIQUE, which destroyed the town of St Pierre in 1902. (1397 m/ 4583 ft)

Peloponnese A broad peninsula of southern GREECE, joined to the northern part of the country by the isthmus of CORINTH.

Pembrokeshire *see* Dyfed.

Penang A state of west MALAYSIA comprising Penang Island and the mainland province of Wellesley.

Pennines A range of hills that runs down the middle of ENGLAND from the border with SCOTLAND to the MIDLANDS, rising to 894 m (2087 ft) at Cross Fell.

Pennsylvania A state of the north-eastern U.S.A. The capital is HARRISBURG. (117 412 sq km/45 333 sq miles; pop. 11 853 000)

Perm' An industrial city in the western URALS of RUSSIA. It was known as Molotov 1940–57. (Pop. 1 049 000)

Perpignan A cathedral town in south-western FRANCE. (Pop. 140 000)

Persepolis The capital of ancient Persia, south-east of TEHRAN, destroyed by Alexander the Great in 330 BC.

Persia *see* Iran.

Persian Gulf *see* Gulf, The

Perth 1 The state capital of Western AUSTRALIA, which includes the port of Freemantle. (Pop. 969 000). **2** A city and former capital of SCOTLAND, 55 km (35 miles) north of EDINBURGH. (Pop. 42 000)

Perthshire A former county of SCOTLAND, now divided between CENTRAL REGION and TAYSIDE.

Peru A republic in western South AMERICA with a coast on the PACIFIC. Formerly the centre of the Inca empire and then a Spanish territory, it gained independence in 1824. The west is mainly desert, rising to the ANDES in the east. Exports include minerals and fish. Spanish and Indian languages are spoken. The capital is LIMA. (1 285 215 sq km/496 222 sq miles; pop. 20 000 000; cur. Sol = 100 centavos)

Peshawar A historic town in north-west PAKISTAN at the foot of the KHYBER PASS. (Pop. 555 000)

Petra An ancient, ruined city, founded in about 1000 BC, in southern JORDAN, and carved out of pink limestone.

Petrograd *see* St Petersburg.

Philadelphia A port and city in south-east PENNSYLVANIA, the fourth largest city in the U.S.A. (Pop. city 1 688 700/metropolitan area 4 768 400)

Philippines A republic in South-East ASIA occupying a scattered group of over 7000 islands, the principal ones being LUZON, MINDANAO, SAMAR and NEGROS. It gained independence from the U.S.A. in 1946. The volcanic mountains on the islands are generally thickly forested, except for where they have been terraced for rice paddies. Exports include electronic goods, agricultural produce, timber and minerals. Pilipino and English are the main languages, and MANILA is the capital. (300 000 sq km/115 830 sq miles; pop. 58 115 000; cur. Peso = 100 centavos)

Phnom Penh The capital of CAMBODIA, in the south of the country. (Pop. 500 000)

Phoenix The state capital of ARIZONA, U.S.A. (Pop. city 853 300/metropolitan area 1 714 800)

Piedmont (Piedmonte) A region of north-west ITALY. The main town is TURIN.

Pierre The capital of SOUTH DAKOTA, U.S.A. (Pop. 121 400)

Pietermaritzburg A city in eastern SOUTH AFRICA and capital of NATAL. (Pop. 180 000)

Pigs, Bay of (Bahia de Cochinos) A bay on the south coast of CUBA where exiled Cubans, backed by the U.S.A., made a disastrous invasion attempt in 1961.

Pilsen *see* Plzen.

Piraeus The main port of GREECE, close to ATHENS, on the AEGIAN SEA. (Pop. 196 400)

Pisa A city in north-western ITALY on the River ARNO, famous for its leaning bell tower. (Pop. 104 300)

Pitcairn Island An island and British colony in the south PACIFIC, where mutineers from H.M.S. *Bounty* settled (after 1790).

Pittsburgh An industrial city in western PENNSYLVANIA, U.S.A. (Pop. city 402 600/metropolitan area 2 172 800)

Plate, River (Rio de la Plata) The huge estuary of the PARANA and URUGUAY Rivers in south-east South AMERICA, with URUGUAY to the north and ARGENTINA to the south.

Plenty, Bay of The broad inlet on the north coast of the North Island of NEW ZEALAND.

Plovdiv A major market town in BULGARIA. (Pop. 373 000)

Plymouth **1** A port and naval base in south-west ENGLAND. (Pop. 255 000). **2** The capital of the island of MONTSERRAT. (Pop. 3200) **3** A town in MASSACHUSETTS, which has grown from the first European settlement in NEW ENGLAND, established by the Pilgrim Fathers of the Mayflower in 1602. (Pop. 37 100)

Plzen (Pilsen) An industrial city in western BOHEMIA, CZECHOSLOVAKIA. Pilsner lager beer was first produced here in 1842. (Pop. 174 100)

Po, River The longest river in ITALY, flowing across the north of the country from the ALPS across a fertile plain to the ADRIATIC SEA. (Length 642 km/ 405 miles)

Pohnpei (Ponape) The island on which KOLONIA, the capital of the FEDERATED STATES OF MICRONESIA, stands.

Pointe-à-Pitre The capital of GUADELOUPE. (Pop. 23 000)

Poitiers A historic university city in south central FRANCE (Pop. 80 000).

Poland A republic in central EUROPE with a coast on the BALTIC SEA. It has had a turbulent history. After forming part of the 'Soviet Bloc' of eastern Europe in the wake of the Second World War, in 1989 the Communist government was replaced by a democratic one. Plains lie to the north, rising to mountains in the south. Exports include iron and steel, ships and coal. Polish is the main language. The capital is WARSAW. (312 683 sq km/120 727 sq miles; pop. 37 600 000; cur. Zloty = 100 groszy)

Polynesia The largest of the three island divisions of the PACIFIC, the others being MICRONESIA and MELANESIA. The group includes SAMOA, the COOK, SOCIETY and MARQUESAS islands and TONGA.

Pomerania A region of north-west POLAND, on the BALTIC coast.

Pompeii An ancient city near NAPLES which was smothered by an eruption of VESUVIUS in AD 79.

Ponape *see* Pohnpei.

Pondicherry The former capital of French INDIA, in the south-east of the country, founded in 1683 and governed by FRANCE until 1954. (Pop. 251 400)

Ponta Delgada A port and the capital of the AZORES, on São Miguel Island. (Pop. 21 200)

Poona (Pune) A historic and industrial city east of BOMBAY, in western INDIA. (Pop. 1 203 400)

Popocatpetl A volcano, twinned with IXTACCIHUATL,

65 km (40 miles) south-east of MEXICO CITY. (5452 m/ 17 887 ft)

Port-au-Prince The main port and capital of HAITI. (Pop. 888 000)

Port Elizabeth A port and industrial city in CAPE PROVINCE, SOUTH AFRICA. (Pop. 585 400)

Port Harcourt The second port of NIGERIA after LAGOS. (Pop. 288 900)

Port Jackson The great natural harbour also called SYDNEY Harbour, in south-west AUSTRALIA.

Portland 1 A port on the ATLANTIC coast of the U.S.A., in MAINE. (Pop. city 61 800/metropolitan area 210 000). **2** A port on the Williamette River in OREGON, U.S.A. (Pop. city 365 900/metropolitan area 1 340 900)

Port Louis The capital and main port of MAURITIUS. (Pop. 160 000)

Port Moresby The capital and main port of PAPUA NEW GUINEA, in the south-east. (Pop. 126 000)

Porto *see* Oporto.

Porto Alegre A port and regional capital of southern BRAZIL. (Pop. city 1 126 000)

Port of Spain The capital and chief port of TRINIDAD AND TOBAGO. (Pop. city 62 700/metropolitan area 443 000)

Porto Novo The administrative capital of BENIN. (Pop. 209 000)

Port Said The port at the MEDITERRANEAN end of the SUEZ CANAL, EGYPT. (Pop. 342 000)

Portsmouth A port and major naval base in southern ENGLAND. (Pop. 192 000)

Port Stanley The capital of the FALKLAND ISLANDS. (Pop. 1000)

Portugal A republic in south-west EUROPE with a coastline on the ATLANTIC. It formerly had an extensive overseas empire, but is now the poorest country in western Europe, although membership of the European Community has boosted the economy. It has coastal plains rising to high mountains in the north and east. Exports include textiles, wine, fish and cork, and tourism is a major industry. The capital is LISBON. (92 082 sq km/35 553 sq miles; pop. 10 100 000; cur. Escudo = 100 centavos)

Port-Vila The capital and chief port of VANUATU. (Pop. 17 500)

Posen *see* Poznan.

Potsdam A city just 25 km (16 miles) south-west of BERLIN, GERMANY. (Pop. 137 700)

Powys A county in mid-WALES created in 1974 out of Breconshire, Montgomeryshire, and Radnorshire. The administrative centre is Llandrindod Wells. (5077 sq km/1960 sq miles; pop. 111 000)

Poznan (Posen) A historic city in central western POLAND. (Pop. 571 000)

Prague (Praha) The capital and principal city of CZECHOSLOVAKIA, situated on the Vltava River. (Pop. 1 235 000)

Praia The capital of CAPE VERDE. (Pop. 4055)

Pressburg *see* Bratislava.

Pretoria The administrative capital of SOUTH AFRICA, 48 km (30 miles) north of JOHANNESBURG in the TRANSVAAL. (Pop. 739 000)

Prince Edward Island The smallest of the provinces of CANADA, an island in the Gulf of ST LAWRENCE. The provincial capital is CHARLOTTETOWN. (5660 sq km/ 2185 sq miles; pop. 123 000)

Principe *see* São Tomé and Principe.

Pristina The capital of the autonomous province of KOSOVO in SERBIA, YUGOSLAVIA. (Pop. 216 000)

Provence A historical region of coastal south-east FRANCE.

Providence A port, and the state capital of RHODE ISLAND, U.S.A. (Pop. city 154 100/metropolitan area 1 095 000)

Prussia A historical state of GERMANY, centring on its capital, BERLIN.

Puebla A major city 120 km (75 miles) south-east of MEXICO CITY, and the capital of a state of the same name. (Pop. city 835 000)

Puerto Rico An autonomous commonwealth in association with the U.S.A. (Puerto Ricans are U.S. citizens). The territory comprises three islands of the Greater Antilles in the CARIBBEAN. The largest island is also called Puerto Rico, and is one of the most densely populated areas of the world. Most of the available land has been cleared for farming and the principal exports include sugar, tobacco, fish and chemicals. Spanish is the main language, and the capital is SAN JUAN. (8897 sq km/3435 sq miles; pop. 3 345 000; cur. U.S. dollar = 100 cents)

Puglia (Apulia) A region of south-east ITALY. The regional capital is BARI. (19 250 sq km/7500 sq miles; pop. 3 848 000)

Pune *see* Poona.

Punjab 1 A state in north-western INDIA. The capital is CHANDIGARH. (50 362 sq km/19 440 sq miles; pop. 16 789 000) **2** A fertile province in the north of PAKISTAN. The capital is LAHORE.(205 344 sq km/79 283 sq miles; pop. 47 292 000)

Pusan A major port, and the second largest city in South KOREA after SEOUL. (Pop. 3 160 000)

Putumayo, River A river of north-west South AMERICA, rising in the ANDES and flowing south-east to join the AMAZON. (Length 1900 km/1180 miles)

Pyongyang (Pyeongyang) An industrial city and the capital of North KOREA. (Pop. 1 700 000)

Pyrenees A range of mountains that runs from the Bay of BISCAY to the MEDITERRANEAN, along the border between FRANCE and SPAIN. The highest point is Pico d'Aneto (3404 m/11 170 ft).

Q

Qacentina *see* Constantine.

Qatar An emirate consisting of a peninsula that thrusts northwards into the GULF from the coast of SAUDI ARABIA. It was made a British protectorate in 1916, but became independent in 1971. A desolate and poor country until 1949, when it started to export oil, it is now one of the wealthiest countries in the world. Arabic is the official language, and the capital is DOHA. (11 437 sq km/4416 sq miles; pop. 311 000; cur. Riyal = 100 dirhams)

Qazvin (Kasvin) A historic town in north-west IRAN. (Pop. 244 300)

Qingdao A city in SHANDONG province in north-eastern CHINA. (Pop. 1 300 000)

Qinghai A province of north-western CHINA. The capital is XINING. (720 000 sq km/280 000 sq miles; pop. 3 720 000)

Qiqihar A manufacturing city in HEILONGJIANG province, CHINA. (Pop. 1 000 000)

Qom (Qum) A holy city in central northern IRAN. (Pop. 424 100)

Quebec The largest province of CANADA, in the east of the country, and also the name of the capital of the province. The majority of the population are French-speaking. (1 358 000 sq km/524 300 sq miles; pop. province 6 438 000/city 57 075)

Queen Charlotte Islands A group of some 150 islands lying 160 km (100 miles) off the west coast of CANADA. (9 790 sq km/3780 sq miles; pop. 5620)

Queen Charlotte Strait A waterway, some 26 km (16 miles) wide, between the north-eastern coast of VANCOUVER ISLAND and the mainland of CANADA.

Queensland The north-eastern state of AUSTRALIA. The state capital is BRISBANE. (1 272 200 sq km/591 200 sq miles; pop. 2 488 000)

Quercy A former province of south-western FRANCE, around Cahors.

Quetta The capital of the province of BALUCHISTAN, PAKISTAN. (Pop. 285 000)

Quezon City A major city and university town, now a part of Metro MANILA, and the administrative capital of the PHILIPPINES from 1948 to 1976. (Pop. 1 165 000)

Quito The capital of ECUADOR, lying just south of the Equator, 2850 m (9350 ft) high in the ANDES. (Pop. 1 110 000)

Qum *see* Qom.

Qwaqwa A non-independent black homeland in SOUTH AFRICA occupied by South Sotho people, bordering LESOTHO. (Pop. 305 000)

R

Rabat The capital of MOROCCO, in the north-west, on the ATLANTIC coast. (Pop. 520 000)

Radnorshire *see* Powys.

Ragusa *see* Dubrovnik.

Rainier, Mount *see* Cascade Range.

Rajasthan A state of north-west INDIA. The state capital is JAIPUR. (342 239 sq km/132 104 sq miles; pop. 34 261 000)

Raleigh The state capital of NORTH CAROLINA, U.S.A. (Pop. city 169 300/metropolitan area 609 300)

Ranchi An industrial town in the state of BIHAR, INDIA. (Pop. 502 800)

Rand, The *see* Witwatersrand.

Rangoon (Yangon) The capital of BURMA, and an important port on the mouth of the Rangoon River. (Pop. 2 549 000)

Rarotonga The largest of the COOK ISLANDS, with the capital of the islands, Avarua, on its north coast. (67 sq km/26 sq miles; pop. 9500)

Ras al Khaymah One of the UNITED ARAB EMIRATES, in the extreme north-east, on the MUSANDAM peninsula. (1036 sq km/400 sq miles; pop. 83 000)

Ravenna A city in north-eastern ITALY, noted for its Byzantine churches. (Pop. 136 500)

Rawalpindi A military town of ancient origins in northern PAKISTAN. (Pop. 928 000)

Recife A city and regional capital on the eastern tip of BRAZIL. (Pop. 1 205 000)

Red River 1 A river of the southern U.S.A., rising in TEXAS and flowing east to join the MISSISSIPPI. (Length 1639km/1018 miles). **2** (Song Hong; Yuan Jiang) A river that rises in south-west CHINA and flows south-east across the north of VIETNAM to the Gulf of TONGKING. (Length 800 km/500 miles)

Red Sea A long, narrow sea lying between the Arabian Peninsula and the coast of north-east AFRICA. In the north it is connected to the MEDITERRANEAN SEA by the SUEZ CANAL.

Reggio di Calabria A port on the toe of southern ITALY. (Pop. 177 700)

Reggio nell'Emilia A town of Roman origins in north-eastern ITALY. (Pop. 130 300)

Regina The capital of the province of SASKATCHEWAN, CANADA. (Pop. 164 000)

Reims *see* Rheims.

Renfrewshire *see* Strathclyde.

Rennes A industrial city in north-eastern FRANCE. (Pop. 241 300)

Reno A gambling centre in NEVADA, U.S.A. (Pop. city 105 600/metropolitan area 211 500)

Réunion An island to the east of MADAGASCAR, an overseas department of FRANCE. The capital is SAINT-DENIS. (2515 sq km/970 sq miles; pop. 530 000)
Reykjavik The capital and main port of ICELAND, on the south-west coast. (Pop. 87 300)
Reynosa A town in north-eastern MEXICO, on the border with the U.S.A. (Pop. 347 000)
Rheims (Reims) A historic city, and the centre of the production of champagne. (Pop. 204 000)
Rhine (Rhein, Rhin, Rijn), River One of the most important rivers of EUROPE. It rises in the Swiss ALPS, flows north through GERMANY and then west through the NETHERLANDS to the NORTH SEA. (Length 1320 km/ 825 miles)
Rhode Island The smallest state in the U.S.A. The state capital is PROVIDENCE. (3144 sq km/1214 sq miles; pop. 968 000)
Rhodes (Rodhos) The largest of the DODECANESE group of islands belonging to GREECE. (1399 sq km/ 540 sq miles; pop. 88 500)
Rhône, River A major river of EUROPE, rising in the Swiss ALPS and flowing west into FRANCE, and then south to its delta on the Golfe de LION. (Length 812 km/505 miles)
Richmond The state capital of VIRGINIA. (Pop. city 219 100/metropolitan area 796 100)
Ridings, The *see* Yorkshire.
Riga A BALTIC port, and the capital of LATVIA. (Pop. 875 000)
Rijeka (Fiume) A port on the ADRIATIC, in CROATIA. (Pop. 193 000)

Rijn, River *see* Rhine, River.
Rimini A popular resort on the ADRIATIC SEA, north-eastern ITALY. (Pop. 129 500)
Rio Bravo *see* Rio Grande.
Rio de Janeiro A major port and former capital (1763–1960) of BRAZIL, situated in the south-east of the country. (Pop. 5 094 000)
Rio Grande (Rio Bravo) A river of North AMERICA, rising in the state of COLORADO, U.S.A., and flowing south-east to the Gulf of MEXICO. For much of its length it forms the border between the U.S.A. and MEXICO. (Length 3078 km/1885 miles)
Rioja, La An autonomous area in the south of the BASQUE region of SPAIN, famous for its fine wine. (Pop. 254 000)
Riyadh The capital and commercial centre of SAUDI ARABIA, founded on an oasis. (Pop. 300 000)
Road Town The capital of the BRITISH VIRGIN ISLANDS. (Pop. 3000)
Roca, Cabo da A cape sticking out into the ATLANTIC in central PORTUGAL, to the west of LISBON, the westernmost point of mainland Europe.
Rockall A tiny, rocky, uninhabited island lying 400 km (250 miles) west of IRELAND, and claimed by the U.K.
Rocky Mountains (Rockies) A huge mountain range in western North AMERICA, extending some 4800 km (3000 miles) from BRITISH COLUMBIA in CANADA to NEW MEXICO in the U.S.A.
Rodhos *see* Rhodes.
Romania A republic in south-eastern EUROPE with a coast on the BLACK SEA. In 1989 a popular revolution

overthrew the repressive Communist regime. The country is dominated by the CARPATHIAN Mountains in the centre, which are surrounded by plains. Exports include machinery and chemicals. The dominant language is Romanian, and the capital is BUCHAREST. (237 500 sq km/91 700 sq miles; pop. 22 890 000; cur. Leu = 100 bani)

Rome (Roma) The historic capital of ITALY, on the River TIBER, in the centre of the country near the west coast. (Pop. 2 831 300)

Rosario An industrial and commercial city on the River PARANA in ARGENTINA. (Pop. 935 500)

Roscommon A county in the north-west of the Republic of IRELAND, with a county town of the same name. (2462 sq km/950 sq miles; pop. county 54 500)

Roseau The capital of DOMINICA. (Pop. 17 000)

Ross and Cromarty A county of north-west SCOTLAND which includes many islands; part of the HIGHLAND region.

Ross Sea A large branch of the ANTARCTIC OCEAN, south of NEW ZEALAND.

Rostock A major port on the BALTIC coast of GERMANY. (Pop. 242 000)

Rostov-na-Donau (Rostov-on-Don) A major industrial city on the River DON, near the north-western extremity of the Sea of AZOV in south-eastern RUSSIA. (Pop. 983 000)

Rotterdam The largest city in the NETHERLANDS and the busiest port in the world. (Pop. city 558 800/ Greater Rotterdam 1 024 700)

Roubaix *see* Lille-Roubaix-Turcoing.

Rouen A port on the River SEINE in northern FRANCE. (Pop. 385 800)

Rousillon *see* Languedoc-Rousillon.

Roxburghshire *see* Borders.

R.S.F.S.R. *see* Russian Soviet Federated Socialist Republic.

Rub al-Khali The so-called 'Empty Quarter', a vast area of sandy desert straddling the borders of SAUDI ARABI, OMAN and YEMEN. (650 000 sq km/251 000 sq miles)

Ruhr, River The river in north-western GERMANY whose valley forms the industrial heartland of western GERMANY. It joins the Rhine at DUISBURG. (Length 235 km/146 miles)

Rushmore, Mount A mountain in the Black Hills of SOUTH DAKOTA, U.S.A., noted for the huge heads of four U.S. presidents (Washington, Jefferson, Lincoln, Theodore Roosevelt) which were carved into its flank 1927–41. (1707 m/5600 ft)

Russia The old name for the Russian Empire, latterly used loosely to refer to the U.S.S.R. or the RUSSIAN FEDERATION.

Russian Federation The largest of the fifteen former constituent republics of the U.S.S.R., which declared sovereignty in 1991. It is a vast country, which also includes 17 autonomous republics, such as CHECHEN-INGUSH and DAGESTAN. Towards the west, the URAL MOUNTAINS run from north to south and these form a theoretical border between EUROPE (to the west) and ASIA (to the east). Most of the population live in the European section, as the eastern part, which stretches across the whole of northern ASIA to the PACIFIC, is largely covered by the wilderness of SIBERIA. The northern coast is on the ARCTIC OCEAN, but there are other shores on the BALTIC SEA to the west, and the CASPIAN and BLACK SEAS to the south-east. An industrial nation, Russia has extensive reserves of oil, gas, gold, coal and iron. The main language is Russian, although many other languages are spoken. The capital is MOSCOW. (17 075 400 sq km/6 592 800 sq miles; pop 142 117 000; cur. Rouble = 100 kopeks)

Rutanzige, Lake *see* Edward, Lake.

Russian Soviet Federated Socialist Republic (R.S.F.S.R.) The former name for the RUSSIAN FEDERATION.

Rutland Once the smallest county of ENGLAND, now a part of LEICESTERSHIRE.

Ruwenzori A mountain range on the border between ZAIRE and UGANDA, also known as the Mountains of the Moon.

Rwanda A landlocked republic in central AFRICA, hemmed in between UGANDA, TANZANIA, BURUNDI and ZAIRE. Formerly administered by BELGIUM, it became independent in 1961. The over-populated country has a weak economy and depends on foreign aid. French and Rwanda are the main languages. The capital is KIGALI. (26 338 sq km/ 10 169 sq miles; pop. 6 480 000; cur. Rwanda franc = 100 centimes)

Ryazan An industrial city 175 km (110 miles) south-east of MOSCOW, RUSSIA. (Pop. 488 000)

Ryukyu Islands (Nansei-shoto) A chain of islands belonging to JAPAN stretching 1200 km (750 miles) between Japan and Taiwan. (Pop. 1 366 600)

S

Saarbrücken An industrial city of western GERMANY, near the border with FRANCE. (Pop. 189 000)

Sabah The more easterly of the two states of MALAYSIA on northern coast of the island of BORNEO. (73 700 sq km/28 450 sq miles; pop. 1 034 000)

Sacramento The state capital of CALIFORNIA. (Pop. city 304 100/metropolitan area 1 219 600)

Sacramento, River The longest river in CALIFORNIA, U.S.A. (Length: 560 km/350 miles)

Sahara Desert The world's largest desert, spanning much of northern AFRICA, from the ATLANTIC to the RED SEA, and from the MEDITERRANEAN to MALI, NIGER, CHAD and the SUDAN.

Sahel The semi-arid belt stretching across AFRICA from SENEGAL to SUDAN, separating the SAHARA from tropical AFRICA to the south.

Saigon *see* Ho Chi Minh City.

St Barthélémy A small island dependency of GUADELOUPE. (Pop. 3000)

St Croix The largest of the U.S. VIRGIN ISLANDS. The main town is Christiansted. (218 sq km/84 sq miles; pop. 50 000)

Saint-Denis The capital of REUNION island. (Pop. 110 000)

Saint-Etienne An industrial city 50 km (30 miles) south-west of LYONS, FRANCE. (Pop. 319 500)

St Eustatius (Statia) An island of the NETHERLANDS ANTILLES, in the LEEWARD ISLANDS. The capital is Oranjestad. (Pop. 1500)

St George's The capital of GRENADA, and the island's main port. (Pop. 30 800)

St Helena A remote island and British colony in the South ATLANTIC. Napoleon Bonaparte was exiled here by the British from 1815 until his death in 1821. (122 sq km/47 sq miles; pop. 5500)

St Helena Dependencies The islands of ASCENSION and TRISTAN DA CUNHA are so-called dependencies of ST HELENA, a British colony.

St Helens, Mount An active volcano in the CASCADE RANGE of western WASHINGTON State, U.S.A. It erupted in 1980 causing widespread destruction. (2549 m/ 8364 ft)

Saint John A port at the mouth of the SAINT JOHN RIVER, on the ATLANTIC coast of NEW BRUNSWICK, CANADA. (Pop. 114 000)

St John The smallest of the main islands of the U.S. VIRGIN ISLANDS. (52 sq km/20 sq miles ; pop. 2400)

Saint John River A river of the eastern U.S.A., which rises in MAINE and flows north-west through CANADA to the Bay of FUNDY. (Length 673 km/418 miles)

St John's 1 The capital and main port of ANTIGUA. (Pop. 30 000). **2** A port and the capital of NEWFOUNDLAND, CANADA. (Pop. 155 000)

St Kitts and Nevis An independent Commonwealth state comprising two small volcanic islands in the eastern CARIBBEAN. Until 1983, when it gained independence, the country formed a British colony which included ANGUILLA. Tourism is a major source of revenue. English is the main language, and the capital, on St Kitts, is BASSETERRE. (261 sq km/

101 sq miles ; pop. 43 900; cur. East Caribbean dollar = 100 cents)

St Lawrence, River A commercially important river of south-east CANADA, which flows north-east from Lake ONTARIO to the Gulf of ST LAWRENCE, forming part of the border between CANADA and the U.S.A. (Length 1197 km/744 miles)

St Lawrence, Gulf of An arm of the ATLANTIC OCEAN in north-eastern CANADA, into which the ST LAWRENCE River flows.

St Lawrence Seaway A navigable waterway that links the GREAT LAKES, via the ST LAWRENCE River, to the ATLANTIC OCEAN.

St Louis A city in eastern MISSOURI, U.S.A., on the River MISSISSIPPI. (Pop. city 429 300/metropolitan area 2 398 400)

St Lucia A volcanic island forming an independent state in the WINDWARD ISLANDS of the CARIBBEAN. It became independent of Britain, within the Commonwealth, in 1979. Its main exports are bananas and coconuts, and it has an important tanker port to the south of the capital, CASTRIES. English and a French patois are spoken. (619 sq km/239 sq miles ; pop. 123 000; cur. East Caribbean dollar = 100 cents)

St Maarten *see* St Martin.

St Martin One of the LEEWARD ISLANDS in the south-eastern CARIBBEAN. It is divided politically into two, one a part of GUADELOUPE (FRANCE); the other (Sint Maarten) a part of the NETHERLANDS ANTILLES. The capital of the French side is Marigot; of the Dutch side Philipsburg. (54 sq km/21 sq miles ; pop. 24 000)

St Paul The state capital of MINNESOTA, twinned with the adjoining city of MINNEAPOLIS. (Pop. city 265 900/ metropolitan area 2 230 900)

St Petersburg A former capital of RUSSIA and the country's second-largest city. It is an industrial city, important cultural centre and major port on the BALTIC SEA. From 1914–24 it was known as Petrograd; then, until 1991, Leningrad.

St Pierre and Miquelon Two islands to the south of NEWFOUNDLAND, CANADA which are an overseas territory administered by FRANCE. (240 sq km/93 sq miles; pop. 6100)

St Thomas The principal tourist island of the U.S. VIRGIN ISLANDS. The capital is CHARLOTTE AMALIE. (83 sq km/32 sq miles; pop. 44 000)

St Vincent, Cape *see* São Vincente, Cabo de.

St Vincent and the Grenadines A state in the WINDWARD ISLANDS of the CARIBBEAN, comprising the island of St Vincent and a chain of lesser islands to the south, the Grenadines. It became independent from Britain, within the Commonwealth, in 1979. Bananas and arrowroot are the main exports. The principal language is English, and the capital is KINGSTOWN. (389 sq km/150 sq miles; pop. 103 000; cur. East Caribbean dollar = 100 cents)

Saipan The largest and most heavily populated of the NORTHERN MARIANAS. The island group's capital, SUSUPE, is on the western side. (122 sq km/47 sq miles; pop. 17 000)

Sakai A port and industrial city on south HONSHU island. (Pop. 818 400)

Sakhalin A large island to the north of JAPAN, but belonging to the RUSSIA. (76 400 sq km/29 500 sq miles; pop. 660 000)

Salamanca An elegant university town in western SPAIN, and the name of the surrounding province. (Pop. town 167 100)

Salem 1 A city in MASSACHUSETTS, U.S.A. (Pop. city 38 600/metropolitan area 259 100). **2** The state capital of OREGON, U.S.A. (Pop. city 90 300/metropolitan area 255 200)

Salerno A port 45 km (28 miles) south of NAPLES, ITALY. (Pop. 155 900)

Saloniki (Thessaloníki) The second largest city in GREECE after ATHENS. (Pop. 706 200)

Salt Lake City The state capital of UTAH. (Pop. city 164 800/metropolitan area 1 025 300)

Salvador A port on the central east coast of BRAZIL and capital of the state of Bahia. (Pop. 1 507 000)

Salvador, El *see* El Salvador.

Salween, River A river rising in TIBET and flowing south through BURMA, forming part of the border with THAILAND, to the ANDAMAN SEA. (Length 2900 km/ 1800 miles)

Salzburg A city in central northern AUSTRIA, and the name of the surrounding state, of which it is the capital. (Pop. city 140 000)

Samar The third largest island of the PHILIPPINES. (13 080 sq km/5050 sq miles; pop. 1 100 000)

Samara see Kuybyshev.

Samarkand An ancient city in UZBEKISTAN. (Pop. 515 000)

Samoa, American An American territory, comprising a group of five islands, in the central South PACIFIC. The capital is PAGO PAGO. (197 sq km/76 sq miles; pop. 36 000)

Samoa, Western A state, comprising two main islands, in the South PACIFIC. It gained independence within the Commonwealth in 1962. Copra, bananas and other vegetable products are the main exports. Samoan and English are spoken, and the capital is APIA. (2831 sq km/1093 sq miles; pop. 164 000; cur. Tala = 100 sene)

Sámos A Greek island 2 km (1 mile) off the coast of TURKEY. (Pop. 31 600)

Samsun A port on the BLACK SEA coast of TURKEY, and the name of the surrounding province, of which it is the capital. (Pop. town 280 100)

San'a The capital of YEMEN, situated in the middle of the country. (Pop. 210 000)

San Antonio An industrial centre in southern TEXAS. (Pop. city 842 800/metropolitan area 1 188 500)

San Diego A major port and industrial city in southern CALIFORNIA. (Pop. city 960 500/metropolitan area 1 063 900)

San Francisco A PACIFIC port and commercial centre in CALIFORNIA. (Pop. city 712 800/metropolitan area 5 684 600)

San Francisco Bay An inlet of the PACIFIC OCEAN in western CALFORNIA, U.S.A., joined to the ocean by the Golden Gate Strait.

San José The capital of COSTA RICA, in the centre of the country. (Pop. 249 000).

San Jose A city in CALIFORNIA, U.S.A., and the focus of 'Silicon Valley'. (Pop. city 686 200/metropolitan area 1 371 500)

San Juan The capital of PUERTO RICO, and a major port. (Pop. 435 000)

San Lorenzo del Escorial *see* Escorial, El.

San Luis Potosi An elegant colonial city and provincial capital in north-central MEXICO. (Pop. city 407 000)

San Marino Europe's smallest republic, situated on the north-eastern side of the peninsula of ITALY, which completely surrounds it. Tourism and the sale of stamps account for much of the country's income. Italian is spoken; the capital is called San Marino. (61 sq km/24 sq miles; pop. 23 000; cur. Italian lira)

San Miguel de Tucumán A regional capital in north-western ARGENTINA. (Pop. 497 000)

San Pedro Sula The second largest city in GUATEMALA. (Pop. 398 000)

San Salvador 1 The capital and major city of EL SALVADOR. (Pop. 884 100) **2** A small island in the centre of the BAHAMAS, the first place in the New World reached by Columbus (1492). (Pop. (850)

San Sebastián A port and industrial city in north-eastern SPAIN. (Pop. 175 600)

Santa Barbara A resort and industrial centre in southern CALIFORNIA. (Pop. city 76 900/metropolitan area 322 800)

Santa Fe The state capital of NEW MEXICO, U.S.A. (Pop. city 52 300/metropolitan area 100 500)

Santander A port and industrial city in north-eastern SPAIN. (Pop. 180 300)

Santiago The capital and principal city of CHILE. (Pop. 4 132 000)

Santiago de Compostela A university city and centre of pilgrimage in north-western SPAIN. (Pop. 93 700)

Santiago da Cuba A port and provincial capital in southern CUBA. (Pop. 345 000)

Santo Domingo The capital and main port of the DOMINICAN REPUBLIC. (Pop. 1 313 000)

Santorini A volcanic island in the CYCLADES group of Greek islands. (84 sq km/32 sq miles; pop. 7100)

Santos The largest port in BRAZIL, 60 km (38 miles) south-east of SAO PAULO. (Pop. 417 000)

São Francisco, River A river of eastern BRAZIL, important for its hydroelectric dams. (Length 2900 km/ 1800 miles)

São Miguel The largest island in the AZORES. (770 sq km/298 sq miles; pop. 131 900)

São Paulo A major industrial city in south-eastern BRAZIL, and capital of the state called São Paulo. (Pop. city 8 500 000/metropolitan area 16 000 000)

São Tomé The capital of SAO TOME AND PRINCIPE. (Pop. 25 000)

São Tomé and Principe A republic of islands, by the Equator, off the west coast of AFRICA in the Gulf of GUINEA. It gained independence from PORTUGAL in 1975. Copra and cocoa are the main exports. Portuguese and local languages are spoken. The capital is SAO TOME. (964 sq km/372 sq miles; pop. 89 000; cur. Dobra = 100 centimes)

São Vincente, Cabo de (Cape St Vincent) The south-western corner of PORTUGAL.

Saône, River A river of eastern FRANCE which merges with the River RHONE at LYONS. (Length 480 km/ 300 miles)
Sapporo A modern city, founded in the late 19th century as the capital of HOKKAIDO island, JAPAN. (Pop. 1 543 000)
Saragossa *see* Zaragoza.
Sarajevo The capital of BOSNIA HERZEGOVINA. (Pop. 448 500)
Saransk An industrial town, capital of the republic of Mordovia in the RUSSIAN FEDERATION. (Pop. 301 000)
Saratov An industrial city and river port on the VOLGA, RUSSIA. (Pop. 894 000)
Sarawak A state of MALAYSIA occupying much of the north-western coast of BORNEO. (125 204 sq km/ 48 342 sq miles; pop. 1 323 000)
Sardinia (Sardegne) The second largest island of the MEDITERRANEAN after SICILY, also belonging to ITALY, lying just south of CORSICA. The capital is CAGLIARI. (24 089 sq km/9301 sq miles ; pop. 1 633 400)
Sargasso Sea An area of calm water in the ATLANTIC between the WEST INDIES and the AZORES, where seaweed floats on the surface. It is a major spawning ground for eels.
Sark *see* Channel Islands.
Saskatchewan A province of western CANADA, in the prairies. The capital is REGINA. (651 900 sq km/ 251 000 sq miles; pop. 968 000)
Saskatchewan, River A river of CANADA, rising in the ROCKY MOUNTAINS and flowing westwards into Lake WINNIPEG. (Length 1930 km/1200 miles)

Saskatoon A city on the SASKATCHEWAN River. (Pop. 154 000)

Saudi Arabia A kingdom in south-west ASIA which occupies most of the Arabian peninsula between the RED SEA and the GULF. The country consists mostly of desert, but it has huge oil reserves which have made it one of the wealthiest nations in the world. The birthplace of Islam, it is a focus of pilgrimage, notably to MECCA and MEDINA. Arabic is the official language. The capital is RIYADH. (2 150 000 sq km/830 000 sq miles ; pop. 11 520 000; cur. Rial = 20 quirsh = 100 hallalas)

Savannah The main port of GEORGIA, U.S.A. (Pop. city 145 400/metropolitan area 323 900)

Savoie (Savoy) A mountainous former duchy in south-east FRANCE, which has been a part of FRANCE since 1860 and is now divided into two departments, Savoie and Haute Savoie.

Scafell Pike *see* Lake District.

Scandinavia The countries on, or near, the Scandinavian peninsula in north-east EUROPE, usually taken to include NORWAY, SWEDEN, DENMARK and FINLAND.

Scapa Flow An anchorage surrounded by the ORKNEY ISLANDS, famous as a naval base.

Schelde, River A river of western EUROPE rising in FRANCE and then flowing through BELGIUM and the NETHERLANDS to the NORTH SEA. (Length 435 km/ 270 miles)

Schlesien *see* Silesia.

Schleswig-Holstein The northernmost state of GERMANY. The capital is KIEL. (Pop. 2 614 000)

Scilly, Isles of A group of islands off the south-west tip of ENGLAND. The main islands are St Mary's, St Martin's and Tresco. (Pop. 2000)
Scotland A country of the U.K., occupying the northern part of GREAT BRITAIN. The capital is EDINBURGH. (78 762 sq km/31 410 sq miles; pop. 5 035 000)
Seattle A port in WASHINGTON State, U.S.A. (Pop. city 490 000/metropolitan area 1 677 000)
Seine, River A river of northern FRANCE, flowing through PARIS to the ENGLISH CHANNEL. (Length 775 km/482 miles)
Selkirkshire *see* Borders.
Semarang A port and textile city on the north coast of JAVA, INDONESIA. (Pop. 503 200)
Sendai A city in the east of HONSHU island, JAPAN. (Pop. 700 200)
Senegal A republic in West AFRICA, with a coastline on the ATLANTIC OCEAN. It was formerly part of French West Africa, but became independent in 1960. Desert lies to the north, and tropical forest to the south. Exports include groundnut oil, fish and phosphates. French is the official language. The capital is DAKAR. (196 192 sq km/75 750 sq miles; pop. 6 971 200; cur. CFA franc = 100 centimes)
Senegal River A West African river that flows through GUINEA, MALI, MAURITANIA, and SENEGAL to the ATLANTIC OCEAN. (Length 1790 km/1110 miles)
Seoul The capital of South KOREA, in the north-west of the country. (Pop. 8 364 000)
Sepik River A major river of PAPUA NEW GUINEA. (Length 1200 km/750 miles)

Seram (Ceram) An island in the MALUKU group, INDONESIA. (17 148 sq km/6621 sq miles)
Serbia (Srbija) A landlocked republic, and the largest republic of YUGOSLAVIA. The capital is BELGRADE. (88 361 sq km/34 107 sq miles; pop. 9 314 000)
Sevastopol' A BLACK SEA port of the UKRAINE. (Pop. 335 000)
Severn, River The longest river in the U.K., flowing through WALES and the west of ENGLAND. (Length 350 km/220 miles)
Seville (Sevilla) A historic, now industrial city in southern SPAIN, and also the name of the surrounding province. (Pop. city 653 800)
Seychelles A republic comprising a group of beautiful tropical islands in the western INDIAN OCEAN, just south of the Equator. The main islands are Mahé and Praslin. It gained independence from the U.K., within the Commonwealth, in 1976. Tourism is a major industry. Both English and French are spoken, and the capital, on Mahé, is VICTORIA. (435 sq km/175 sq miles; pop. 66 000; cur. Seychelles rupee = 100 cents)
Sfax The second city of TUNISIA. (Pop. 232 000)
s'Gravenhage *see* Hague, The.
Shaanxi A province on north-western CHINA. The capital is XI'AN. (190 000 sq km/73 000 sq miles; pop. 28 070 000)
Shandong A province of northern CHINA, with its capital at JINAN. (150 000 sq km/58 000 sq miles; pop. 72 310 000)
Shanghai The largest and most westernized city in

CHINA. An important port, it is situated on the delta of the CHANG JIANG (Yangtze) River. (Pop. 11 860 000)

Shannon, River A river of the Republic of IRELAND, and the longest river in the BRITISH ISLES. It flows south-west into the ATLANTIC OCEAN near LIMERICK. (Length 386 km/240 miles)

Shanxi A province of northern CHINA, with its capital at TAIYUAN. (150 000 sq km/58 000 sq miles; pop. 24 472 000)

Sharjah The fourth largest of the UNITED ARAB EMIRATES. Its capital city is also called Sharjah. (159 000 sq km/61 000 sq miles; pop. emirate 184 000/ city 126 000)

Shatt al Arab A waterway flowing into the GULF along the disputed border between IRAN and IRAQ, formed where the Rivers EUPHRATES and TIGRIS converge some 170 km (105 miles) from the coast.

Sheffield A major industrial city in South YORKSHIRE, ENGLAND. (Pop. 545 000)

Shenandoah, River A river, of great significance during the American Civil War, that flows through northern VIRGINIA, U.S.A. (Length 90 km/55 miles)

Shenyang The capital of LIAONING province, CHINA. (Pop. 4 000 000)

Shetland Islands A group of some 100 islands off the north coast of mainland SCOTLAND. The capital is Lerwick. (1426 sq km;550 sq miles; pop. 28 000)

Shijiazhuang The capital of HEBEI province. (Pop. 973 000)

Skikoku The smallest of the four main islands of JAPAN. (Pop. 4 227 200)

Shiraz A provincial capital of IRAN, south-east of TEHRAN. (Pop. 801 000)

Shropshire A county of west central ENGLAND; the county town is Shrewsbury. (3490 sq km/1347 sq miles; pop. 390 000)

Siam *see* Thailand.

Siberia A huge tract of land, mostly in northern RUSSIA, that extends from the URAL MOUNTAINS to the PACIFIC coast. It is renowned for its inhospitable climate, but parts of it are fertile, and it is rich in minerals.

Sichuan (Szechuan) The most heavily populated of the provinces of CHINA, in the south-west of the country. The capital is CHENGDU. (570 000 sq km/220 sq miles; pop. 97 740 000)

Sicily (Sicilia) An island hanging from the toe of ITALY, and the largest island in the MEDITERRANEAN. The capital is PALERMO. (25 708 sq km/9926 sq miles; pop. 5 065 000)

Siena (Sienna) A historic town of TUSCANY, in central ITALY. (Pop. 60 500)

Sierra Leone A republic in West AFRICA with a shoreline on the ATLANTIC. It gained independence from the U.K., within the Commonwealth, in 1971. Humid coastal plains rise to mountains in the north and east. Diamonds, minerals and coffee are exported. The official language is English. The capital is FREETOWN. (71 740 sq km/27 691 sq miles; pop. 3 980 000; cur. Leone = 100 cents)

Sierra Madre Occidental The mountain range of western MEXICO.

Sierra Madre Oriental The mountain range of eastern MEXICO.

Sierra Nevada 1 A mountain range in southern SPAIN. **2** A mountain range in eastern CALIFORNIA, U.S.A.

Sikkim A state in north-eastern INDIA. The capital is Gangtok. (7096 sq km/2739 sq miles; pop. 316 400)

Silesia (Schlesien) A region straddling the borders of CZECHOSLOVAKIA, GERMANY and POLAND.

Simla A hill station in HIMCHAL PRADESH, northern INDIA. (Pop. 80 200)

Simpson Desert An arid, uninhabited region in the centre of AUSTRALIA.

Sinai A mountainous peninsula in north-eastern EGYPT, bordering ISRAEL, between the Gulf of AQABA and the Gulf of SUEZ.

Sind A province of south-eastern PAKISTAN. The capital is KARACHI. (140 914 sq km/54 407 sq miles; pop. 19 029 000)

Singapore A republic in South-East ASIA consisting of one main island and many smaller ones, which lie to the south of the Malay peninsula, just north of the Equator. It became an independent nation, within the Commonwealth, in 1965. Singapore has few natural resources of its own, but the capital, also called Singapore, is a hugely successful financial and commercial centre, with one of the world's busiest ports. Malay, Chinese, English and Tamil are spoken. (620 sq km/239 sq miles; pop. 2 590 000; cur. Singapore dollar = 100 cents)

Siracusa *see* Syracuse.

Síros *see* Cyclades.

Sirte, Gulf of A huge indent of the MEDITERRANEAN SEA in the coastline of LIBYA.

Sivas An industrial town in central TURKEY. (Pop. 197 300)

Skagerrak The channel, some 130 km (80 miles) wide, separating DENMARK and NORWAY. It links the NORTH SEA to the KATTEGAT and BALTIC SEA.

Skiathos The westernmost of the Greek SPORADES islands. (Pop. 4200)

Skopje The capital of the republic of MACEDONIA in southern YUGOSLAVIA. (Pop. 506 500)

Skye An island off the north-west coast of SCOTLAND; the largest of the Inner HEBRIDES. The main town is Portree. (1417 sq km/547 sq miles; pop. 8000)

Slavonia (Slavonija) A part of CROATIA, south-east of ZAGREB, mainly between the DRAVA and Slava Rivers.

Sligo A county on the north-west coast of the Republic of IRELAND, with a county town of the same name. (1796 sq km/693 sq miles; pop. county 55 400)

Slovakia The eastern region of CZECHOSLOVAKIA, one of the country's two constituent republics. The capital is BRATISLAVA. (49 032 sq km/19 931 sq miles; pop. 5 013 000)

Slovenia A republic bordering AUSTRIA, HUNGARY, ITALY and CROATIA, which declared independence from YUGOSLAVIA in 1991. The capital is LJUBLJANA. (20 251 sq km/7817 sq miles; pop. 1 891 900)

Smolensk An industrial city in RUSSIA, on the River DNIEPER. (Pop. 326 000)

Smyrna *see* Izmir.

Snake, River A river of the north-west U.S.A., which

flows into the COLUMBIA River in WASHINGTON State; it is used for irrigation and to create hydroelectric power. (Length 1670 km/1038 miles)

Snowdonia A mountainous region in the north of WALES. The highest peak is Mount Snowdon (1885 m/ 3560 ft)

Snowy Mountains A range of mountains in south-eastern AUSTRALIA, where the River Snowy has been dammed to form the complex Snowy Mountains Hydroelectric Scheme. The highest peak is Mount KOSCIUSKO (2230 m/7316 ft).

Society Islands A group of islands at the centre of FRENCH POLYNESIA. They are divided into the Windward Islands, which include TAHITI and Moorea; and the Leeward Islands, which include Raiatea and Bora-Bora. (Pop. 142 000)

Socotra An island in the north-western INDIAN OCEAN, belonging to YEMEN. (Pop. 12 000)

Sofia (Sofiya) The capital of BULGARIA, in the west of the country. (Pop. 1 093 800)

Solent, The A strait in the ENGLISH CHANNEL that separates the Isle of WIGHT from mainland ENGLAND.

Solomon Islands An independent state in the south-west PACIFIC consisting of a long archipelago in which GUADACANAL is the main island. It became independent of British protection, within the Commonwealth, in 1978. Fishing and agriculture are the main industries. English is the official language, although many other languages are spoken. The capital is HONIARA. (29 785 sq km/11 500 sq miles; pop. 280 000; cur. Solomon Islands dollar = 100 cents)

Somalia A republic in north-eastern AFRICA with coastlines on the INDIAN OCEAN and the Gulf of ADEN. It is a poor, arid country that has been ravaged by famine and by wars (with ETHIOPIA), and it is heavily dependent on foreign aid. Somali is the main language. The capital is MOGADISHU. (637 657 sq km/ 246 199 sq miles; pop. 7 822 900; cur. Somali shilling)

Somerset A county in the south-west of ENGLAND; the county town is Taunton. (3458 sq km/1335 sq miles; pop. 440 000)

Somme, River A river of northern FRANCE, the scene of a devastating battle during the First World War. (Length 245 km/152 miles)

Song Hong *see* Red River.

Sounion, Cape A cape overlooking the the southern AEGEAN SEA, 60 km (37 miles) south-west of ATHENS, GREECE.

South Africa A republic occupying the southernmost tip of AFRICA with coastlines on the INDIAN and ATLANTIC OCEANS. Formerly a British dominion, it left the Commonwealth and became a republic in 1961. The bulk of the country lies on a plateau which is ringed with mountains to the south and east. The land is blessed with many natural resources, but it does not have oil. The political system (formerly institutionalized as *apartheid*), whereby the white minority had considerable advantage over the black majority, has caused South Africa problems internally and internationally. Exports include gold, diamonds, fruit, vegetables and meat. The official languages are English and Afrikaans, but other languages are also used.

There are two capitals: PRETORIA (administrative) and CAPE TOWN (legislative). (1 221 042 sq km/471 445 sq miles; pop. (including black homelands) 33 340 000; cur. Rand = 100 cents)

Southampton A major port in southern ENGLAND. (Pop. 206 000)

South Australia A state in central southern AUSTRALIA, on the GREAT AUSTRALIAN BIGHT. ADELAIDE is the state capital. (984 380 sq km/380 069 sq miles; pop. 1 347 000)

South Carolina A state in the south-east of the U.S.A., with a coast on the ATLANTIC OCEAN. The state capital is COLUMBIA. (80 432 sq km/31 055 sq miles; pop. 3 347 000)

South China Sea An arm of the PACIFIC OCEAN between south-east CHINA, MALAYSIA and the PHILIPPINES.

South Dakota A state in the western U.S.A. The state capital is PIERRE. (199 552 sq km/77 047 sq miles; pop. 708 000)

Southern Alps A range of mountains on the South Island of NEW ZEALAND.

Southern Ocean *see* Antarctic Ocean.

South Georgia An island in the South ATLANTIC, and a dependency of the FALKLAND ISLANDS. (3755 sq km/ 1450 sq km)

South Glamorgan A county in south WALES. The administrative centre is CARDIFF. (416 sq km/161 sq miles; pop. 384 700)

South Island *see* New Zealand.

South Pole The most southerly point of the Earth's axis, in ANTARCTICA.

South Sandwich Islands A group of islands in the South ATLANTIC which are dependencies of the FALKLAND ISLANDS. (340 sq km/130 sq miles)
Soviet Union *see* Union of Soviet Socialist Republics.
Soweto A group of black townships to the south of JOHANNESBURG, SOUTH AFRICA. (Pop. 829 400)
Spa A spa town in BELGIUM which was the origin of the general term 'spa'. (Pop. 10 000)
Spain A kingdom in south-west EUROPE on the Iberian peninsula with coasts on the ATLANTIC and MEDITERRANEAN. The bulk of the country lies on a plateau with mountains to the north and south-east. Wine, fruit, machinery and iron are exported, and the country also has a thriving tourist industry. The capital is MADRID. (504 782 sq km/194 897 sq miles; pop. 38 820 000; cur. Peseta = 100 centimos)
Spitsbergen A large island group in the SVALBARD archipelago, 580 km (360 miles) to the north of NORWAY. (39 000 sq km/15 060 sq miles; pop. 2000)
Split The largest city on the coast of DALMATIA, CROATIA. (Pop. 236 000)
Sporades (Sporadhes) *see* Dodecanese.
Spratly Islands A group of islands in the SOUTH CHINA SEA between VIETNAM and BORNEO. Occupied by JAPAN during the Second World War, they are now claimed by almost all the surrounding countries.
Springfield 1 The state capital of ILLINOIS, U.S.A. (Pop. city 101 600/metropolitan area 190 100). **2** A manufacturing city in MASSACHUSETTS, U.S.A. (Pop. city 150 300/metropolitan area 515 900)
Srbija *see* Serbia.

Sri Lanka An island republic of southern ASIA, lying off the southernmost tip of INDIA. Formerly known as Ceylon, it gained independence from the U.K. in 1948 and became a member of the Commonwealth in 1972. A fertile country, famous for its tea, it suffers from a protracted civil war between the native Sinhalese and the Tamil population. Tea, rubber and timber are exported. Sinhalese, Tamil and English are the main languages. The capital is COLOMBO. (65 610 sq km/ 25 332 sq miles; pop. 16 500 000; cur. Sri Lankan rupee = 100 cents)
Srinagar The capital of the state of JAMMU and KASHMIR, northern INDIA. (Pop. 606 000)
Staffordshire A MIDLANDS county of ENGLAND. The county town is Stafford. (2716 sq km/1949 sq miles; pop. 1 018 000)
Stalingrad *see* Volgograd.
Stanley *see* Port Stanley.
Stanley Falls *see* Boyoma Falls.
Stanleyville *see* Kisangani.
Statia *see* St Eustatius.
Stettin *see* Szczecin.
Stockholm The capital of SWEDEN, and an important port on the BALTIC SEA. (Pop. 1 435 500)
Stockton-on-Tees A town in the county of CLEVELAND, ENGLAND. (Pop. 173 000)
Stoke-on-Trent A major city in the 'Potteries' of the MIDLANDS of ENGLAND. (Pop. 250 000)
Strasbourg An industrial city and river port in eastern FRANCE, the capital of the ALSACE region, and the seat of the European Parliament. (Pop. 378 500)

Stratford-upon-Avon A town in WARWICKSHIRE, ENGLAND, the home of William Shakespeare (1564–1616). (Pop. 22 000)

Strathclyde An administrative region in western SCOTLAND, with its administrative centre in GLASGOW. It was created in 1975 out of the former counties of Ayrshire, Lanarkshire, Renfrewshire, Bute, Dunbartonshire and parts of Stirlingshire and Argyllshire. (13 856 sq km/5350 sq miles; pop. 2 373 000)

Stromboli A island with an active volcano in the EOLIAN ISLANDS, to the north of SICILY. (Pop. 400)

Stuttgart A major industrial centre and river port of the NECKAR river in south-western GERMANY. (Pop. 600 000)

Sucre The legal capital of BOLIVIA. (Pop. 70 000)

Sudan A republic in north-east AFRICA with a coast on the RED SEA. It was made an Anglo-Egyptian condominion in 1899 but became independent in 1956. Much of the land is covered by desert and most of the population live in the towns that dot the banks of the River NILE. Ravaged by civil wars, a chronic refugee problem and drought, the Sudan struggles to feed its people. Exports include cotton and gum arabic. Arabic is the official language, and the capital is KHARTOUM. (2 505 813 sq km/967 500 sq miles; pop. 22 350 000; cur. Sudanese pound = 100 piastres = 1000 millièmes)

Sudd A vast swampland on the White NILE in SUDAN.

Sudetenland *see* Sudety.

Sudety (Sudetenland) A mountainous region straddling the border between CZECHOSLOVAKIA and POLAND.

Suez Canal A canal in north-east EGYPT, linking the MEDITERRANEAN to the RED SEA. It was completed in 1869.
Suez (El Suweis) A town situated at the southern end of the SUEZ CANAL (Pop. 195 000)
Suez, Gulf of A northern arm of the RED SEA that leads to the SUEZ CANAL.
Suffolk A county in EAST ANGLIA, ENGLAND. The county town is Ipswich. (3800 sq km/1467 sq miles; pop. 619 000)
Sulawesi (Celebes) A large, hook-shaped island in the centre of INDONESIA. (179 370 sq km/69 255 sq miles; pop. 10 409 600)
Sulu Archipelago A chain of over 400 islands of the south-west PHILIPPINES, stretching between the Philippines and BORNEO.
Sulu Sea A part of the PACIFIC OCEAN which lies between the PHILIPPINES and BORNEO.
Sumatra The main island of western INDONESIA. (473 607 sq km/182 860 sq miles; pop. 28 016 200)
Sumba One of the LESSER SUNDA ISLANDS, INDONESIA, to the south of SUMBAWA and FLORES. (11 153 sq km/4306 sq miles; pop. 251 100)
Sumbawa One of the LESSER SUNDA ISLANDS, INDONESIA, between LOMBOK and FLORES. (15 448 sq km/5965 sq miles; pop. 195 000)
Sunda Islands *see* Lesser Sunda Islands.
Sunda Strait The strait, 26 km (16 miles) across at its narrowest, which separates JAVA and SUMATRA.
Sunderland An industrial town in TYNE AND WEAR, ENGLAND. (Pop. 200 000)

Superior, Lake The largest and most westerly of the GREAT LAKES. (82 400 sq km/31 800 sq miles)

Surabaya The second largest city of INDONESIA after JAKARTA, on the north-east coast of JAVA. (Pop. 2 470 000)

Surat A port on the west coast of INDIA, in western GUJARAT. (Pop. 913 800)

Surinam A country in north-east South AMERICA, with a coast on the ATLANTIC. It became fully independent of the NETHERLANDS in 1975. The most fertile region lies along the coast; inland there are forested mountains. Bauxite and alumina are the chief exports. Dutch is the official language, and the capital is PARAMARIBO. (163 265 sq km/63 037 sq miles; pop. 384 000; cur. Surinam guilder = 100 cents)

Surrey A county of central southern ENGLAND. The county town is Guildford. (1655 sq km/639 sq miles; pop. 1 012 000)

Sussex, East A county in south-east ENGLAND; the county town is Lewes. (1795 sq km/693 sq miles; pop. 655 000)

Sussex, West A county in south-east ENGLAND; the county town is Chichester. (1989 sq km/768 sq miles; pop. 660 000)

Susupe The capital of the NORTHERN MARIANAS, on the island of SAIPAN. (Pop. 8000)

Suva The capital and main port of FIJI. (Pop. city 74 000/metropolitan area 133 000)

Suzhou A city in JIANGSU province, CHINA. (Pop. 900 000)

Svalbard An archipelago in the ARCTIC OCEAN to the

north of NORWAY, which includes SPITSBERGEN. A convention (1920) granted sovereignty to NORWAY, but all signatories can exploit the mineral reserves. (62 049 sq km/23 958 sq miles; pop. 3500)

Sverdlovsk *see* Ekaterinburg.

Swansea A port in south WALES. (Pop. 168 000)

Swaziland A landlocked kingdom in southern AFRICA which became independent of the U.K. in 1968, while still remaining within the Commonwealth. It is almost completely surrounded by, and dependent on, SOUTH AFRICA, with just a short border with MOZAMBIQUE. It is a wooded, mountainous country and agricultural produce is one of its main exports. English and Swazi are the principal languages. The capital is MBABANE. (17 400 sq km/6705 sq miles; pop. 691 000; cur. Lilangeni = 100 cents)

Sweden A kingdom in north-west EUROPE on the eastern side of the Scandinavian peninisula, with a jagged coast on the BALTIC SEA and the Gulf of BOTHNIA. Much of the land is forested; to the east runs a range of mountains and to the south there are plains where the winters are marginally less harsh. Exports include timber, wood pulp, iron and machinery. The language is Swedish, and the capital is STOCKHOLM. (449 793 sq km/173 665 sq miles; pop. 8 340 000; cur. Krona = 100 öre)

Switzerland A federal republic in west central EUROPE, high in the ALPS and surrounded by FRANCE, GERMANY and ITALY. Tourism is a major industry, and exports include jewellery, machinery and chemicals. In addition, Switzerland has important banking and financial centres. It has been a neutral country since 1516. German, French, Italian and Romansch are spoken. The capital is BERNE. (41 293 sq km/15 493 sq miles; pop. 6 510 000; cur. Swiss franc = 100 centimes)

Sydney The largest city and port in AUSTRALIA, and the capital of NEW SOUTH WALES. (Pop. 3 332 600)

Syracuse 1 A city in the centre of NEW YORK State. (Pop. city 164 200/metropolitan area 650 5000).

2 (Siracusa) An ancient seaport on the east coast of SICILY, ITALY. (Pop. 119 200)

Syrdar'ya, River A river of central ASIA, flowing through KAZAKHSTAN to the ARAL SEA. (Length 2860 km/1780 miles)

Syria A republic in western ASIA with a coastline on the MEDITERRANEAN SEA. The fertile plains on the coast rise to mountains, and much of the eastern part of the country is desert. Oil and foodstuffs are the main exports. Arabic is the national language and the capital is DAMASCUS. (185 180 sq km/71 498 sq miles; pop. 11 000 000; cur. Syrian pound)

Szczecin (Stettin) A port in north-west POLAND. (Pop. 390 200)

Szechwan *see* Sichuan.

T

Table Mountain A flat-topped mountain overlooking CAPE TOWN in south-west SOUTH AFRICA. (1087 m/ 3567 ft)

Tabriz A city in north-west IRAN. (Pop. 599 000)

Tadzhikistan (Tajikistan) A former republic of southern central U.S.S.R., occupying the mountainous region on the border with CHINA and AFGHANISTAN. It declared independence in 1991. The capital is DUSHANBE. (143 100 sq km/55 250 sq miles; pop. 5 100 000)

Taegu The third largest city of South KOREA, in the south-east of the country. (Pop. 1 608 000)

Tagus (Tajo; Tejo), River A major river of south-west EUROPE, which rises in eastern SPAIN and flows west and south-west through PORTUGAL to the ATLANTIC OCEAN west of LISBON. (Length 1007 km/626 miles)

Tahiti The largest of the islands of FRENCH POLYNESIA in the South PACIFIC. The capital is PAPEETE. (1005 sq km/388 sq miles; pop. 96 000)

T'ai-chung A major commercial and agricultural centre in western TAIWAN. (Pop. 608 000)

T'ai-pei The capital and largest city of TAIWAN, in the very north of the island. (Pop. 2 272 000)

Taiwan An island republic in the East CHINA SEA, which claims to be the legitimate Republic of China since the Nationalist government fled here from the mainland in 1949. This fertile, tropical island, 160 km (100 miles) off the Chinese mainland, was formerly called Formosa. It has developed rapidly over the last three decades to become a major industrial nation of the Far East, exporting manufactured goods such as electronic equipment, clothing and toys, as well as food. The official language is Mandarin Chinese. The capital is T'AI-PEI. (16 174 sq km/13 967 sq km; pop. 20 000 000; cur. New Taiwan Dollar = 100 cents)

Taiwan Strait The stretch of water that separates TAIWAN from mainland CHINA.

Taiyuan The capital of SHANXI province, CHINA. (Pop. 1 838 000)

Taklimakan Desert The largest desert in CHINA, consisting mainly of sand, in the west of the country.

Takoradi A main port of GHANA, in the south-west of the country. (Pop. 165 000)

Tallahassee The state capital of FLORIDA, U.S.A. (Pop. city 112 000/metropolitan area 207 600)

Tallinn A port on the BALTIC SEA, and the capital of ESTONIA. (Pop. 458 000)

Tamil Nadu A state in south-east INDIA. The state capital is MADRAS. (130 357 sq km/50 839 sq miles; pop. 48 298 000)

Tampa A port and resort on the west coast of FLORIDA, U.S.A. (Pop. city 275 000/metropolitan area 1 811 000)

Tampere (Tammerfors) The second largest city in FINLAND after HELSINKI, in the south-west of the country. (Pop. 167 000)

Tana (Tsana), Lake A lake in the mountains of north-west ETHIOPIA, and the source of the Blue NILE. (3673 sq km/1418 sq miles)

Tanganyika *see* Tanzania.

Tanganyika, Lake The second largest lake in AFRICA after Lake VICTORIA, in the GREAT RIFT VALLEY, between TANZANIA and ZAIRE, although BURUNDI and ZAMBIA also share the shoreline. (32 893 sq km/ 12 700 sq miles)

Tangier (Tanger) A port on the north coast of MOROCCO, on the Strait of GIBRALTAR. (Pop. 188 000)

Tangshan An industrial and coal-mining city in HEBEI province, CHINA. (Pop. 1 087 000)

Tanzania A republic of East AFRICA with a coastline on the INDIAN OCEAN, which was formed in 1964 when the former British colony of Tanganyika joined up with ZANZIBAR to form a single independent state, within the Commonwealth. The landscape is composed primarily of plateaux and grasslands, rising into mountains in the south and north-east. The economy is mainly agricultural, and exports include cotton, coffee, sisal, and diamonds. The official language is Swahili, but English is also spoken. The capital is DODOMA. (945 200 sq km/364 943 sq miles; pop. 22 440 000; cur. Tanzanian shilling = 100 cents)

Taranto A port and naval base on the south coast of ITALY, on the Gulf of TARANTO. (Pop. 245 000)

Taranto, Gulf of An inlet of the MEDITERRANEAN SEA between the 'toe' and the 'heel' of ITALY.

Tarawa The main atoll and capital of the group of islands forming KIRIBATI. (Pop. 23 000)

Tarragona A port of ancient origins on the MEDITERRANEAN coast of north-eastern SPAIN, and the name of the surrounding province. (Pop. city 111 700)

Tarsus An agricultural centre in south-east TURKEY, the birthplace of St Paul. (Pop. 160 000)

Tashkent The capital of UZBEKISTAN, in the north-east, near the border with KAZAKHSTAN. (Pop. 1 987 000)

Tasmania An island state to the south of AUSTRALIA, separated from the mainland by the BASS STRAIT. The capital is HOBART. (68 332 sq km/26 383 sq miles; pop. 435 000)

Tasman Sea A branch of the PACIFIC OCEAN that separates AUSTRALIA and NEW ZEALAND.
Tatar Republic (Tatarstan) An autonomous republic of the RUSSIAN FEDERATION, south-west of MOSCOW, around the River VOLGA. In 1992 it voted to become a sovereign state. The capital is KAZAN'. (68 000 sq km/ 26 250 sq miles; pop. 394 000)
Tatra Mountains A range of mountains that lines the border between POLAND and CZECHOSLOVAKIA. The highest peak is Gerlachovka (2663 m/8737 ft).
Tatung *see* Datung.
Tayside An administrative region of SCOTLAND formed in 1975 out of the former counties of Angus, Kinross-shire and part of Perthshire. The administrative centre is DUNDEE. (7511 sq km/2900 sq miles; pop. 392 000)
Tbilisi The capital of GEORGIA, in the centre of the republic. (Pop. 1 140 000)
Tegucigalpa The capital of HONDURAS, in the south of the country. (Pop. 473 700)
Tehran The capital of IRAN, in the central north of the country. (Pop. 6 000 000)
Tel Aviv-Jaffa The largest city of ISRAEL, former capital and the main financial centre. It was combined with the old port of Jaffa in 1950. (Pop. 324 000)
Tenerife The largest of the CANARY ISLANDS. The capital is Santa Cruz. (2058 sq km/795 sq miles; pop. 558 000)
Tennessee A state in southern central U.S.A. The state capital is NASHVILLE (109 412 sq km/42 244 sq miles; pop. 4 762 000).
Tennessee, River A river which flows south-west from

the APPALACHIAN MOUNTAINS of NORTH CAROLINA and then through ALABAMA, TENNESSEE and KENTUCKY to join the OHIO River. It is an important source of irrigation and hydroelectric power. (Length 1049 km/ 652 miles)

Tevere, River *see* Tiber.

Texas A state in the south-west of the U.S.A., bordering MEXICO. It is the nation's second largest state. The capital is AUSTIN. (678 927 sq km/262 134 sq miles; pop. 16 370 000)

Thailand A kingdom on the mainland part of South-East ASIA, with a long piece of territory running down the Malay peninsula across the Isthmus of KRA. Known as SIAM until 1939 and from 1945 to 1949, it is the only South-East Asian nation to have remained free of foreign colonial rule. The country is mainly composed of well-watered and fertile plains, rising to mountains in the north and to an arid plateau in the north-west. Agriculture is the main occupation, and Thailand exports rice and rubber, but it is increasingly turning to manufacturing. Tourism is also a major source of income. The main language is Thai, and the capital is BANGKOK. (513 998 sq km/198 45 sq miles; pop. 53 400 000; cur. Baht = 100 satang)

Thailand, Gulf of A branch of the SOUTH CHINA SEA lying between the Malay peninsula and the coasts of THAILAND, CAMBODIA and VIETNAM.

Thames, River A major river of southern ENGLAND flowing eastwards from its source in the Cotswold Hills, past LONDON to its estuary on the NORTH SEA. (Length 338 km/210 miles)

Thar Desert A desert in north-west INDIA, covering the border between RAJASTHAN and PAKISTAN.

Thebes The ruins of an ancient city on the River NILE in central EGYPT. It was the capital of Ancient Egypt for about 1000 years from 1600 BC.

Thessaloníki *see* Saloniki.

Thimphu (Thimbu) The capital of BHUTAN, in the west of the country. (Pop. 8922)

Thon Buri A city on the west side of the River CHAO PHRAYA, oppposite BANGKOK, in THAILAND. (Pop. 919 000)

Thousand Islands A group of over 1000 islands scattered in the upper ST LAWRENCE River, between the U.S.A. and CANADA.

Tianjin (Tientsin) A major industrial city in HEBEI province, the third largest city in CHINA after SHANGHAI and BEIJING. (Pop. 7 390 000)

Tiber (Tevere), River A river of central ITALY, rising to the east of FLORENCE and flowing south to ROME and then to the MEDITERRANEAN SEA. (Length 405 km/ 252 miles)

Tibet (Xizang Autonomous Region) A region of south-west CHINA, consisting of a huge plateau high in the HIMALAYAS. Formerly a Buddhist kingdom led by its spiritual leader, the Dalai Lama, it was invaded by China in 1949 and has been gradually desecrated. (1 221 600 sq km/ 471 660 sq miles; pop. 1 893 000)

Tierra del Fuego The archipelago at the southern tip of South AMERICA belonging the ARGENTINA and CHILE, and separated from the mainland by the Strait of MAGELLAN.

Tientsin *see* Tianjin.

Tigray A province of northern ETHIOPIA, bordering ERITREA, whose people have been fighting a separatist war against the central government. The capital is Mekele. (Pop. 2 045 000)

Tigris, River A major river of the MIDDLE EAST, rising in eastern TURKEY, flowing through SYRIA and IRAQ and joining the EUPHRATES to form a delta at the SHATT AL ARAB waterway as it enters the GULF. (Length 1900 km/1180 miles)

Tijuana A border city and resort in north-west MEXICO, at the northern end of the BAJA CALIFORNIA. (Pop. 567 000)

Timbuktu A town in central MALI at the edge of the SAHARA DESERT. (Pop. 20 000)

Timişoara An industrial city in south-west ROMANIA. (Pop. 288 000)

Timor An island at the eastern end of the LESSER SUNDA ISLANDS, INDONESIA. The eastern half of the island was a possession of PORTUGAL, but was annexed in 1975 by INDONESIA. (30 775 sq km/11 883 sq miles; pop. 3 085 000)

Timor Sea The arm of the INDIAN OCEAN between the north-west coast of AUSTRALIA and the island of TIMOR.

Tipperary A county in the south of the Republic of IRELAND. It includes the town of Tipperary, but Clonmel is the county town. (4255 sq km/1643 sq miles; pop. 135 000)

Tiranë (Tirana) The largest city and the capital of ALBANIA, in the centre of the country. (Pop. 220 000)

Tiruchchirappalli (Trinchinopoly) An industrial city in central TAMIL NADU in southern INDIA. (Pop. 609 500)
Titicaca, Lake The largest lake in South AMERICA, in the ANDES, on the border between BOLIVIA and PERU. (8135 sq km/3141 sq miles)
Tobago An island to the north-east of Trinidad, forming part of the republic of TRINIDAD and TOBAGO. (Pop. 40 000)
Togo A republic of West AFRICA with a small coast on the Gulf of GUINEA. It became independent of FRANCE in 1960. The land is crossed by high, forested uplands, with grasslands to the north and south. The majority of the population live from agriculture; coffee and cocoa are among the main exports, but phosphates are also a major source of revenue. The official language is French, and the capital is LOMÉ. (56 700 sq km/ 20 900 sq miles; pop. 3 110 000; cur. CFA franc = 100 centimes)
Tokyo The capital of JAPAN, a port on the east coast of HONSHU island. Its original name was Edo (until 1868). (Pop. city 8 353 700/Greater Tokyo 11 680 000)
Toledo 1 A historic city of central SPAIN, on the River TAGUS. (Pop. 60 100). **2** A city and GREAT LAKE port in OHIO, U.S.A. (Pop. city 343 900/metropolitan area 610 800)
Tonga A kingdom comprising an archipelago of some 150 volcanic and coral islands in the South PACIFIC, in POLYNESIA. Formerly known as the Friendly Islands, the country became independent of British protection in 1970, and joined the Commonwealth. The main exports are copra and vegetable products. The official

language is Tongan, and the capital is NUKU'ALOFA. (675 sq km/261 sq miles; pop. 109 000; cur. Pa'anga = 100 seniti)

Tongking (Tonkin) *see* Mien Bac.

Tonle Sap A lake in central CAMBODIA which swells and quadruples in size when the River MEKONG floods. ((in flood) 10 400 sq km/4000 sq miles)

Topeka The state capital of KANSAS, U.S.A. (Pop. city 119 000/metropolitan area 159 000)

Toronto The largest city of CANADA, and the capital of ONTARIO, situated on Lake Ontario. (Pop. 2 999 000)

Torres Strait The strait which separates the north-eastern tip of AUSTRALIA from NEW GUINEA.

Tortola The main island of the British VIRGIN ISLANDS.

Toulon A major naval base and port in south-east FRANCE, on the MEDITERRANEAN. (Pop. 418 000)

Toulouse A city of south-west FRANCE, on the GARONNE River. (Pop. 551 000)

Touraine A former province of north-west FRANCE, around TOURS.

Tours A town in western FRANCE, on the River LOIRE. (Pop. 268 000)

Trabzon (Trebizond) A port on the BLACK SEA in north-eastern TURKEY. (Pop. 156 000)

Trafalgar, Cape The south-western tip of SPAIN.

Transkei A Bantu homeland in eastern CAPE PROVINCE, SOUTH AFRICA, declared independent by South Africa in 1976. The capital is Umtata. (41 000 sq km/ 15 831 sq miles; pop. 3 300 000)

Transvaal A province of northern SOUTH AFRICA. The capital is PRETORIA. (Pop. 8 950 500)

Transylvania A region of central and north-western ROMANIA.

Trebizond *see* Trabzon.

Trieste A port on the ADRIATIC SEA in north-east ITALY, close to the border with YUGOSLAVIA. (Pop. 251 000)

Trichinopoly *see* Tirchchirappalli.

Trinidad and Tobago A republic in the south-eastern CARIBBEAN, just off the coast of VENEZUELA, consisting of two main islands, Trinidad (by far the larger) and TOBAGO to the north-east. Formerly a British colony, the country became independent in 1962, and joined the Commonwealth. The country's revenue used to be derived from the plantations producing sugar cane, cocoa, coffee and fruit, but exports of oil and gas, found on or around Trinidad, now provide most of the national income. English, Hindi, Spanish and French are spoken. The capital is PORT OF SPAIN. (5128 sq km/1980 sq miles; pop. 1 200 00; cur. Trinidad and Tobago dollar = 100 cents)

Tripoli 1 The capital and main port of LIBYA, in the north-west. (Pop. 620 000). 2 A port in northern LEBANON. (Pop. 175 000)

Tristan da Cunha A group of four remote, volcanic islands in the middle of the South ATLANTIC OCEAN, which form part of the ST HELENA DEPENDENCIES. (100 sq km/40 sq miles; pop. 325)

Trivandrum A port on the southern tip of INDIA, and the state capital of KERALA. (Pop. 520 000)

Trujillo A city and provincial capital in north-west PERU. (Pop.750 000)

Tsana, Lake *see* Tana, Lake.

Tsushima Strait *see* Korea Strait.

Tucson A city in southern ARIZONA, U.S.A. (Pop. city 365 400/metropolitan area 594 800)

Tulsa A city in north-eastern OKLAHOMA, on the ARKANSAS River. (Pop. 375 000/metropolitan area 725 000)

Tunis The capital and main port of TUNISIA. (Pop. 550 000)

Tunisia A republic in central north AFRICA with a coast on the MEDITERRANEAN and the Gulf of GABES. A French protectorate from 1881, it gained its independence in 1955. The south is mainly desert, while the north is dominated by the ATLAS MOUNTAINS. The fertile regions of the north produce grain, vegetables, olives and citrus fruits, but the country's main income is derived from oil and oil products, and phosphates. The official language is Arabic; the capital is TUNIS. (164 000 sq km/63 380 sq miles; pop. 7 540 000; cur. Dinar = 100 millimes)

Turin (Torino) A major industrial town on the River PO, and the capital of the PIEDMONT region, in north-west ITALY. (Pop. 1 103 500)

Turkey A republic that bridges the division between EUROPE and ASIA. Asian Turkey represents by far the greater part, occupying a huge peninsula between the BLACK SEA and the MEDITERRANEAN SEA; a small portion of the country, however, lies to the west of the BOSPHORUS and the Sea of MARMARA, in Europe. The land is generally rugged but well-watered and fertile, and agriculture is the main industry. Exports include cotton, fruit, grain and tobacco, and textiles. The official language is Turkish. The capital is ANKARA. (780 576 sq km/302 380 sq miles; pop. 44 736 957; cur. Lira = 100 kurus)

Turkmenistan A former republic in the south of the U.S.S.R. bordering AFGHANISTAN and IRAN, and with a shoreline on the CASPIAN SEA. It declared sovereignty in 1990. The capital is ASHKHABAD. (488 100 sq km/ 186 400 sq miles; pop. 3 600 000)

Turks and Caicos Islands A British colony in the north-eastern WEST INDIES consisting of some 14 main islands. The capital is Cockburn Town on Grand Turk. (430 sq km/166 sq miles; pop. 7400)

Turku (Åbo) A port in south-west FINLAND, on the Gulf of BOTHNIA. (Pop. 161 400)

Tuscany A region of central western ITALY. The capital is FLORENCE. (Pop. 3 600 000)

Tuvalu A country of the South PACIFIC consisting of nine islands known formerly known as the Ellice Islands, which became independent of the U.K. in 1978, within the Commonwealth. The main occupations are fishing and agriculture, and exports include copra and postage stamps. Tuvaluan and English are spoken, and the capital is FUNAFUTI. (26 sq km/ 10 sq miles; pop. 8000; cur. Tuvaluan or Australian dollar = 100 cents)

Tver *see* Kalinin.

Tyne and Wear A metropolitan county in north-east ENGLAND, created in 1974 out of parts of Durham and Northumberland. The administrative centre is SUNDERLAND. (540 sq km/208 sq miles; pop. 1 145 000)

Tyrol A province of western AUSTRIA, in the ALPS. The capital is Innsbruck. (Pop. 586 200)
Tyrone A county in the west of Northern IRELAND. The county town is Omagh. (3266 sq km/1260 sq miles; pop. 160 000)
Tyrrhenian Sea A part of the MEDITERRANEAN SEA between SICILY, SARDINIA and mainland ITALY.

U

U.A.E. *see* United Arab Emirates.
Udaipur A historic city in southern RAJASTHAN, INDIA. (Pop. 233 000)
Ufa An industrial city and capital of BASHKIRIA, in the RUSSIAN FEDERATION. (Pop. 1 048 000)
Uganda A landlocked republic of East AFRICA, which gained independence from the U.K., within the Commonwealth, in 1962. Lake VICTORIA lies to the south-east, and mountains to the south-west; the centre of the country is a plateau of grasslands. The main exports are coffee, tea and cotton, but the economy has been slow to recover from the devastating rule of Idi Amin (1971–79) and the ensuing chaos and civil war. English is the official language, and the capital is KAMPALA. (235 886 sq km/91 075 sq miles; pop. 15 000 000; cur. Uganda shilling = 100 cents)
Ujung Padang A major port in the south-west of SULAWESI, INDONESIA. It was formerly known as Makassar. (Pop. 709 000)
U.K. *see* United Kingdom.

Ukraine Formerly the westernmost republic of the U.S.S.R., bordering ROMANIA and POLAND; it declared itself independent in August 1991. The capital is KIEV. (603 700 sq km/233 100 sq miles; pop. 51 700 000)
Ulan Bator The capital of MONGOLIA, in the central north of the country. (Pop. 440 000)
Ulan-Ude The capital of the BURYAT REPUBLIC, in the RUSSIAN FEDERATION. (Pop. 330 000).
Ulster One of the four ancient provinces into which IRELAND was divided, covering the north. It is often used to refer to Northern IRELAND, but three counties of Ulster are in the Republic of IRELAND (DONEGAL, MONAGHAN and CAVAN).
Ul'yanovsk A city of the eastern URALS, in RUSSIA, on the River VOLGA. (Pop. 525 000)
Umbria A landlocked region of central, eastern ITALY, bordering TUSCANY. (Pop. 816 000).
Umm al Qaywayn One of the seven UNITED ARAB EMIRATES, on the GULF. Its capital is also called Umm al Qaywaym. (518 sq km/200 sq miles; pop. emirate 14 000/town 3000)
Union of Soviet Socialist Republics (U.S.S.R.) The name of a vast union of Communist republics that once stretched from EUROPE to the BERING STRAIT, from the ARCTIC CIRCLE to the borders of southern ASIA, covering one sixth of the world. It was established in 1922, replacing the old Russian Empire. Ruled from its capital, MOSCOW, it included the R.S.F.S.R. (the Russian Federation) and fourteen other republics, including the UKRAINE, GEORGIA, TURKMENISTAN, UZBEKISTAN, ARMENIA,and KAZAKHSTAN. Since 1990 most of these

republics, as well as the three BALTIC Republics, LATVIA, LITHUANIA and ESTONIA, have chosen to become independent. In 1991 an umbrella organization called the COMMONWEALTH OF INDEPENDENT STATES was set up to replace the centralized role of the U.S.S.R. (22 402 200 sq km/ 8 649 538 sq miles; pop. 275 000 000; cur. Rouble = 100 kopecks)

United Arab Emirates (U.A.E.) A group of seven emirates that lines the coast of the southern GULF. The seven (ABU DHABI, DUBAI, AL FUJAYRAH, AJMAN, SHARJAH, UMM AL QAYWAYN, and RAS AL KHAYMAH) formed a British protectorate before becoming independent in 1971. The land is mainly desert, but it has huge oil reserves, which have made the U.A.E. extremely wealthy. The country is ruled centrally from the capital, Abu Dhabi. The main language is Arabic. (83 600 sq km/32 000 sq miles; pop. 1 380 000; cur. Dirham =100 fils)

United Kingdom (U.K.) The United Kingdom of Great Britain and Northern Ireland occupies the greater part of the BRITISH ISLES, and consists of ENGLAND, SCOTLAND and WALES (Great Britain) and the northern part of IRELAND (NORTHERN IRELAND). The term United Kingdom has been used since 1801, but the country is often more loosely referred to as Britain. One of the earliest countries to industrialize, and formerly the hub of a major world empire, it has long been a significant manufacturing and trading nation. It is a member of the European Community, and exports include oil and oil products, vehicles and machinery, iron and steel, and textiles. The capital is LONDON.

(244 119 sq km/94 255 sq miles; pop. 57 000 000; cur. Pound sterling = 100 pence)

United States of America (U.S.A.) A federal republic occupying the southern half of North AMERICA, as well as the separate states ALASKA to the north-west of CANADA, and HAWAII in the PACIFIC OCEAN. There are 50 states, of immense variety, from the fertile and temperate east coast, to the deserts of the south-west, from the Great Plains of the centre, to the humid, sub-tropical south-east. The U.S.A. is now the major world power, and the mainspring of numerous multinational companies, and it has a significant cultural influence worldwide. It exports machinery, electrical equipment, chemicals, grain, petroleum products and foodstuffs. The main language is English, but Spanish is also widely spoken, as well as many other languages. The capital is WASHINGTON D.C. (9 372 614 sq km/ 3 618 772 sq miles; pop. 241 000 000; cur. Dollar = 100 cents)

Upper Volta *see* Burkina-Faso.

Uppsala An old university town in eastern central SWEDEN. (Pop.154 000)

Ural Mountains (Urals) A mountain range in western RUSSIA. Running north to south from the ARCTIC to the ARAL SEA, the Urals form the traditional dividing line between EUROPE and ASIA. The highest point is Mount Narodnaya (1894 m/3500 ft).

Uruguay A republic in south-east South AMERICA, with BRAZIL to the north and ARGENTINA to the south and west, and a coast on the ATLANTIC OCEAN. The land is primarily made up of plateaux and grasslands, used for raising cattle and sheep. The main exports are meat and meat products, and wool. The official language is Spanish. The capital is MONTEVIDEO. (176 215 sq km/68 037 sq miles; pop. 2 950 000; cur. Peso = 100 centésimos)

Urümqi (Urumchi) The capital of the XINJIANG AUTONOMOUS REGION of north-west CHINA. (Pop. 1 200 000)

U.S.A. *see* United States of America.

U.S.S.R. *see* Union of Soviet Socialist Republics.

Utah A state in the west of the U.S.A. The state capital is SALT LAKE CITY. (212 628 sq km/82 096 sq miles; pop. 1 645 000)

Utrecht A historic city in the central NETHERLANDS. (Pop. city 231 000/Greater Utrecht 498 900)

Uttar Pradesh The most populous state of INDIA, in the north of the country. The capital is LUCKNOW. (294 364 sq km/113 654 sq miles; pop. 110 865 000)

Uzbekistan A former republic of south-central U.S.S.R., to the north of TURKMENISTAN. It declared sovereignty in 1990. The capital is TASHKENT. (449 600 sq km/ 173 546 sq miles; pop. 20 300 000)

V

Vadodara (Baroda) An industrial city in south-east GUJARAT, INDIA. (Pop. 745 000)

Valencia 1 A port on the MEDITERRANEAN coast of SPAIN, and the capital of the province of the same name. (Pop. city 752 000). **2** An industrial city in northern VENEZUELA. (Pop. 540 000)

Valladolid An industrial city in north-west SPAIN. (Pop. city 330 200)

Valle d'Aosta A French-speaking region of north-west ITALY. The capital is Aosta. (Pop. 114 000)

Valletta The capital of MALTA. (Pop. 14 000)

Valparaíso The main port of CHILE, in the centre of the country. (Pop. 267 000)

Van, Lake A salt lake in eastern TURKEY. (3675 sq km/ 1419 sq miles)

Vancouver A major port and industrial centre in south-east BRITISH COLUMBIA, CANADA, on the mainland opposite VANCOUVER ISLAND with access to the PACIFIC OCEAN. (Pop. 1 268 000)

Vancouver Island The largest island off the PACIFIC coast of North AMERICA, in south-west CANADA. The capital is VICTORIA. (32 137 sq km/12 408 sq miles; pop. 390 000)

Vanuatu A republic consisting of a chain of some 80 volcanic and coral islands in MELANESIA, in the south-west PACIFIC. Espiritu Santo and Efâte are the two largest islands. Formerly known as the New Hebrides, the country gained independence from the U.K. and FRANCE in 1980 and joined the Commonwealth. The principal economic activities are fishing, cattle ranching, and the production of copra. The main languages are Pidgin, English and French, and the capital, on Efâte, is PORT-VILA. (14 760 sq km/5700 sq miles; pop. 138 000; cur. Vatu)

Varanasi (Benares) A holy Hindu city on the banks of the River GANGES in UTTAR PRADESH, north-eastern INDIA. (Pop. 798 000)

Vatican City State A tiny independent state in ROME, ITALY, centring upon the Vatican, palace of the popes. The capital is Vatican City. (0.44 sq km/0.17 sq miles; pop. 1000; cur. Vatican City lira, or Italian lira)

Veglia *see* Krk.

Veneto A region of north-eastern ITALY, centring upon VENICE. (Pop. 4 367 000)

Venezuela A republic in north-eastern South AMERICA with a coast on the CARIBBEAN SEA and the ATLANTIC OCEAN. Most of the population live in the towns and cities along the coast; to the south are remote highlands crossed by tributaries of the ORINOCO River. The northern spur of the ANDES cuts into the north-east of the country. The economy is underpinned by the rich oil reserves around Lake MARACAIBO. The main language is Spanish, and the capital is CARACAS. (912 050 sq km/352 000 sq miles; pop. 18 340 000; cur. Bolívar = 100 céntimos)

Venice (Venezia) A historic port built on islands at the head of the ADRIATIC SEA in north-eastern ITALY. The principal thoroughfares are canals. (Pop. 346 000)

Vermont A state in the north-east of the U.S.A., bordering CANADA. The state capital is MONTPELIER. (24 887 sq km/9609 sq miles; pop. 535 000)

Verona A historic and industrial city in the VENETO, northern ITALY. (Pop. 260 000)

Versailles A town just to the west of PARIS, FRANCE, which grew up around the palace built there by Louis XIV in the 1660s. (Pop. 96 000)

Vesuvius An active volcano to the south-east of NAPLES, in south-west ITALY, notorious for having buried POMPEII in ash during an eruption in AD 79. (1281 m/4203 ft)

Vianchan *see* Vientiane.

Victoria 1 A state in south-eastern AUSTRALIA. The state capital is MELBOURNE. (227 620 sq km/87 884 sq miles; pop. 4 054 000). **2** A port on the south-eastern coast of VANCOUVER ISLAND, south-west CANADA, and the capital of BRITISH COLUMBIA. (Pop. 233 000). **3** A port and the capital of HONG KONG, in the north-west of Hong Kong Island. (Pop. 1 026 900) **4** The capital of the SEYCHELLES, on the island of Mahé. (Pop. 25 000)

Victoria, Lake The largest lake in AFRICA, and the second largest freshwater lake in the world after Lake SUPERIOR. Its shoreline is shared by UGANDA, KENYA and TANZANIA. (69 485 sq km/26 828 sq miles)

Victoria Falls One of the greatest waterfalls in the world, where the River ZAMBEZI tumbles some 108 m/355 ft, on the border between ZAMBIA and ZIMBABWE.

Vienna (Wien) The capital of AUSTRIA, on the River DANUBE, in the north-east of the country. (Pop. 1 531 000)

Ventiane (Viangchan) The capital of LAOS, on the River MEKONG in the north-east of the country, near the border with THAILAND. (Pop. 177 000)

Vietnam A republic on the mainland of South-East ASIA, with a long coast on the SOUTH CHINA SEA. A French colony until the Second World War, it was divided into two, North Vietnam and South Vietnam, in 1954. Over the next two decades Communists, supported by North Vietnam, waged a war with the government of South Vietnam, which was supported by the U.S.A., until the U.S.A. withdrew its forces after 1973. This led to fall of South Vietnam's capital SAIGON (renamed HO CHI MINH CITY) and victory for the North. The country was unified in 1976. With highly fertile land and rich reserves in minerals, Vietnam is potentially one of the wealthiest countries of South-East Asia, but the economic policies of the the government have led many of its people to despair. The main exports are coal, clothing and agricultural products. Vietnamese, Chinese, French and English are spoken, and the capital is HANOI (337 870 sq km/130 452 sq miles; pop. 61 950 000; cur. Dong = 10 hao= 100 xu)

Vilnius The capital of LITHUANIA. (Pop. 536 000)

Virginia A state in the east of the U.S.A., with a coast on the ATLANTIC OCEAN. The capital is RICHMOND (103 030 sq km/39 780 sq miles; pop. 5 706 000).

Virgin Islands, British A British Crown colony in the eastern CARIBBEAN, to the east of PUERTO RICO. The British islands are in the east of the Virgin Island group. Sixteen of the islands are inhabited, including Virgin Gorda and Tortola, the site of the capital, ROAD TOWN. (103 sq km/50 sq miles; pop. 12 000)

Virgin Islands, U.S. A territory of the U.S.A. in the eastern CARIBBEAN, to the east of PUERTO RICO. The U.S. islands are in the west and south of the Virgin Island group. The main islands are St John, St Croix and St Thomas – the site of the capital, CHARLOTTE AMALIE. (344 sq km/133 sq miles; pop. 100 000)

Visayan Islands A group of islands in the centre of the

Philippines, which includes NEGROS, CEBU, Leyte, Masbate, Panay, Bohol, Panay and Samar.

Vistula, River A river of central and northern POLAND, flowing northwards through CRACOW and WARSAW to the BALTIC SEA. (Length 1090 km/677 miles)

Vladivostok A major port on the PACIFIC coast in the Far East of RUSSIA, 50 km (30 miles) from the border with CHINA. (Pop. 590 000)

Vlissingen *see* Flushing.

Volga, River A largely navigable river of western RUSSIA, flowing south from its source, to the north-east of MOSCOW, to the CASPIAN SEA. It is the longest river in EUROPE. (Length 3690 km/2293 miles)

Volgograd A port and major industrial city on the River VOLGA. It was called Stalingrad from 1925 to 1961. (Pop. 990 000)

Volta, Lake A major artificial lake that occupies much of eastern GHANA, formed by the damming of the Volta River, and fed by the White and Black Volta Rivers. (8480 sq km/3251 sq miles)

Voronezh An industrial city 450 km (280 miles) south of MOSCOW, RUSSIA. (Pop. 842 000)

Voroshilovgrad A major industrial city of the eastern UKRAINE in the DONETS BASIN. Formerly called Lugansk, it was renamed in 1970 after Kliment Voroshilov, President of the U.S.S.R. (1953–60). (Pop. 491 000)

W

Waikato, River The longest river in NEW ZEALAND, flowing north-west from the centre of North Island to the TASMAN SEA. (Length 350 km/220 miles)

Wales A principality in the south-west of GREAT BRITAIN, forming a part of the U.K. CARDIFF is the capital. (20 768 sq km/8017 sq miles; pop. 2 749 600)

Wallis and Fortuna Islands Three small islands forming an overseas territory of FRANCE in the south-west PACIFIC, to the north-east of FIJI. The capital is Mata-Utu. (367 sq km/143 sq miles; pop. 13 500)

Warsaw (Warszawa) The capital of POLAND, on the River VISTULA, in the eastern central part of the country. (Pop. 1 641 000)

Warwickshire A county of central ENGLAND. The county town is Warwick. (1981 sq km/765 sq miles; pop. 475 000)

Washington A state in the north-west of the U.S.A., on the border with CANADA, and with a coast on the PACIFIC. The capital is OLYMPIA. (172 416 sq km/66 570 sq miles; pop. 4 409 000)

Washington D.C. The capital of the U.S.A., on the Potomac River. It stands in its own territory called the District of Columbia (D.C.), between the states of VIRGINIA and MARYLAND, close to the ATLANTIC coast. (179 sq km/69 sq miles; pop. city 622 800/metropolitan area 3 429 400)

Waterford A county in the south of the Republic of IRELAND. The county town is also called Waterford. (1838 sq km/710 sq miles; pop. county 89 000)

Weimar A historic city in southern central GERMANY. (Pop. 65 000)

Wellington The capital of NEW ZEALAND, a port in the south-west of North Island. (Pop. 342 000)

Weser, River A river in the north-west of GERMANY, flowing through BREMEN and BREMERHAVEN to the NORTH SEA. (477 sq km/196 sq miles)

West Bank A piece of disputed territory to the west of the River JORDAN, including a part of JERUSALEM, which was taken by ISRAEL from JORDAN in the Arab-Israeli war of 1967, and has been occupied by Israel since then. New Israeli settlements here have incited growing resentment among the Palestinian population. (5858 sq km/2262 sq miles)

West Bengal A state in eastern INDIA, bordering BANGLADESH. CALCUTTA is the capital. (88 752 sq km/ 34 258 sq miles; pop. 54 581 000)

Western Australia A state occupying much of the western half of AUSTRALIA,. The capital is PERTH. (2 527 636 sq km/975 920 sq miles; pop. 1 300 000)

Western Isles The regional authority covering the Inner and Outer HEBRIDES of western SCOTLAND. The administrative centre is Stornaway, on the Isle of Lewis. (2900 sq km/1120 sq miles; pop. 32 000)

Western Sahara A disputed territory of western AFRICA, with coastline on the ATLANTIC OCEAN. Consisting mainly of desert, it is rich in phosphates. It was a Spanish overseas province until 1975, and is now claimed by MOROCCO, against the wishes of an active separatist movement. The main town is Laayoune. (266 770 sq km/103 000 sq miles; pop. 200 000)

Western Samoa *see* Samoa, Western.

West Glamorgan A county in South WALES, created in 1974 from part of Glamorgan and the borough of SWANSEA, with Swansea as the administrative centre. (817 sq km/315 sq miles; pop. 368 000)

West Indies A general term for the islands of the CARIBBEAN SEA.

West Midlands A metropolitan county of central ENGLAND, created in 1974, with its administrative centre in BIRMINGHAM. (889 sq km/347 sq miles)

West Virginia A state of eastern U.S.A. The capital is CHARLESTON. (62 341 sq km/24 070 sq miles; pop. 1 936 000)

Westmeath A county in the central north of the Republic of IRELAND. The county town is Mullinagar. (1764 sq km/681 sq miles)

Wexford A county in the south-east of the Republic of IRELAND. The county town is also called Wexford. (2352 sq km/908 sq miles; pop. county 13 293)

White Sea An arm of the BARENTS SEA off north-west RUSSIA which is almost enclosed by the bulge of the KOLA peninsula.

Whitney, Mount A mountain in the Sequoia National Park in eastern CALIFORNIA, with the highest peak in the U.S.A. outside ALASKA. (4418 m/14 495 ft)

Wichita A city in southern KANSAS, U.S.A., on the ARKANSAS River. (Pop. city 283 500/metropolitan area 428 600)

Wicklow A county in the south-west of the Republic of IRELAND. The county town is also called Wicklow. (2025 sq km/782 sq miles; pop. county 87 000)

Wiesbaden An old spa town in western GERMANY, and capital of the state of HESSEN. (Pop. 272 000)

Wight, Isle of An island and county off the south coast of ENGLAND, separated from the mainland by the SOLENT. The county town is Newport. (380 sq km/ 147 sq miles; pop. 120 000)

Wiltshire A county in central southern ENGLAND. The county town is Trowbridge. (3481 sq km/1344 sq miles; pop. 510 000)

Winchester A historic city in southern ENGLAND, and the county town of HAMPSHIRE. (Pop. 31 000)

Windward Islands *see* Leeward and Windward Islands.

Winnipeg The capital of MANITOBA, CANADA, in the south of the state. (Pop. 585 000)

Winnipeg, Lake A lake in the south of MANITOBA, CANADA, which drains into the HUDSON BAY via the Nelson River. (23 553 sq km/9094 sq miles)

Wisconsin A state in the north central U.S.A., bordering Lake SUPERIOR and Lake MICHIGAN. The state capital is MADISON. (141 061 sq km/54 464 sq miles; pop. 4 775 000)

Witwatersrand (The Rand) A major gold-mining and industrial area of south TRANSVAAL, SOUTH AFRICA.

Wollongong A major port and industrial centre in NEW SOUTH WALES, AUSTRALIA, 80 km (50 miles) south of SYDNEY. (Pop. 235 000)

Wolverhampton An old industrial town in the WEST MIDLANDS of ENGLAND. (Pop. 255 000)

Worcestershire *see* Hereford and Worcester.

Wroclaw (Breslau) An industrial city on the River ODER in south-west POLAND. (Pop. 631 000)

Wuhan (Hankow) The capital of HUBEI province, south-east CHINA (Pop. 3 885 000)
Wyoming A state in the west of the U.S.A. The state capital is CHEYENNE. (253 597 sq km/97 914 sq miles; pop. 509 000)

X

Xi Jiang The third longest river in CHINA, flowing across the south-west of the country from YUNNAN to its delta on the SOUTH CHINA SEA near GUANGZHOU (Canton). (Length 2300 km/1437 miles)
Xiamen (Amoy) A port on the east coast of CHINA, in FUJIAN province. (Pop. 1 006 000)
Xining An industrial city and the capital of QINGHAI province, in western CHINA (Pop. 860 000)
Xinjiang (Sinkiang) Uygur Autonomous Region A region of north-west CHINA, bordering MONGOLIA, RUSSIA, AFGHANISTAN, PAKISTAN and INDIA. It is also known as Dzungaria. The capital is URUMQI. (1 646 799 sq km/ 635 829 sq miles; pop. 12 830 000)
Xizang Autonomous Region *see* Tibet.

Y

Yaren The capital of NAURU. (Pop. 400)
Yamoussoukro The new capital of COTE D'IVOIRE, in the centre of the country. (Pop. 45 000)
Yangon *see* Rangoon.

Yamuna (Jumna), River A major river of north INDIA, a tributary of the GANGES. (Length 1376 km/855 miles)
Yangtze Kiang *see* Chang Jiang.
Yaoundé The capital of CAMEROON, in the south-west of the country. (Pop. 500 000)
Yellow River *see* Huang He.
Yellow Sea A branch of the PACIFIC OCEAN between the north-east coast of CHINA and the peninsula of KOREA.
Yemen A republic of the south-west Arabian peninsula, with coasts on the RED SEA and the Gulf of ADEN. Until recently, there were two separate nations: North Yemen; and South Yemen, which became an independent republic in 1967 after the British abandoned their garrison in ADEN. In 1990, however, the two Yemens decided to form a single country, ruled jointly from the capital, SAN'A. The landscape of the north is mountainous and fertile, whereas the south is mainly mountainous desert. The main exports are coffee, cotton and fish. The official language is Arabic. (482 682 sq km/186 374 sq miles; pop. 8 500 000; cur. Yemeni rial = 100 fils)
Yerevan An industrial city and the capital of ARMENIA, close to the border with TURKEY. (Pop. 1 114 000)
Yinchuan The capital of NINGXIA-HUI AUTONOMOUS REGION, in north central CHINA. (Pop. 635 000)
Yogyakarta (Jogjakarta) A city of south-central JAVA, and a cultural centre. (Pop. 400 00)
Yokohama The main port of JAPAN, and the country's second largest city after neighbouring TOKYO, on the south-east coast of HONSHU island. (Pop. 3 012 900)
Yorkshire An old county of north-east ENGLAND which

used to be divided into the East, West and North Ridings. In 1974, however, the county was redivided into North Yorkshire (administrative centre: Northallerton; 8309 sq km/3207 sq miles; pop. 666 000); West Yorkshire (administrative centre: Wakefield; 2039 sq km/787 sq miles; pop. 2 038 000); and South Yorkshire (administrative centre: Barnsley; 1560 sq km/602 sq miles; pop. 1 302 000).

Yucatán A state on a broad peninsula of south-east MEXICO. (Pop. 1 100 000)

Yugoslavia A federal republic of south-east EUROPE. It was created in 1918, and became a single republic after the Second World War under the Communist leadership of Marshal Tito. The six constituent republics were SERBIA, SLOVENIA, CROATIA, MONTENEGRO, MACEDONIA, and BOSNIA HERZEGOVINA. Serbia was always the dominant republic, and the seat of the capital, BELGRADE. In 1991 Slovenia and Croatia became independent, and Bosnia and Macedonia may follow suit. The economy is largely agricultural, but exports include chemicals, machinery, textiles and clothing. The main languages are Serbo-Croat and Macedonian. (255 804 sq km/ 98 766 sq miles; pop. 23 000 000; cur. Yugoslav dinar = 100 paras)

Yukon Territory A mountainous territory in north-west CANADA centring upon the River Yukon, and including the River KLONDIKE. (536 372 sq km/207 076 sq miles; pop. 23 500)

Yünnan A province in south-western CHINA. The capital is KUNMING. (436 200 sq km/168 400 sq miles; pop. 34 000 000)

Z

Zagreb The capital of CROATIA. (Pop. 1 180 000)
Zagros Mountains A mountain range in south-west IRAN, running parallel to the border with IRAQ. The highest point is Zard Kuh. (4548 m/14 918 ft)
Zaïre A republic in southern central AFRICA, landlocked but for a small strip of land that reaches the ATLANTIC coast. Formerly the Belgian Congo, it became independent of BELGIUM in 1960. The country centres upon the basin of the River ZAIRE, with dense rainforests rising to highlands in the east. Most of the population is engaged in agriculture and fishing, but the country's main revenue comes from exports of copper, diamonds, timber and coffee. The official language is French but Swahili, Lingali and other African languages are also spoken. The capital is KINSHASA. (2 344 116 sq km/905 063 sq miles; pop. 34 670 000; cur. Zaïre = 100 makuta)
Zaïre (Congo), River A major river of central AFRICA (the second longest river in Africa after the NILE) and, with its tributaries, forming a massive basin. It rises as the Lalualaba in the south of ZAIRE, then flows north and north-west, and finally south-west, forming the border between Zaïre and the CONGO before entering the ATLANTIC OCEAN. (Length 4800 km/3000 miles)
Zambezi, River A river of southern AFRICA. It rises in ZAMBIA, then flows south to form the border with ZIMBABWE and then south-east across MOZAMBIQUE to the INDIAN OCEAN. (Length 2740 km/1700 miles)
Zambia A landlocked republic of southern central

AFRICA, set mainly on a high plateau well watered by rivers. Formerly the British protectorate of Northern Rhodesia, it became independent within the Commonwealth in 1964. The major occupation is farming and agriculture, but Zambia also has valuable mineral wealth and exports copper, in particular, as well as cobalt, coal, zinc, lead and manganese. The official language is English, and the capital is LUSAKA. (752 617 sq km/290 sq miles; pop. 6 660 000; cur. Kwacha =100 ngwee)

Zanzibar An island lying just off the east coast of AFRICA, in the INDIAN OCEAN. Settled by Arab traders, it was a major commercial centre by the 17th century. It became a British protectorate in 1890, and joined neighbouring Tanganyika in 1964 to form the independent republic of TANZANIA. The main town is the port also called Zanzibar. (2461 sq km/950 sq miles; pop. 556 000)

Zaporozh'ye A major industrial city on the River DNIEPER in the UKRAINE. (Pop. 844 000)

Zaragoza (Saragossa) A historic and industrial city in north-eastern SPAIN, on the River EBRO, and the name of the surrounding province. (Pop. city 590 000)

Zealand (Sjaelland) The largest island of DENMARK, on which the capital, COPENHAGEN is sited. (7014 sq km/2708 sq miles; pop. 1 855 500)

Zermatt A popular ski resort in south-west SWITZERLAND, close to the MATTERHORN. (Pop. 3200)

Zhangjiakou A city in HEBEI province, in north-east CHINA. (Pop. 630 000)

Zhejiang A province of eastern CHINA, with a coast on

the East China Sea. The capital is HANGZHOU. (102 000 sq km/39 780 sq miles; pop. 37 920 000)

Zhengzhou The capital of HENAN province, in east central CHINA. (Pop. 1 271 000)

Zibo An industrial city in SHANDONG province, north-eastern CHINA. (Pop. 2 000 000)

Zimbabwe A landlocked republic of central southern AFRICA. Formerly a part the British colony of Rhodesia, it became Southern Rhodesia when it declared unilateral independence, with white minority rule, in 1965; after a civil war it became fully independent in 1980 and joined the Commonwealth. The country consists primarily of high plateaux, rising to highlands in the east, with forests in the south-east. The economy is based mainly on agriculture and mining. Exports include agricultural produce, gold, cotton and asbestos. The official language is English, but Shona and Ndebele are spoken. The capital is HARARE. (390 600 sq km/150 810 sq miles; pop. 8 660 000; cur. Zimbabwe dollar = 100 cents)

Zululand *see* KwaZulu.

Zürich The largest city in SWITZERLAND, in the north-east of the country, and a major industrial and financial centre. (Pop. 422 000)